C0-AWM-614

ML
455
.C 651

The Evolution

OF

Modern Orchestration

BY

LOUIS ADOLPHE COERNE, Ph.D.

New York

THE MACMILLAN COMPANY

1908

All rights reserved

Copyright, 1908,

By THE MACMILLAN COMPANY

Set up and electrotyped.   Published September, 1908

ML
455
.C651

Stanhope Press
F. H. GILSON COMPANY
BOSTON, U.S.A.

CONTENTS

PART I. — PRELIMINARIES.

PART II. — THE CLASSIC ERA.

PART III. — ROMANTICISM.

PREFACE

IT is not the purpose of this work to write a treatise on instrumentation or to prepare a pedagogical analysis of orchestration only, but rather to trace the evolution of the orchestra and of orchestration in connection with the history of music proper. Special emphasis will be laid upon what may be termed the IMPELLING FORCES to which the development of orchestration is due. This necessitates a considerable repetition of familiar facts that do not lend themselves to further original treatment. The restatement of such facts, however, would seem to form an indispensable background for the main theme, which is thereby exposed with all its attending phases of logical evolution.

In addition to extended studies of orchestral scores themselves, the standard works of Berlioz, Gevaërt, Riemann, Parry, and others have, as a matter of course, been referred to. The subject under discussion has already been admirably handled by Lavoix in his voluminous work entitled "Histoire de L'Instrumentation," but it was unquestionably done through French glasses, and the scores of not one German romanticist are submitted to careful analysis beyond those of Weber and Wagner. "Parsifal" had not been produced at the time when Lavoix's book went to press, nor had such representative composers as Brahms, Saint-Saëns, Tschaikowsky, Dvořák then won their full meed of recognition. It is obvious, therefore, that the orchestration especially of the nineteenth century offers a fertile field for further profitable research. Again, the present writer is not aware of the existence of any comprehensive work in the English language upon the *history* of the orchestra and of orchestration.

Throughout these pages the achievements of the more prominent composers are set forth in such manner as to indicate not only the distinctive features of their orchestration but of their general creative ability as well. In each case, the general style of composition and its significance as a contribution to musical literature are first enlarged upon. This is followed by an examination of the differentiated treatment of the strings, the wood, the brass, presented in logical sequence. A final analysis is then made of the individual method of orchestration as a whole, together with its relative value in the evolution of orchestration.

In the Appendix to this book will be found a few musical illustrations selected from representative orchestral scores.

LOUIS ADOLPHE COERNE.

CAMBRIDGE, MASSACHUSETTS, U. S. A.
April 30, 1905.

v

28841

INTRODUCTORY NOTE

It was inevitable that in an age marked like the present by specialization in all the arts and in all branches of learning as well, the need would one day be felt of a history of orchestration. In attempting to supply it with this book Dr. Coerne has filled a want in English musical literature. Of treatises devoted to the art of writing for the orchestra there is no lack. Berlioz, the greatest master of the art before Wagner, wrote such a treatise, which while it was still looked upon as in many respects a model, was revised and brought down to date by Richard Strauss; but invaluable as this treatise is and as are the more voluminous treatises of the Belgian Gevaërt, the German Hofmann and the Englishman Prout, they are after all study-books for the creative musician, and only by laborious comparison of their illustrative examples, or the scores of composers, can the historical inquirer learn aught of the evolution of the art to which they are devoted. Even then his view is restricted, practically, to the music composed since the closing decades of the eighteenth century. The explanation of this fact is that while the art of music is always spoken of as young in the handbooks, that of orchestration is much younger. The student of orchestration, say the teachers, can derive little benefit from a study of scores older than those of Haydn and Mozart because some of the instruments of their predecessors are obsolete and so is their manner of writing for the instruments still in use. This, however, brings small comfort to the historical investigator who is quite as desirous to know what the orchestra was like prior to Haydn and Mozart, and the Mannheim symphonists, as he is to learn the steps by which it reached its present marvellous efficiency. It is the help which it extends in this direction which makes the "Histoire de l'Instrumentation" of M. Lavoix, to which our author acknowledges indebtedness, valuable; but that work is accessible only to students who have knowledge of the French language.

Moreover, there are interesting signs of a return to some of the orchestral instruments which had fallen into disuse when the modern art of orchestration came into existence. It is not only a pious regard and reverence for Bach and Händel, especially the former, which is prompting conductors when performing their works to restore instruments to the orchestra which were considered hopelessly obsolete only a few decades ago, but also a growing appreciation of the fact that modern substitutes for them have largely failed of their mission. Two facts of large importance confront the careful observer of musical phenomena today: the

art of composition has reached that degree of technical perfection, or high virtuoso-
ship which in the history of all the arts introduces a decay of true creativeness.
We have, therefore, on the one hand excessive admiration for technique *per se*,
and on the other a growing reaction towards old ideals.   Of this latter fact I thought
I saw significant evidences in 1900 when as a member of the International Jury
at the Paris Exposition new specimens of a considerable number of archaic
musical instruments came into my hands for examination, among them a bass
flute for the return of which Mr. Frederick Corder expresses an ardent longing in
his admirable essay on Instrumentation in the new edition of Grove's " Dictionary
of Music and Musicians."   Since then, too, we have heard the harpsichord in our
concert-rooms, seen the oboe d'amore adopted by Richard Strauss, the alto flute by
Felix Weingartner, and observed the establishment in America as well as Europe of
orchestral and chamber concerts in which music of the seventeenth and earlier
centuries is played upon instruments for which it was written.   We shall in all
likelihood some day have to extend our treatises on orchestration to include some
of the instruments now considered obsolete, and be grateful for all references to
them in historical works like the present one.

Dr. Coerne, the author of this book, is an American composer born in Newark,
N. J., who has achieved the distinction of having an opera of his writing performed
in a European opera-house.   His " Zenobia " was brought forward in Bremen on
December 1, 1905.   It was the first instance of the performance in Europe of a
grand opera composed by a native of the United States.   The score of this opera
and the subject-matter of this book were accepted as a thesis by Harvard University
which conferred the degree of Ph. D. on the author in June, 1905.   It was the first
time that the university bestowed the degree for special work in music.

H. E. KREHBIEL.

New York, *April*, 1908.

THE EVOLUTION OF
MODERN ORCHESTRATION

PART I. — PRELIMINARIES.

CHAPTER I.

THE CRADLE OF INSTRUMENTAL MUSIC. (HISTORICAL REVIEW.)

I.

PRIMITIVE men were no doubt impelled to give utterance to their feelings by a desire for awakening sympathetic response in their fellow beings. Vocal manifestation of feeling developed into incipient melody, hence rudimentary scales. Gestures of dancing suggested rhythm. A fusion of both melody and rhythm led to contrast, and contrast implies symmetry of design. To emphasize rhythm combined with euphony, musical instruments were needed. Relics of certain species of these instruments are analogous to subsequent species of civilized nations.

Another source whence music can be traced is in the religious rites of the pagans.

Ancient history reveals diversified and wide-spread musical activity. The oldest representations of musicians are to be found on Egyptian monuments. Through contact with Oriental nations, Egypt possibly founded her system of intellectual music on extraneous principles. On the other hand, she probably influenced the music of the Hebrews, certainly that of the Greeks. Exemplification of Oriental instrumentalists is seen on Assyrian bas reliefs. One of these, in the possession of the British Museum, represents performers on a drum, a double-pipe, a primitive species of the dulcimer, and seven harps. The preponderance of stringed instruments suggests sensitive appreciation for modulated quality of tone. Constant reference to Hebrew music is, of course, to be found in the Scriptures. The classification of singers for temple worship during the reign of Solomon and of David, and the especial importance attached to song with instrumental accompaniment will at once recur to the mind.

Greece during her ascendency elevated music to a plane of importance only secondary to that of her sister art, poetry, whose handmaiden she became. Indeed, though both vocal and purely instrumental music were practised independently, prominence was bestowed upon the welding together of poetry and music as embodied in the Athenian tragedies. The Greeks possessed but a theoretical knowledge of harmony. Instrumental accompaniment probably duplicated the vocal melody in unison or octave, and may have added some simple harmonic intervals such as the fourth or fifth.

With the disorganization of Greece, music was transplanted to Rome, and, being no longer looked upon as an art, sank into degeneracy. Nevertheless, the fundamental principles governing the science of music as promulgated by the Greek theoreticians were rescued from oblivion by early Roman writers. And these principles, leavened by fragments of melancholy and contemplative strains of Hebraic melody, devolved from the early Christian neophytes, were destined to constitute the rock upon which all subsequent Western ecclesiastical music, even to the present day, has been built.

Review thus far tends to show that the objective of prehistoric and ante-Christian musical thought was primarily the emotional expression of human feeling. The growth of musical art was, moreover, amazingly dilatory as compared with that of the other fine arts.

II.

The next step to record is that of incipient harmonic effects, musical notation, the principles of design. And for centuries the art was now developed exclusively under the beneficent patronage of the Roman Church — persistently along vocal lines. For the Church adolescent discountenanced anything suggestive of pagan worship, or traceable to depraved Roman orgies. Consequently instrumental evolution lay quiescent. This was the age of dreary speculation, of highly ingenious and elaborately scientific artifice. Yet the results were but puerile. For even such rudiments of modern musical grammar as are readily mastered in our day by a mere child, were far beyond the perspective of the early scholastic monks, who arrived at a few tangible results only by the most circuitous methods. Nevertheless progress, though sluggish, is to be traced in logical sequence.

Beginning with the establishment of singing-schools by Pope Sylvester, and the Antiphons and Hymns of Ambrosius in the fourth century, it is but necessary to recall the documents of Boëtius and of Isadore in the sixth century, the reforms of the Gregories in the seventh and eighth, the *sequentiae* of Notker in the ninth. More specific were the crude attempts at harmony in the ninth and tenth centuries as typified by Hucbald's organum; Guido d'Arezzo's notation in the eleventh; finally the adoption of mensural writing asattributed to Franco de Cologne, thirteenth, and Johannes de Muris, fourteenth century.

Thus under the guardianship of the Church, and upon a basis of what has ever been known as the Gregorian Chant, a decade of centuries had been consumed in learning to perceive and to apply the fundamentals of melody and of harmony, to discover an adequate interpreter, notation, and an accurate though flexible regulator, rhythm.

III.

Meanwhile the Folk-song, already mentioned in its primogenial character, reasserted itself as the annotator of lyric poetry, through the activity of the troubadours from the eleventh to the fourteenth centuries. Of these, the name of Adam de la Hale is, of course, best known. Just as combined Oriental and Greek traditions formed the substructure of the early ecclesiastical modes, so a fusion of the Gregorian Chant and the Folk-song resulted in the establishment of a second, and in this case more distinctly accretive nucleus. This was of incalculable service, primarily to subsequent secular music as a whole, eventually to instrumentation as a side issue. For the soul of the Folk-song finds expression in the melodic. And this natural mode of expressing natural emotion, amplified not alone by the peoples of the Romance nations and of the Teutonic races, but also quite especially by such as were of Celtic origin, infused life, color, and variety into the stiff and formal church style then in vogue. Again, *la gaie science* required the art of accompaniment; consequently this long-neglected acquirement began to awake from its lethargy. So we find the troubadours accompanying their songs with a variety of instruments such as the crwth, the rebec, the lute, the harp, the viol.

The Folk-song has in the end proved to be the most enduring mode of expressing feeling, representing, as it does, the natural growth of a nation. Influenced by local temperament, climate, history, on every hand its distinctly indigenous characteristics have stood out in peaceful contrast to the eclectic polyphony of coexisting scientific attempts. And, as we know, although the Folk-song was eclipsed for a time by other forms, it was destined to play an important rôle. For its loftiest mission was realized not only in connection with the German Singspiel of the eighteenth century, but also through its application by the great classicists of the same period as contrasting theme for the Sonata-piece.

IV.

Continuing our chronological review, we trace the propagandism of Italian theoretical principles through France into the Netherlands. Here, during the fifteenth and early sixteenth centuries, polyphonic vocal music was reared on the exalted pedestals of noble Gothic architecture. From Dufay — the connecting link between the French and Flemish Schools — through Ockeghem, Josquin des Près, Willaert, to Lasso, the supremacy of musical composition was conceded to the Low Countries, although simultaneous musical activity in Italy was by no means retrogressional. As for the labors of such men as Dunstable in England and Isaak in Germany, the former was not in the direct line either of technical or of æsthetic evolution, whereas the latter was trained in Italy and wrote in the Flemish style.

The concentrated results of this era consisted of the consecutive development of the technicalities of counterpoint, growing regard for euphony and expressive verbal interpretation, finally, the ascendency of objective emotionalism. Lasso, embodying in his works the highest ideals of polyphonic writing, transplanted them into Germany. Simultaneously, Palestrina, the greatest purist of Italian vocal writing, was at the zenith of his glory. France had produced Goudimel and Claude le Jeune. The music of England was prominently connected with such names as Merbecke, Tallys, Byrd, Morley. The Reformation was exercising a powerful influence upon the art of music in the development of the Chorale.

And thus in the second half of the sixteenth century, this wonderful array of coexisting phases of choral art stood prepared for something greater. Pure choral music had been perfected. The era of instrumental music was at hand. For in spite of the rare æsthetic beauty, the intricate yet lucid voice-leading, the admirable handling of human voices *en masse* that signalize the works of Palestrina and Lasso, two essential elements, indispensable for further creative expansion, were lacking — rhythm and form. To attain these, new means and methods were necessary. Two possibilities presented themselves: solo singing, and instrumental music. Although both of these combined had been subjected to quasi-scientific experiment since time immemorial, the style of writing for them possessed as yet but little individuality. There was indeed much to be done before a permanent basis for modern tonality and modern instrumentation could be secured. The old modal system was still at the root of both sacred and secular music. Harmony was but the adventitious corollary of counterpoint. Only simple diatonic intervals were in use. Incipient harmony could not inspire men to think rhythmically. Pure church music was monotonous and vague. True, secular music in erudite form was influenced by the Folk-song, and showed some progress in rhythmic and simple harmonic effects. These in turn reacted favorably upon the sacred forms. Nevertheless, any attempt at developing motives as the synthetic germs of a composition was not to be thought of until the following century in connection with instrumental forms.

The pith of the conditions prevalent at the close of the era has been happily stated by Parry when he says: "It is as though the art was still in too nebulous a state for the essential elements to have crystallized into separate and definite entities."

(Summary on page 26.)

CHAPTER II.

THE DAWN OF INDEPENDENT INSTRUMENTATION.

I.

THE awakening interest for instrumental music received its incentive from two distinctive sources — the organ, and accompaniment to solo singing. As a natural corollary to centuries of ecclesiastical supremacy in musical composition, the organ had taken first rank among instruments and was, comparatively speaking, the most advanced, both as to mechanical construction and correlative technique of its performers. Hence the organ was destined to become a spontaneous yet covert connecting link between pure choral and pure instrumental music.

The initiative in this progression is due to the direct heirs of the Flemish School — the Venetian organists. Both Andreas Gabrieli (1510), pupil of Willaert, and Merulo (1533) had begun to add ornamental embellishments to their accompaniments, and although coherence was lacking, the step once taken led to extended experiments. Thus the treatment of further instruments employed in religious worship instinctively received more careful attention. Little by little composers awoke to the realization that the servile imitation of *a capella* polyphonic choral writing hitherto employed, was unsuited to the characteristics of differentiated individual instruments or combinations of instruments. True, the artistic value of these early attempts was but small, and would almost appear as an incompatibility, taking into consideration the fact that their authors were erudite in the subtleties of canonical device. Nevertheless, several tangible results are to be noted. As has been said, instrumental writing acquired a certain amount of individuality. Through search for balance of tone there was inaugurated a selective process as to the permanent value of each specific *genre* of an instrument. Instrumental adaptation of choral imitation led to contrast. Expansibility of musical thought was quickened. Thus Flemish influence was kept alive in that the incipient forms of their Venetian disciples, inherited by the subsequent violinist-composers, matured into the cyclic sonata.

Conspicuous are the organ works of Frescobaldi (1583–1644), the great predecessor of Bach. His labors also directly influenced subsequent clavier music as developed by Kuhnau in the following century. Credit is due to Giovanni Gabrieli (1587) for systematic attempts at orchestration and a distinctive style of writing for the violin. This latter, however, had to wait for the development

5

of technique, which, as we shall see, was concurrent with the progress of solo singing. And thus the year 1600, epoch-making in the rehabilitation of the drama, can be likewise referred to as a general starting point for independent instrumentation.

II.

The second and more powerful incentive that instrumentation received was from monody, in connection with which its function as accompaniment in simplified form was demonstrated. The *jons et origo* of declamatory recitative are, of course, to be traced to the attempted reforms of the Florentine camerata. Monody was the cradle of opera and oratorio, and became in turn the foster child of her progeny. Now these histrionic roots were diversified and far reaching.

In the first place, during the two centuries preceding the era under discussion, the miracle plays and representations of similar purport had had recourse to musical support, though of a nature disjointed and irrelevant.

Secondly, the efforts of the troubadours, minstrels, and minnesingers embodied solo-singing to instrumental accompaniment, and contained elements of the dramatic.

Lastly, a newly awakened veneration for everything pertaining to classic Greece revealed the nobility of her drama. This was the *causa vera* to be espoused! And the evolution of this renaissance, which reached a climax in 1600, must be traced to the history of the Medici.

Toward the close of the fifteenth century, when three generations of that family had brought Florence to the height of her glory, art had received a new impulse under the fostering care of Lorenzo. Moreover, science had acquired the doctrines of the Greek scholars fleeing from Turkish oppression. And the brief interim of asceticism under the sway of the Dominican monk, Savanarola, was followed by the restoration to power of the Medici. A non-clerical influence in all matters pertaining to art made itself felt, and the founding of the Platonic Academy by Cosimo the Great added fuel to the already existing predilection for the drama as exploited by the Ancients.

Hence the aim of the amateur poet and composer, Bardi, and his coterie was to produce a drama which should faithfully conform to the purity and idealism of classic models. And they sought diligently for a clue to original renditions of Attic tragedy, the Dorian choral lyrics, the song-lyrics of Anacreon, Sappho. But their conception thereof was based on a fallacy, so that were one to judge the fruits of their labors solely for their intrinsic value, the verdict would be disappointing.

On the other hand, the step they took was a gigantic one forward in its revolutionary after-results. For the quintessence of recitative and lyrical solo was contained in Galilei's and Caccini's declamatory recitatives with accompaniment of lute or viol; in Peri's and Caccini's "Dafne" and "Euridice" — the first genuine music dramas in the monodic style; in Cavalieri's allegory or incipient oratorio "L'Anima e Corpo." All these attempts were infinitely more expressive and effective than the sombre selections with which A. Gabrieli and Merulo had been wont to enliven festive secular occasions. Bardi and Corsi, in the face of conservatism and skepticism, had sought to reinstate the principles founded upon the Greek Dithyramb. Inspired by the enthusiasm of these two amateurs, the professionals, Peri and Cavalieri, succeeded simultaneously in discovering two rational operatic designs, capable of sequent dramatic treatment.

Finally, the very nature of the monodic principle was inseparable from instrumental accompaniment, and the primary causes that led to monody, namely, expression and dramatic effect, would in themselves insist upon a keener appreciation for instrumental combination as to selection, distribution of parts, dynamics, color-scheme. This is borne out to a limited extent in the later works of both Peri and Cavalieri, whose instrumentation, though crude, paved the way for their greater contemporary and eventual successor, Monteverde. Even though the bulk of the figured bass accompaniment was assigned to the harpsichord, "Euridice" called into requisition one viol, three flutes, and a triplet of instruments of the lute variety. Cavalieri made use of practically the same combination, and even recommended that a violin should duplicate the vocal melody throughout.

In contradistinction to these essays at dramatic scoring should be mentioned the instrumentation of Striggio (1535), whose *intermezzi* or comedies interspersed with music were written in the madrigal style. Nor should the *concertante* sacred song of Viadana (1564) or the instrumental effects of Gibbons (1583) be overlooked. But Striggio, some thirty odd years before "Euridice" was produced, had not only forestalled but surpassed his immediate successors by the employment of an orchestra of which more than half were stringed instruments; again, seven of these were played with a bow. So that, considering the primitive methods then in use, the constitution of Striggio's orchestra was unique. It consisted of six lutes, seven viols, two gravicembali, six flutes, eight cornetti and tromboni, all of variated types and sizes.

The above enumeration brings to mind the pre-existence of a rather heterogeneous assortment of now partially obsolete instruments with which we are more or less familiar. Therefore, before proceeding from the subject of instrumentation to that of orchestration proper as inaugurated by Monteverde, a review of the structural and mechanical evolution of instruments themselves would seem in place.

(Summary on page 26.)

CHAPTER III.

EVOLUTION OF MUSICAL INSTRUMENTS.

THE first serious attention bestowed upon the mechanism of instruments and the selection of those whose qualities should justify permanent retention occurred during the sixteenth century, and, as we have seen, the causes that led up to this were extraneous. In glancing over the names and descriptions of the many varieties of instruments already in existence before this development began, the mind becomes easily confused. Many species of stringed instruments such as lutes, viols, clavichords, harpsichords, not to mention brass instruments, the schalmei, cromornes, abounded on every hand; but the deeper the student of instrumental evolution delves into comparative research, the more he finds authorities at variance. However, the lineage of the three great representatives of stringed instruments as are in use to-day — instruments played with a bow, the harp, the pianoforte, may fairly be traced simultaneously.

I.

Prehistoric origin of stringed instruments, in spite of extant relics, is a matter of conjecture. History, on the other hand, suggests various sources in various ages. Of greatest recorded antiquity are the Egyptian lute and harp, which were struck with a plectrum or plucked by the fingers. These migrated through Arabia into Spain, thence to Southern Italy, and became diffused over all Europe. The Greek lyra or kithara, having originally but four strings, was also played with a plectrum, and became the heirloom of the Romans. But to discover the origin of instruments played with a bow is a more difficult matter. A number of theories are plausible. Like all other instruments they were probably invented simultaneously by many isolated barbaric races. The bow and arrow were undoubtedly suggestive, and it is to be presumed that primitive types of the lyre family whose strings were originally plucked, were fitted to uncouth sounding-boards and played upon with a bow. The Hindoos possessed such instruments, and it is possible that their admission into Europe was concurrent with that of the lute and harp. In defence of this supposition, one might point to the dance of the women attending the Jongleurs. Now the dance is no uncertain revealer of racial characteristics. But not only the dance itself, but also certain features of the accompaniment, as well as the types of instruments peculiar to the Jongleurs

8

bear the impress of Orientalism. As far as is known, neither the Greeks nor the Romans possessed instruments played with a bow.

From the Middle Ages on, the study of instrumental evolution is, of course, based upon authentic history. The most direct line of descent for bowed-instruments is probably from either the Celtic crwth or the Oriental rebab to the vielle or viola of the Middle Ages (Spanish vihuela, Latin fidula), of which the last representative was the gamba; and the viola da gamba was the predecessor of the violoncello. The early viols were of manifold types, there being, for instance, as many as seven viole da braccia and six viole da gambe. The violin owes its existence to a gradual metamorphosic development of the early tenor viola, during the latter part of the fifteenth and early sixteenth centuries. Skill in the manufacture of these instruments was of an advanced order in the Netherlands prior to the advent of the great Italian violin makers, whose efforts were eventually crowned by the immutable sovereignty of the Cremonese creations at the commencement of the eighteenth century. The introduction of the contrabasso was likewise of slow growth. For as late as the seventeenth and eighteenth centuries there still existed bass instruments of the lute family, such as the double-necked theorbo and the largest bass lute, the chitarrone, which were struck with a plectrum. But growing appreciation for the wonderful possibilities concealed in the infant violin proper, of technique, tone, color, delicacy, and variety of shading, reacted upon the secondary bowed-instruments, and they in turn were rapidly perfected. Hence, by a judicious selection of the superior and a suppression of the inferior types of viols were the violas and violoncellos evolved; and the theorbo and chitarrone were permanently supplanted by the double-bass, constructed on the same general principles as the violin.

Although the ideal balance of tone and expressive powers as embodied in the modern string orchestra justifies the perspicuity of this selective process in every way, it would seem to be a matter for regret that a certain species of viols, the viola d'amore, should have become practically obsolete. Its seven strings were supplemented by seven concealed under strings, designed to vibrate sympathetically. One might say that this principle has been incorporated in the modern grand pianoforte by means of the " una corda " pedal. But since Meyerbeer resuscitated the viola d'amore in " Les Huguenots " in 1836, the only living composer who has assigned to it a conspicuous rôle is, to the present writer's knowledge, Mr. C. M. Loeffler in his symphonic poem " La Mort de Tintagiles," after Maeterlinck, indeed the original score contained parts for *two* solo viole d'amore though one part has since been rewritten for a violin.

II.

The evolution of the harp is obvious, whereas that of the pianoforte is more complex. The prototype of the modern pianoforte in its embryonic state traces its ancestry to all the various types of stringed instruments taken collectively. Specifically, the primitive acoustic monochord of Pythagoras might be looked upon as a plausible starting point. Add to this a keyboard and its attendant devices as applied to church organs in the earlier centuries of the Christian era, and the prototype is complete. Be that as it may, there was developed during the fourteenth and fifteenth centuries a family of widely known instruments embodying advanced qualities of mechanism, styled " Hackbrett," synonym for cembalo, tympanon, although it is best known as the dulcimer. According to Dr. Riemann, it originated apparently in Germany, since for a time it was called in Italy by the name of Salterio tedesco. The instrument consisted of a flat trapezium-shaped sounding-board on which steel strings were set, and was played upon by two hammers held one in each hand of the performer. In improved form, it is still extant in the hands of the gypsies. But already at the beginning of the sixteenth century was the clavichord established as its successor. The clavichord, according to Hipkins, was derived from the polychord with four strings, which in turn was developed from the monochord " to facilitate the melodic division of the Gregorian tones." Directly appeared still another instrument styled clavicembalo or harpsichord, of which the psaltery, a triangular harp, was undoubtedly the ancestor. The spinet and virginal differed from the harpsichord only as to shape; and in England, virginal was the general term for spinet and harpsichord. The cardinal point of dissimilarity between the mechanical construction of the clavichord and the harpsichord was that the strings of the former were caused to sound by means of metal tangents, which struck against the strings and then pressed them up, whereas the strings of the latter were plucked by hard quills set in wooden jacks. But of far greater importance was the difference of tone-quality. The tone of the clavichord was delicate, subdued, — incapable of energetic utterance, but so expressive that it was a favorite with great musicians; that of the harpsichord was crisp, short, uniform. A radical readjustment of mechanism was found necessary in order to combine in one instrument euphony and variation of dynamic force. Therefore in the beginning of the eighteenth century hammer-action was invented, and the pianoforte, derived from the dulcimer, came into existence. Despite this fact, both the clavichord and the harpsichord continued to hold their own beyond the boundaries of that century. And so we see that the perfected modern pianoforte, being but the outcome of a variety of instruments already in existence three hundred years ago, was unable to supersede them until the nineteenth century.

Turning our attention again to instruments belonging to the orchestra proper, we find an inexhaustible subject in the evolution of the two other great families, the wood and the brass. Most of the above-advanced hypotheses in respect to origin and migration of strings are equally pertinent to the wind. But the inference that the genesis of these latter instruments antedates that of the lyre and lute is surely justified in that conch shells and the horns of animals must have offered the most natural means for producing artificial musical tones. Again, the construction of stringed instruments suggests a more advanced stage of intellectuality. Finally, there have been preserved to us from antiquity a far more numerous and varied array of comparatively natural instruments such as the Egyptian mem and sebi, — respectively vertical and horizontal flutes, of which the former was more common and still exists in the guise of the modern Arab flute. One of the most simple species of horn was the " Schofar " or ram's-horn, used in the temple worship of the Hebrews. The Assyrians as well as the Egyptians possessed trumpets, probably of brass. The war trumpets of the Romans were of bronze. The deep-toned trumpet or tuba was straight; the high-toned lituus was bent; and the buccina, large trumpet or trombone, was curved.

III.

The principle of both single and double reeds was understood by the Greeks. As a result of the researches of Professor A. A. Howard, an accurate description of their representative instruments, the auloi, Latin tibiae, is to be found in "Harvard Studies in Classical Philology," Vol. 4. His article presents strong arguments in favor of the belief that instrumental polyphony was actually practised by the Greeks. Performers upon the auloi played almost invariably upon two pipes at once. The instruments were supplied with finger-holes, were capable of producing both the diatonic and chromatic scales, and may be divided into three classes corresponding, in a general way, to the three types of wood-winds as are in use to-day. All of them had a tube of cylindrical bore, but most of them were supplied with a double mouthpiece like the modern oboe, so that these species of the auloi can be regarded as the prototype of the preferred double-reeds that prevailed during the Middle Ages when they went under the name of schalmei. This nomenclature is confusing; in explanation it should be said that not until after the original schalmei had developed into the pommer, thence to the oboe, was the single-reeded predecessor of the clarinet known by this name. Colloquialism refers to the schalmei in its later application.

Another double-reed that came into temporary existence during the Middle Ages was the variety of cromornes. They differed from the schalmei principally as to form — Krummhorn.

The successors of the original schalmei are described in detail by Praetorius, who wrote in the first decade of the seventeenth century. Of the six varieties of pommer mentioned by him, the treble pommer became transformed into the hautbois (high wood); the alto pommer into the cor Anglais (cor anglè, bent horn), — known during the seventeenth and eighteenth centuries as the oboe da caccia; and out of the bass pommer, likewise styled bombarde, emanated the fagotto (bundle of fagots). As a commentary to the above enumeration one should take note of a quite remarkable tendency which was, indeed, already in vogue during the Hellenic age. Namely, that from each parent instrument whether string, wood, or brass, there germinated a complete family representing the four ranges of the human voice. And again from these the process of tribal expansion was carried yet further. Moreover it must be remembered that before the Middle Ages, the art of combining human voices in polyphony was but in a nascent state, and probably existed in classic Greece not at all. Therefore families of instrumental species cannot have been constructed for the purpose of obtaining homogeneous *harmonic* effects. An extensive *range* of con-natural tone-color was then the objective. It will be found that this tendency was uniform throughout the history of instrumental evolution. Of course when we reach the sixteenth century, we find that the advantage of distributing the components of harmony among the members of assimilated instruments began to be appreciated. It is possibly due to this natural evolution that innovators in orchestration at first accustomed themselves to the use of pure tone-color rather than of mixed tints. Thus in the sixteenth century, the flûte à bec, predecessor of the modern flute, was employed in groups of four. Praetorius makes mention of no less than eight different kinds as prevalent in his day. Our chief representative of the single reed, the clarinet, which was not invented until the end of the seventeenth century, owes its origin to a primitive form of instrument with clarinet mouthpiece: — the mediæval chalemiax or chalumeau, whence the phonetic rendition, schalmei. The now obsolete basset-horn belongs properly to this genealogy. It was frequently used during the time of its development by the composers of the latter eighteenth and early nineteenth centuries. From it were devolved the short-lived alto and tenor clarinets, and the better qualities of all three are now embodied in the subsequently perfected bass-clarinet. Mention is also due to the saxophone, invented by Sax in 1840. It should be classed under the heading of wood instruments rather than of brass, since its tone-quality partakes somewhat of the nature of the clarinet. It has a single-reed mouthpiece, and the fingering is akin to that of the clarinet; but the over-blowing produces the octave as in the flute and oboe, whereas in the clarinet the twelfth is produced. Sax made seven different sized saxophones, of which four are commonly in use, and that particularly in French and American military bands.

IV.

The history of brass instruments is extensive; at the same time their development is easy to trace. But it must be remembered that only those instruments possess pedigree from which upper harmonics are produced, *i. e.* those constructed with long tube and narrow bore. Even this statement must be qualified in that the French horn is of modern extraction. Only trumpets and trombones, therefore, are directly descended from the early Roman instruments with cup-shaped mouthpieces, such as the lituus and buccina. And in the Middle Ages there existed side by side two such families, — the Zinken, and the trombe and tromboni. The Zink or cornetto had a wooden tube pierced by sounding holes, and was constructed in different sizes. The larger species was, at the close of the sixteenth century, transformed into the Serpent, which had a bell of brass. This instrument is still in use in some Italian military bands. The Zinken were extant in the hands of the "town musicians" even into the eighteenth century. Akin to them are the simple Alpine Horn and the Lur of Norway.

In the Middle Ages the trumpet was generally made of brass, and the tube was at first unbent. The principle of sliding tubes for the purpose of procuring additional tones to the natural ones of an instrument was of ancient origin. It was applied to trumpets as well as to trombones, a practice still in force in England. The obvious advantage of this device was that a complete chromatic scale could be obtained, impossible for all other brass instruments at a time when crooks and valves were unknown. The earlier name for the trombone, *i. e.* bass trumpet, was sackbut, but the original appellation, buccina, has been perpetuated in the German Bosaun, now Posaune.

In the sixteenth century, the tromba, synonym for clarino, trummet, together with the three *genres* of trombones as used by the subsequent great classicists, was already perfected as a sliding-tube instrument. Or one might include both instruments under one heading by speaking of the tromba as a treble trombone. However, in order to obtain more efficient high brass instruments, constant experiments were made. The earlier improvements had obviated the clumsy length of brass instruments by bending and rebending their tubes. Then followed the application to the brass of the finger-hole system of the wooden Zinken. Finally, in the eighteenth century, the introduction of removable crooks improved the trombe as far as quality of tone is concerned. But the highest point of evolution was arrived at early in the nineteenth century, when the perfection of the chromatic valve principle revolutionized not only the mechanism but also the manner of writing for trumpets as well as for horns and bugles.

As has been intimated above, the history of the French horn is short. There is but a slight analogy between it and the *cor de chasse* of the Middle Ages, an instrument that possessed but few tones.   The genuine French horn made its appearance in the first half of the seventeenth century, and the stages of its development may be regarded as centennial.   In the eighteenth century was added the crook principle, in the nineteenth, the valve system.   These improvements were attendant upon those made upon trumpets.   Like the trumpet, the "natural" horn was conducive to purity of tone, the chromatic horn to greater practicability without material loss of purity.

The family of bugles belong more properly to the subject of military bands, but a word is due to their evolution on account of the orchestral importance of one of their members — the bass tuba.   The bugle-horn, also known as the sax-horn, is constructed on acoustic principles diametrically opposed to those of the trombe family in that the bore is wider and the tube shorter, whereby the principle of obtaining harmonics is reversed.

The date of Beethoven's birth signalized the first application of key mechanism to wood instruments.   Simultaneously, experiments were made upon the now obsolete brass Zinken.   The new instrument was called *bugle à clefs,* and was the forerunner of a group of different sized opheicleides, of which the lowest supplanted the sixteenth century Serpent.   Subsequently the opheicleide itself was superseded by the bass tuba, a more noble instrument of the same general family.

V.

The evolution of instruments of percussion requires but brief mention.   Sound-producing apparatus devoid of definite pitch belongs to the initial attempts of primitive men to assist vocal expression of emotional feeling, to accompany religious orgies, or to encourage their warriors on the march.   The modern orchestra includes the best of these primitive species, transformed into perfected types of genuine artistic value, and has also drawn into requisition various instruments originating in countries that are far apart.   Most commonly used are the bass-drum, the cymbals, and the triangle.   The family of drums further includes the long side-drum and the small military drum.   With the cymbals and triangle belong the tam-tam or Chinese gong, the Oriental and Spanish tambourine, the Spanish and Neapolitan castanets, and the Turkish crescent or bell-rattle.   The use of all such instruments is, of course, the exception rather than the rule.   Their mission is primarily to suggest "local" coloring or to emphasize rhythm for dancing.

Instruments of percussion possessing definite and variable pitch are represented primarily by the kettle-drums, which are constant and indispensable members of the orchestra.   The early Hackbrett or dulcimer might also be classed under this heading, which further includes the various sets of bells, such as the carillon or Glockenspiel of Chinese origin, together with the Stahlspiel or Lyra, and the Xylophone.

This sketch demonstrates the fact that the early evolution of instruments went hand in hand with that of music in general and is subject to identical hypotheses. With the dawn of secular music, the development of instrumental construction and mechanism is focused upon the sixteenth century, with emphasis upon the anterior practice of employing complete homogeneous groups.

In order to cover the entire ground, this survey of the development of musical instruments has necessarily transgressed the bounds of the sixteenth century perspective. And since we are about to recontinue a critical review of the orchestra as inherited by Monteverde, it will be well to remember that in his day the only orchestral instruments in the modern sense of the word were violins and viols, harps, flutes, pommers, cornetti, trumpets, trombones. In combination with these, lutes, guitars, organs, the clavichord and the harpsichord were still employed.

(Summary on page 26.)

CHAPTER IV.

BEGINNINGS OF ORCHESTRATION.

I.

(*) CLAUDIO MONTEVERDE (1567–1643) is justly styled the founder of the modern orchestra; but although modern orchestral organization owes its substratum of solidity and balance of tone to him, only indirectly was he led to attain this end, for his paramount objective was artistic expression. Naturally, the employment of artistically grouped instruments appealed to him as the most flexible conveyance for expressive thought. Again, Monteverde was instinctively a dramatic writer, so that as a matter of course the histrionic efforts of the Florentine experimentalists attracted him. Finally, when Monteverde entered upon his dramatic career after having already become celebrated as a writer of madrigals and of other vocal forms, pure choral music as perfected by Palestrina and Lasso was at its zenith, and instrumentation in its elementary state was inseparable from the drama, — it being understood that the early attempts at oratorio in the *stilo rappresentativo* were built on the same general principles as the early operas, without differentiation in musical or instrumental treatment. Nor were the incipient efforts at orchestral accompaniment to religious worship of sufficient importance to be taken into consideration. Therefore, *Monteverde's* contribution to the chain of æsthetic and practical musical development consists of his successful search after expressive and dramatic effects and his reconstruction of the orchestra. He also broke away from the Church Modes, employed a system of harmony nearer akin to our own, made free use of the Chord of the Dominant Seventh, and introduced bolder harmonies and unprepared dissonances. These harmonic innovations were already noticeable in his earlier vocal compositions.

As we have seen, Peri contributed much to his successors from a dramatic standpoint, but as for expression, the Florentine *pseudo* music dramas consisted of a monotonous and long-spun succession of primitive and dreary *recitativi* with but little support other than a *basso continuo* and meagre chords, whereas Monteverde, absorbed in the discovery of means by which he might emphasize expression, developed true creative talent in a diversity of ways. For although his chord successions were still crude and his perspective for design but slightly evolved, his realization of the importance of stage effects led him to intensify the

(*) See Appendix of Musical Illustrations, Examples 1 to 5.

dramatic action, to vary the tone-color, to extend the functions of the accompaniment to the voice, and to relieve the monotony of constant *recitativo* by a more liberal and artistic use of the *arioso*.

These innovations were destined to wield far-reaching influence. Though admiration for the earlier pure choral style was soon rekindled in Italy, it was not long before the two styles, the old and the new, were combined, as embodied in the oratorios of Carissimi; and Schütz, who had been taught by Giovanni Gabrieli of Venice, transplanted these Italian methods into Germany. But the direct line of development from Monteverde's dramatic theories is to be traced through Cavalli, and from him through Lulli, into France, thenceforth the permanent home for histrionic displays; for Italy turned to a more careful consideration of melodic beauty and taste for design, whereas the disciples of Schütz, though cultivating the new principles especially in oratorio, still retained their German characteristics.

Turning to Monteverde's labors in the field of instrumentation, we find, in place of the very rudimentary and heterogeneous combinations heretofore employed, a well-defined and fairly logical assortment of instruments, the nuclei of which were strings, and it is the establishment of this nucleus that is epoch making. True, his first dramatic attempt, "Orfeo," was scored for organs, harpsichords, lutes, harps, guitars, trombones, trumpets, flutes, and various members of the viol family, including so-called little French violins, [a] constituting an orchestra of thirty-six men, of whom nearly one third were performers upon brass instruments. On the other hand, it is necessary to take several contingencies into consideration. In the first place, this orchestra, like Cavalieri's, was concealed behind the scenes, instructive in its suggestion for the modern sunken orchestra at Bayreuth. Again, it has been supposed that the loud-voiced trumpets were muted, a device sometimes employed for special effects in modern scoring. (As to this supposition, however, the present writer is of the opinion that the instruments actually employed were the *cornetti muti* or soft-speaking trumpets of wood, and that in translation, the word "muted" has been erroneously applied.) Finally, although Monteverde was not, like Peri and Cavalieri, content to depend entirely upon the performers to supply the necessary chords and embellishments, nevertheless in the art of instrumentation he was but a pioneer, and most of his accompaniments were light and of a primitive nature. The very simplicity of his rudimentary method of scoring is proof that neither he nor his contemporaries could have realized the resonant powers of so formidable an aggregation of brass when properly handled; and just this non-realization was propitious for the early development of the orchestra, in that, by negative means, noisy trivialities were excluded from the scores of the early masters. But in antithesis to this undue preponder-

[a] Ex. 2.

ance of metallic tone-quality, the employment of no less than seventeen instruments played with a bow was an immense stride forward, especially when we consider the fact that within the same decade lutes and the harpsichord had constituted the body of embryo orchestras.

At the close of the sixteenth century there were still many varieties of the viol family, but the value of the erroneously styled "little French violin" is said to have been first appreciated by Monteverde, who introduced it into his orchestra where its inestimable value was at once recognized. Profiting by this felicitous innovation, he continued to emphasize the importance of the string band, enlarged it, and, by a judicious suppression of the weaker members of the viol family, established a body of strings that conforms, at least approximately, to the violins, violas, 'cellos, and basses of the present day.

Having once for all instituted a rational and permanent foundation for obtaining solidity of tone combined with facility of execution, it was a matter of course that the brass should ultimately appear in more logical proportion to the strings. The progress of the wood-wind was of slower growth, largely due to technical imperfections and mechanical difficulties of performance. But, considering the means at his disposal, a commendable appreciation for contrasted groups of instruments is embodied in the pages of his later works, — indeed, already in "Orfeo" can be traced this tendency to enhance the dramatic situation by means of judicious tone-coloring. Oft-quoted illustrations are the accompaniment of Pluto's songs by four trombones, the lament of Orpheus by bass viols, the chorus of spirits by *organi di legno*. And in his riper works, intelligent instrumentation and characteristic orchestration progress simultaneously. The introduction of the *tremolo*, *pizzicato*, and other dramatic and expressive devices is attributed to him. He showed some system of scoring, which included more specific instructions for the performers than had hitherto been the custom. [b] And the fact that he distinguished between vocal and instrumental effects is of historic value in that it paved the way for the advent of purely orchestral composition. [1]

(b) Ex. 1.

[1] Monteverde's admitted position at the dawn of orchestration constitutes so vast a point of departure in scientific method, that the unprejudiced writer of to-day must, toward Monteverde rather than toward anyone else, weigh and sift opinions as to his intention, however much these opinions combat each other. The statements of the present writer that Monteverde was the first to suggest instrumental characterization in his music — the same being evidenced in the scores that have come down to us — are supported by the majority of investigators. There are, however, others who have followed the same trail and whose conclusions are as worthy of future credence. These declare that it is only a fantastic conceit, which grew out of the circumstance that in the list of characters and instruments in the prefatory matter of the score of Monteverde's "Orfeo," there is a chance association like Pluto's name standing opposite the trombones, etc., which, falsely reasoned, has placed Monteverde in an epoch-making niche where he should not be.

II.

It is remarkable that the direct successors of Monteverde should have been more or less blind to the latent powers of this newly vitalized organism, — this prototype of the modern orchestra. Even Carissimi (1604) cannot be included among the progressive writers for the orchestra, indeed, his art of scoring stands lower than Monteverde's. Of course, in the development of oratorio, his dramatic influence was of great importance. He caused the monodic style to advance rapidly, by infusing into *recitativo* and the *aria* more spontaneity, into instrumental accompaniment greater interest. Though inferior to Monteverde in originality, Carissimi evinced a keener appreciation for plastic and tonal effects. His eminent pupil, Cesti (1620), is likewise to be remembered less for his instrumentation than for his further development of *recitativo* and the *da capo aria* in connection with the operatic stage.

On the other hand, Cavalli (1600), apart from the fortuitous influence his sojourn at the court of Louis XIV had upon Lulli, inherited a more decided talent for orchestration from Monteverde, whose pupil he was. His interesting experiments in writing accompaniments for two violins and a bass established a precedent that survived the test of many years. Like Monteverde, his instincts were strongly dramatic, but perhaps his connection with St. Mark's Church modified his style of writing for the orchestra. For more especially his *a capella* sacred works are imbued with considerable warmth of expression, and show sentient regard for melody, rhythm, and form. And thus, even as Carissimi displayed but little feeling for purely instrumental effects, though holding a unique position as a composer of oratorio, so Cavalli must be regarded as primarily a dramatic writer, — indeed, among the immediate successors of Monteverde, he alone succeeded in substantially furthering dramatic development in Italy, that is to say, the development of dramatic ideals as had been attempted by the Florentine neophytes of Greek tragedy. For as Langhans expresses it: "After him Italian opera gradually diverges from the path originally taken, and sacrifices the antique simplicity aimed at by its founders to the ever increasing demand for sensuous charm. The alliance of poetry and music, dissolved in the Middle Ages and renewed but a few decades before, is again broken off, and the equilibrium that had just been acquired is sacrificed anew to the claims of music."

III.

But while the nature of Italian music after Cavalli's time was subject to variable influences, France took up the cause of drama with enthusiasm, and in this field LULLI (1633–1687) looms up as the sole dictator of his age. Favored by the extravagant demands for display and spectacular effects prevalent at the court of Louis XIV, Lulli proceeded to develop dance forms as had been inaugurated by his predecessor, Cambert, whose position he usurped. The *ballet de cour*, already in vogue in France, consisted of dances, dialogues set to music, combined with dramatic episodes. Out of this native form of entertainment, modern French opera was destined to germinate. Having found this a suitable prototype as a basis for his operas, Lulli proceeded to imbue it with exotic principles. Like Monteverde, he discarded the ecclesiastical modes. Again, he adhered strictly to the requirements of his text, and developed declamatory recitative as promulgated by Cavalli. And to the reactive influence of the Italian monodic theorem upon French literature during this brilliant period of Corneille, Molière, Racine, does France owe the excellence of her declamation.

But, considering the versatility of the man, once again a disappointing analogy to the peculiarly prominent deficiency of Carissimi and Cavalli confronts us. For Lulli's orchestration was, like that of Meyerbeer two hundred years later, sensational rather than of enduring worth. By no means is Lulli's universal genius as organizer, composer and orchestrator to be undervalued, nor is the importance of his influence upon subsequent French music to be lost sight of. But it is evident that the direct evolution of really stable instrumentation was benefited, during this period, more by the crowning achievements of Scarlatti, and by the labors of the secondary Italian composers, who devoted themselves more especially to purely instrumental music, and thereby sowed the seed for subsequent purely orchestral music in Germany. It is true that credit is due to Lulli for having introduced into his orchestra a large variety of instruments, which he used with considerable skill, although all of them were not suitable for permanent retention; but it would appear to the present writer that Lavoix, in his "Histoire de L'Instrumentation," page 216, is, perhaps, somewhat extravagant in his eulogy of Lulli's orchestration, especially since he previously makes but passing reference to that of Scarlatti. Again, similar use of solo effects and of contrasted groups of instruments as cited by Lavoix is also to be found in the scores of Lulli's predecessors and contemporaries in Italy. Indeed one might say that in general the efforts of these early composers to obtain genuinely characteristic tone-color are apt to be overestimated, for, as Lavoix himself subsequently acknowledges in regard to Lulli: — "Il faut l'avouer, c'était encore au violon qu'il avait confié ses scènes symphoniques les plus délicates et les plus expressives." Finally, even though strings formed the basis of his orchestra, augmented by wind instruments both wood and brass, the irrepressible harpsichord, solicitous for the welfare of her flock, and fearful lest emancipation from her protectorate should result in chaos, still closely followed the harmonic delineations of the legitimate orchestral instruments, supporting them, as it were, in concentual leading-strings! Had Lulli and his contemporaries understood the art of judiciously distributing the notes of a chord throughout the orchestra, not to mention the proper choice in number and species of instrument, this custom would have soon fallen into disuse; and, as we know, not until this did take place one hundred years later, was it possible to obtain ideal solidity, balance of tone, contrast, and variety. By a coincidence, the year of Beethoven's birth sounded the death-knell of the orchestral harpsichord, for in the opera "Mitridate," written in that year, Mozart was the last of the great composers to employ it as a regular component of the orchestra.

To Lulli, therefore, orchestration was but a secondary issue, in spite of the importance he attached to it. Form, on the other hand, was permanently benefited by his labors, whereas, in musical history, he occupies the second of the four pedestals sustaining the arch that spans the realm of pure music drama, and retires into the mythical haze of Hellenic tragedy.

IV.

As intimated above, further survey of the field of instrumentation in Italy discovers commendable activity, such as was displayed by Legrenzi; by Steffani and Clari; by the violinists Torelli, Vivaldi, and especially Corelli; finally, by the greatest musician both active and creative of the seventeenth century, Scarlatti.

The labors of Legrenzi (1625) are worthy of consideration on account of his logical development of the constituency of the orchestra. As Maestro at San Marco, Venice, he increased the number of instrumentalists at that church to over thirty. It is noteworthy that he employed almost exclusively violins and viols, supported in the bass by four theorbos (*i. e.* bass instruments of the lute family). The wood-wind was represented by a solitary bassoon, whereas two cornets and three trombones replaced Monteverde's earlier assortment of brass. And thus, already in the seventeenth century was found a man whose perspicuity in the choice of a modest band of loud-voiced instruments commended itself for some of the mightiest climaxes of Beethoven's immortal works.

The significance of chamber music as fostered by Steffani (1655) and Clari (1669) is, of course, well known in musical history. And the wonderful impetus given to the art of violin-making, by stimulating a development of executive technique, brought forth fruit that culminated in the regency of a number of famous violinist-composers. Among these, Torelli (died 1708), for the creation of the *concerto grosso*, Vivaldi (died 1743), for the development of harmonic design and figuration characteristic of his instrument, and Corelli (1653–1713), for combining principles of harmony with contrapuntal devices, rendered invaluable service to the nascent architecture of modern string writing. For by exploring the possibilities of the violin, by establishing its superiority as a solo instrument, by demonstrating not only its potentiality but also its limitations in relation to other instruments, there arose, in consequence, a more delicate perception as to the necessary constitution of an evenly balanced string band. This acquirement was accompanied by improved methods of writing for the strings.

No composer of his time combined these requirements more successfully than Corelli, for the types of composition which occupied his attention were the precursors of the classic sonata, and his contributions thereto mark the starting point of genuinely artistic instrumental music. Corelli's relation to chamber music and the concerto is as that of Monteverde to the orchestra. Neither of them was a radical reformer; they both proceeded along the more conservative lines of evolution, selection, elaboration. The scaffolding of their respective spheres of activity had already been reared by that countless throng of forgotten and unappreciated workers, whose mission it is to make smooth the path for the greater lights, that appropriate and mould into collectaneous form the puny though individual originality of the lesser. But whereas nothing more than a pious interest in an historic heirloom has preserved Monteverde's efforts from falling into oblivion, those of Corelli have been perpetuated by reason of their intrinsic merit.

V.

The highest development of productive musical art during the seventeenth century culminated in[*] SCARLATTI (1659–1725). And orchestration was aided by him to no small degree. Of course, his name is primarily coupled with the Neapolitan operatic principles, — principles that ultimately led to baneful results, in spite of having enriched the world with sensuous and beautiful melody. Only a cursory review of Scarlatti's expansive activity is permissible as being mostly irrelevant to our subject. Reared in the characteristic atmosphere of Carissimi's cantatas and oratorios, impelled by poetic instinct and fondness for melodic design, he enlarged upon the *da capo aria*, the *recitativo accompagnato*, and in general paid careful attention to the external structure of the separate numbers in his operas. Above all, Scarlatti became the knight errant though eventually the thrall of *il bel canto*.[a] Now highly developed vocal phraseology demands judicious accompaniment, and good orchestral accompaniment requires a nice adjustment of dynamic force combined with skill in writing. It was fortunate, therefore, that Scarlatti possessed both these attributes; and through the channels of this important

[*] See Appendix of Musical Illustrations, Examples 6 to 9.

[a] Ex. 7.

branch of orchestration, independent orchestration received permanent form. Let us see how this metamorphosis took place.

Retrospection shows us that Peri, initiating a rudimentary dramatic style in place of Flemish polyphony, contributed but slightly to the advancement of instrumental accompaniment. He and his collaborators wrote little more than a figured bass for the harpsichord, and at performance they evoked the aid of the adventitious efforts of a motley aggregation of instrumentalists. The printed scores of Schütz are equally primitive. In France, the lyrical stage piece of Perrin and Cambert, "La Pastorale" (produced in 1659 — the year of Scarlatti's birth) showed some slight improvement in the art of scoring; but it has been said that even Lulli composed his operas at the spinet, and at times delegated various details of instrumentation to his secretary. Monteverde established a nucleus of strings. Cavalli developed three-part writing for two violins and a bass. Legrenzi regulated the "distribution" of instruments. Corelli and his contemporaries advanced technique of performance and cultivated instrumentation in the miniature.

The task allotted to Scarlatti was, therefore, not difficult. He accepted the already established supremacy of strings, but soon realized that three-part writing did not produce even balance of tone. Consequently, he adopted a manner of writing which comprised a division of the violins into firsts and seconds. He added, moreover, an individual part for the violas, and thereby established a canon of phonetics that has been accepted by all erudite composers since his time. It is true that these characteristics of orchestration cannot be said to have originated with him, but his persistent use thereof established a precedent of permanent value. In three-part writing, not only the violoncellos and basses progressed simultaneously in unison or octaves, but also the viola, if present, reënforced the bass in slavish delineation. It is obvious that this practice was the result either of sophism or of indifference and ignorance. And the fact that as late as the eighteenth century no less a composer than Haydn and even Mozart should have continued to frequently employ three-part writing for the strings is certainly a paradox, and tends to prove how circuitous the process of evolution is. However, Haydn and Mozart had such perfect command of florid counterpoint, that no matter what the distribution of string parts might be, the results were invariably effective.

Four instead of three notes of a chord being now properly dispersed among the strings,[b] Scarlatti proceeded to enrich his orchestra by a logical employment of wind instruments in pairs. The harpsichord, of course, continued to hold its own, but the Händelian principle of long held notes in the wind against more agile string passages is already to be found in his scores, a principle of which Lulli

[b] Ex. 6.

was also cognizant. But Scarlatti's orchestra was more plastic than Lulli's, and his overtures more purely instrumental.

As has been stated, Italian culture of the violin and the increasing regard in which that instrument was held, led to the development of execution as well as to an appropriate style of writing for it on a well defined harmonic basis. These improvements were, moreover, further reflected by a more earnest attention to the progress of other instruments, both as to mechanism and technique. As a result, musical performances improved rapidly, and the isolated, purely instrumental numbers of the opera, heretofore utterly disregarded by the public, began to excite comment. Whereupon Scarlatti, keen to perceive any nascent inclination on the part of his audience, turned to a more careful consideration of the overture. His motives for doing so may not have been of the highest, but the results were directly beneficial in that by eliciting warm approval, these overtures were eventually performed as concert numbers apart from the opera. Though short in form, they consisted of three or four distinct, well-rounded movements, and were destined to become the prototype of the classic symphony.

In specifically instrumental music, Scarlatti paved the way for Bach and Händel by writing for two violins and a violoncello, treated as soli instruments to an accompaniment of a string orchestra.

Finally, the components of his orchestra — represented in his most felicitous scoring by violins, violas, 'cellos, double-basses, two oboes, two bassoons, two horns — were practically identical with those of the early classicists.

So we see that the orchestra as bequeathed by Scarlatti was based upon a well organized body of strings, supported by a modest array of wood and brass instruments. Differentiated style of choral and instrumental writing was accentuated, and although polyphonic mannerism was still prevalent in orchestration, a tendency for individualistic instrumentation was at least apparent. On the other hand, the latent passion of the violoncello, when emancipated from the double-bass, was as yet unknown; and the harpsichord, by reënforcing the inner harmonies, covered the deficiencies of the wind instruments. That the mechanism of the latter should have remained in so immature a condition at a time when the delicate organism of the ideal string quartet had already been perfected, is but the result of natural causes. For when the supremacy of the viols was once for all established, it was of primary importance that *their* efficiency, above all others, should be enhanced; and thus subsidiary instruments were for the time subjected to at least comparative neglect.

The varied labors of Purcell (1658) were without the zone of eclectic progression. Although he adapted the cyclic style of Corelli, and kept in touch with the music of Lulli, whom, it is claimed, he even excelled in instrumentation, he remained true to the traditions of the English Church and English drama.

VI.

While examining the progress of orchestration, the parallel growth of organ and clavier music should not be forgotten. A comprehensive glance at the series of important writers in these branches will suffice to refresh the memory.

A distinctive style, initiated by the earlier Italian composers, Merulo, Andreas and Giovanni Gabrieli, was first exploited by Frescobaldi (1583). He promulgated a novel style of organ playing and contributed to the development of the fugue. After him, organ composition became the prerogative of the Germans, and the seventeenth century is represented by Scheidt, Froberger, Kerl, Reincken, Buxtehude, finally Pachelbel (1653). In Germany, Italy, and France, the subsequent chief exponents of clavier music were respectively Kuhnau, Domenico Scarlatti, and Couperin. Coincidentally, all three were born in the same decade as Bach.

By thus comparing the prodigious activity displayed in every branch of music, we find, as the ultimata of this epoch, that homogeneity in general had given place to a system of related tonalities, vitalized rhythm, diversified figuration, and a rational mode of expression. Moreover there were two distinct elements to build upon, — polyphony, as embodied in the contrapuntal *sonata da chiesa*, and the popular dance, the pivot of the *sonata da camera*. These two styles were capable either of further unassociated development or of reconciliation. By still further adding to such an amalgamation the principle of reiteration and thematic development of a single thought as the motive for a composition, we have as a resultant the cyclic form — first the Suite, earliest of complex forms, then the Sonata.

Musical art was now ready for a master hand who should weld its component parts firmly together. And that master was Bach.

(Summary on page 27.)

SUMMARY OF PART I

CHAPTER I. THE CRADLE OF INSTRUMENTAL MUSIC.

I. Two impelling forces: emotional expression of human feeling and pagan religious rites, account for musical development among primitive men.

Authentic history traces higher development through Egypt and the Orient to the Hellenic races, when poetry and music became conjoined.

II. Under the protectorate of the Roman Church, melody acquired plastic form, and systems of harmony, notation, and measure were established.

III. The lyrics of the troubadours revived a cult for individual emotionalism — the inherent characteristic of the Folk-song, which now influenced, and finally dominated the Gregorian Chant.

IV. Polyphonic choral art of the Netherland School developed consecutively contrapuntal technique, euphony, objective emotionalism, and culminated in the works of Lasso, when it was rivalled if not eclipsed by the creations of Palestrina. But the style of this era lacked rhythm and form. These essentials, together with tonality and a distinctive secular style, were subsequently to be developed in connection with solo singing and independent instrumental music.

CHAPTER II. THE DAWN OF INDEPENDENT INSTRUMENTATION.

I. A desire for increased vitality and florid figuration led to embellished organ accompaniment. This process devolved to other instruments. Hence instrumentation acquired individuality, contrast, expansibility.

II. Search for intensified expression and dramatic effects led to attempts at monody. The principles of monody are to be traced to the Miracle Plays, the Troubadours, the Greek tragedies. A semblance of these tragedies as transfused into Florentine monody led to recitative and lyric solo. These contained the germ of opera and oratorio, for which accompaniment was a requisite. In consequence, selective acumen for species, balance, quality, variety, developed orchestration.

CHAPTER III. EVOLUTION OF MUSICAL INSTRUMENTS.

From primitive stringed instruments played with a bow, such as the Celtic crwth and the Oriental rebab, devolved the vielle, thence the subsequent varieties of viols proper, finally, at the end of the sixteenth century, the modern string quartet.

The pianoforte owes its origin to the monochord and psaltery with key-board attachment, as developed from the dulcimer of the fourteenth and fifteenth centuries, the clavichord and harpsichord of the sixteenth to the Hammerklavier of the eighteenth century. The clavichord was derived from the monochord, the harpsichord from the psaltery, the pianoforte from the dulcimer. The strings of the dulcimer were played upon by hammers held in the hand; the clavichord strings were mechanically pressed up; those of the harpsichord were plucked by quills; whereas the pianoforte is supplied with hammer-action.

The invention of wind instruments probably antedates that of strings. Emanating from the ancient Egyptian vertical flute, the flûte à bec of the Middle Ages matured into the modern horizontal flute. Akin to the single-reed species of the Greek aulos, Latin tibia, were the popularized schalmei, predecessors of the pommer and oboe families. The single-reeded modern clarinet, that came into existence the end of the seventeenth century, was an outgrowth of the chalemiax of mediævalism.

From the Roman lituus and buccina devolved side by side the trombe and Zinken of the Middle Ages. Experimental development through the stages of bent tubes, slide mechanism, finger holes, removable crooks, chromatic valves, perfected the valve-trumpet, the bugle-horn, the slide-trombone.

Instruments of percussion are the parents of all other instruments. Certain species subsequently became distinctly characteristic of certain distinct races; those most effective are now incorporated in the modern orchestra. Of significant importance are the kettle-drums by reason of their unalloyed artistic value.

CHAPTER IV. BEGINNINGS OF ORCHESTRATION.

MONTEVERDE'S creative genius led to three tangible results: — (1) Dramatic expression; (2) the founding of a serviceable orchestra based on bowed instruments; (3) diversity of style between vocal and instrumental composition.

(1) In writing for the stage, he aimed at an intensification of dramatic effects, variety in tone-color, a freer accompaniment, and relief from the monotony of recitative by the employment of a primitive arioso form. The fruits of these dramatic efforts were reaped by Carissimi in Italy, Schütz in Germany, Lulli in France.

(2) The founding of a serviceable orchestra was the result of his expressive and dramatic instinct fostered by the attempts of the Florentine experimentalists, — orchestral music and the drama being, moreover, at that time practically inseparable. His orchestration emphasized the value of strings, readjusted the balance of the wind, and suggested contrasted choirs of instruments.

(3) Diversity of style between vocal and instrumental music pointed the way to independent orchestral composition.

It was not the greatest of his successors that directly furthered the cause of orchestration. Carissimi in oratorio, Lulli in opera, only incidentally enriched instrumental accompaniment as a means to an end. Of greater stability were the orchestral efforts of the secondary composers of this era, of whom Cavalli, Legrenzi, Corelli are the most important. Cavalli established the precedent of three-part string writing, Legrenzi of equilibrium and a fairly adequate supply of strings, whereas their superior, Corelli, by developing violin technique, made possible a style of writing that ultimately matured into the classic sonata. Further originality was displayed in the chamber music of Steffani and Clari, in the *concerto grosso* of Torelli, in the combined harmonic and rhythmic effects of Vivaldi.

In direct lineage from Monteverde, SCARLATTI stands as the second great orchestral innovator. His three principal achievements were: — (1) Balance of tone in the strings by the judicious distribution of the four notes of a chord; (2) numerical suppression of overpowering wind-instruments, and a logical usage of the same in pairs; (3) enlargement of the exterior and thematic development of the interior construction of his overtures. Incidentally, through readjustment of dynamic force, the viola gained individuality, and the strings were enabled to stand out in relief against the wind.

The general tendency of the era was one of universal musical progress in specialized instrumental writing. Homogeneity yielded to systematic harmonic progressions and well defined rhythm. Upon this basis, a unification of the dance movement, polyphony, and thematic treatment was effected in the following century.

PART II. — THE CLASSIC ERA.

CHAPTER V.

BACH, HÄNDEL, AND THEIR CONTEMPORARIES.

An attempt to portray in a felicitous manner the progress of orchestration during the classic era is apt to carry one between Scylla and Charybdis. On the one hand lies the temptation to enlarge upon the biography and extraneous achievements of the great masters, on the other, the danger of superficiality. Minuteness of detail as aimed at in the previous chapter when the beginnings of orchestration rested in the hands of a comparatively small number of men is here incompatible, in view of the desire for conciseness. Moreover, extended panegyrics would of necessity consist of but a flatulent plagiarism upon the voluminous and admirably written works already in existence. The safe course to pursue is therefore to survey the era as a whole in its relation to the orchestra, merely touching upon a very few of the distinctive characteristics peculiar to the most celebrated exponents.

Naturally one turns to that unbroken chain of Teutonic peers, beside whom all contemporary efforts were puny. Of these six, — Bach, Händel, Gluck, Haydn, Mozart, Beethoven, it might be said that only the last three were direct evolutionists of the symphonic orchestra; for Gluck was absorbed in exploring the *dramatic* characteristics of instrumentation, and as to Bach and Händel, in spite of their titanic contributions to music itself, neither of them can be regarded as an orchestral innovator, though this statement savors of heresy. [2]

[2] It should be borne in mind that the "heresy" of the present writer is chargeable only when consideration of Bach's music comes before or takes the place of what Bach did in the development of *orchestration*, which is the first consideration of this book. Of course, it is beyond question that in his instrumentation as distinct from orchestration, Bach added to the possibilities of the instruments existing at that time, — notably as shown by the obbligato wind parts, the gamba and 'cello solos, etc., in the Masses, the Passions and the Church Cantatas. These prove a much larger appreciation of orchestral color than was known in music for three-quarters of a century after him. Nevertheless it must not be forgotten that for many years Bach's music obtained for itself only restricted recognition, which therefore justifies the above made statement that Bach was not a direct evolutionist of the symphonic orchestra.

I.

BACH (1685–1750), comparatively a recluse, was but little known to his contemporaries. His mode of life, however, was only partially responsible for this neglect, for the fact that a German imitation of Neapolitan methods was in predominance at that time, is of especial significance. Thus Haydn and Mozart, who might have reaped incalculable benefit from his experience, were unfamiliar with the greater portion of his works. This fact alone is sufficient to disconnect his name from the direct lineal chain of orchestral evolution. However, in view of the stupendous posterior influence his music was destined to wield, one cannot thus summarily pass over his contributions to orchestration.

Tersely stated, the ideal of this polyphonic giant revealed itself in subtle expression as concealed in his filigree of mercurial counterpoint, in the portrayal of inner feeling, and in profound religious fervor. A Teuton to the core, he stands as the symbolic exponent of organ and Protestant Church music. His arias are imbued with dramatic intensity and lyric pathos, and if at times portions of them seem archaic, one must remember that his art had assimilated the earlier church style and was but the corollary of it. His Passion Music not only still exists, but retains its full vitality. His church style is that of the organ, and the organ was for him the intermediary to orchestration.

Although Bach's instrumentation was by no means equal to the substance of his wonderful conceptions intended for orchestration, he did not neglect to study the prevalent Italian style of scoring, and was, to say the least, a progressive orchestrator, even if not an innovator. In his great organ works, the employment of chromatic and enharmonic modulation, the perfection of the fugue, the development of earlier strict forms eventually caused vocal music to yield precedence to instrumental. And Bach transplanted this polyphonic style into the orchestra with the result that the treatment of each individual instrument was distinctly melodic. Now this interwoven texture of austere polyphony, though resulting in a complete negation of analyzed tone-color, contained the essence of effective orchestral solo writing, as typified in his *concerti grossi*. Bach frequently employed the organ as the centre of his orchestra, though the instrument was never aggressive. Around it were clustered differentiated groups of the usual variety, whose mission it was to add specific unities of color rather than volume of sound.

But when Bach had occasion to introduce episodes of simplicity by way of contrast to his usual polyphony, his scoring for wood-wind was not so felicitous, and in loud passages, even when adequately represented, they were prone to be eclipsed by the strings. It is true that he was frequently hampered by a paucity of instrumentalists, but subsequent renditions of his orchestral works tend to prove that he failed to extract the best results from the wind. In uniting choral writing with the organ, Bach must evidently have been aware of the acoustic phenomenon that a literal redoubling of vocal and organ parts results in the complete absorption of the latter. For in his choral masterpieces, where the organ and orchestra are simultaneously used, we find, as a means of insuring contrast, passages wherein entire chords in the orchestra are employed as passing notes against held chords in the chorus and organ.

Bach's orchestration, therefore, stands for polyphony; melodic treatment in the voice-leading of each and every part both inner and outer; contrasted choirs of affiliated instruments for giving variety to the various sequent movements in relation to each other, rather than for episodic contrast or variety in the separate movements by themselves.

A striking contrast to Bach's secluded and uneventful career is to be found in that of his illustrious contemporary.

II.

HÄNDEL (1685–1759), the man of the world, represents the realistic, and the æsthetics of melodic form. As suzerain of oratorio, he handled the orchestra primarily as subsidiary to the voices. Unlike Bach, his influence upon organ and clavier music was small. And the value of his forty insipid Italian operas lies only in the experience it gave him in manipulation of vocal forces, and the benefits derived from keeping in touch with a cosmopolitan public. His oratorios are the composite of the orthodox style of the church, the traits of the Neapolitan School deprived of their meretricious tendencies, and a precocious expressive and dramatic instinct, the birthright of his own genius. Ultimately was added to this composite the inspiration offered by the English anthem and the talent of Purcell. Indeed, although the centripetal ideal that guided him was spontaneous and original, it must be acknowledged that in the setting of his brilliants is to be found an extraneous aggrandizement, resulting, not from eclecticism, but from plagiarism. Thus unvarnished phrases of Corelli and Alessandro Scarlatti were boldly transfused into the works of Händel when his own Muse failed him. This Italian influence betrays itself in the comparative simplicity of his modulations, and in his but moderate use of striking dissonances. The skeleton of his harmonic structures was reared on a simpler basis than Bach's; on the other hand, the massed effects of his choral polyphony have never been surpassed.

His instrumental forms were likewise Italian, and his orchestration, though masterly, was not so conspicuously original as that of his immediate great successors. Strings as the nuclei were supported by a large number of reeds. In orchestras which included twenty-five strings, frequently no less than five oboes and five bassoons would be employed. Even our modern mighty aggregation of from fifty to sixty strings would hardly bear the adjunct of ten reeds, — indeed, three oboes, one English horn, three bassoons, one contra-bassoon (eight in all) would represent the maximum if tonal equilibrium were to be preserved. However, two extenuating circumstances for this Händelian custom should not be overlooked. His method of writing for the wood did not embody those characteristics subsequently discovered by Haydn and Mozart; again, the instruments themselves lacked power. The criterion of Händel's orchestration rests almost exclusively in his oratorios. Here the mission of instrumental accompaniment was to support, strengthen, intertwine; for Händel was in quest of solidity, sonority, vitality, — terms which in this connection might be considered the synonym for the above three.

His usual method for full scoring was to double the violin parts with oboes, and the basses with bassoons. Clarinets had as yet no status; flutes added ornamentation; the brass was fully represented in logical proportion, though it was then the custom to write high trumpet parts. Next to the violins, the oboe was Händel's as well as Bach's favorite solo instrument. The organ played an important rôle in his oratorios, and he employed the harp freely for historic representations. Together with Bach, he was practically the last to make use of the theorbos. At least passing reference is due to his trios, which constitute so important a contribution to the literature of chamber music. His contrapuntal overtures and interludes, where the wood-wind are allowed greater freedom, display considerable variety. Finally, at this period the harpsichord was fortunately losing its fallacious value as a musical component of the orchestra, being retained rather as a means for conducting.

But as already stated, Händel learned to regard the orchestra not as an unenthralled entity, but rather as the chief ally of oratorio, for which the corner stone was Italian melody, the foundations comparatively simple harmonic progressions, and the superstructure the human voice, surrounded by an orchestral trellis. And the resultant was a massive tonal edifice.

The Contemporaries of Bach and Händel.

Before proceeding to a survey of Gluck's revolutionary accomplishments, it would seem in place to analyze the artistic progress of the lesser lights of this period. And since the crisis of Gluck's life was not reached until a century after the birth of those two giants, Bach and Händel, even though they were his direct predecessors and eventual contemporaries, chronological dates must needs give place to the logic of evolution.

III.

Italy.   In the previous chapter, the progress of orchestration in relation to its beneficent guardian, the drama, was traced from the improvements initiated by Monteverde through those of Scarlatti.   These new doctrines were, of course, assiduously seized upon by the latter's contemporaries and immediate successors. But indeed it was not until the advent of Spontini as late as the first part of the nineteenth century that Italian orchestration was again represented by an exponent of more than secondary importance, taking into consideration the achievements of Rameau in France, not to mention the great German masters.   For Pergolesi excelled particularly in string writing, whereas Cherubini's scoring shows German influence rather than Italian.   Nevertheless, Neapolitan propagandism exerted world-wide influence, and was directly fostered by such men as Buononcini, Durante, Porpora, Leo, Logroscino, all of whom were born in the last quarter of the seventeenth century;   to the same chronological period belongs also Lotti (1667), a worthy representative of the Venetian School, who, although primarily a composer of sacred music of marked individuality, wrote a number of operas for Venice as well as several for Dresden and Vienna.   Having resided for two years in Dresden, he aided the diffusion throughout Germany of operatic and orchestral principles that were conspicuously Italian even if not specifically those of Naples.   Like him, Durante devoted himself almost exclusively to sacred writing.   Leo, though producing many dramatic works as well as oratorios and chamber music, aided the advance of Italian art more as the teacher of Jomelli and Piccini than by his creations.   Both G. Buononcini and the singing teacher, Porpora, were through the irony of fate led to aid artistic evolution by negative means, so to speak, since the trend of their ambitions brought them face to face with the genius of Händel, upon whom their machinations acted but as a stimulus. For, as will be remembered, Buononcini's defeat in London was followed fifteen years later by a second unsuccessful rivalry instigated by Porpora's faction.   Logroscino is to be remembered for his development of opera-buffa and of the Finale as subsequently applied by Piccini.   But it is clearly evident that none of these representative Italian composers contributed materially to orchestration with the exception that their instrumental accompaniments acquired greater freedom.

The brief career of Pergolesi (1710–1736) was consummated during the interim dating approximately from Gluck's birth to Haydn's.   His fame is confined not alone to his sacred works, such as the Stabat Mater, but to his dramatic productions as well, of which the finest example is, of course, "La serva padrona," of opera-buffa propinquities.   His proclivity for employing an orchestra of strings alone, as exemplified in the above mentioned representative works, was fortunate in that thereby he was able to concentrate his thoughts upon finish and detail, such as served as a valuable model for the period in which he was living, when string writing was as yet at an immature stage.

IV.

Germany. In Germany itself Italian influences predominated, and interest was centered chiefly upon the opera, in connection with which Scarlatti's tenets of writing for the orchestra were diligently copied. German dramatic activity paved the way to the establishment in 1678 of a permanent opera house in Hamburg, which enjoyed uninterrupted existence for sixty years. Most prominent among the composers for and directors of this enterprise were Theile (1646), Keiser (1674), Mattheson (1681), and Telemann (likewise 1681). Of these, Keiser accrued the greatest temporary popularity by reason of his prolific and sensational though shallow versatility. His orchestration, which was of the lightest kind, included various alternating groups of instruments. Fétis states that Keiser employed in his opera "Frédegonde" sometimes the strings alone, or the clavichord together with plucked stringed instruments and a bass. Again, the voice was accompanied by a single violin, an oboe and a bass, oboes alone, or a flute and viols. These combinations present nothing new; they were but in accordance with the customs of the times. Telemann also was possessed of a reputation sufficient to overshadow in his day that of Bach. Though the importance of his activity has since been reduced to insignificance, credit is at least due to him, not alone for his dramatic writings, but also for his contribution to concert and chamber music, which frequently revealed strong German tendencies, all too rare in the midst of Neapolitan sovereignty. So-called symphonies, overtures, concertos, quartets and the like are included in Telemann's exhaustless list of compositions, and in view of his intimacy with Bach, these works must have wielded at least transitory influence upon the experimental stage of that master's instrumentation and orchestral form. Händel likewise for three years devoted his energies to writing operas for the Hamburg stage; but this was in his youthful days, and, as has been already intimated, these attempts were but puerile and can have no possible bearing upon the art of orchestration.

Emanuel Bach (1714–1788) was also unquestionably attracted by the doctrines of this histrionic circle, although he was never directly associated with it. (Incidentally, therefore, it should be noted that he was not the successor of Telemann as director in operatic lines, a statement erroneously set forth by one historian of repute; he did succeed him as church musical director but not until later in life. In support of this correction it is but necessary to call attention to the fact that in 1738, the very year in which the degeneracy of the Hamburg operatic experiments culminated in the relinquishment of the enterprise, Emanuel Bach, being but twenty-four years old, went to Berlin, where two years later he became chamber cembalist to Frederick the Great.) The results of his efforts are of value to posterity in that he was instrumental in causing musical composition to be established on a more decidedly harmonic rather than contrapuntal basis. For although he honestly endeavored to fathom the profundity of his illustrious father, the subtle influence of his courtly surroundings and the effervescent superficiality of Neapolitanism could not but have its effect upon his art. Again, his early training was such as to foster a regard for what has been called the "gallant" style, and, as Dr. Riemann states it: "to this very tendency he owes his greatness, for by it he became the father of modern instrumental music, the precursor of Haydn, Mozart, and Beethoven in the department of the sonata, symphony, etc., which he clothed in more pleasing modern dress;" and thus "the son of the last master of the old school became the founder of the new school."

Passing reference is due to three further German contemporaries of Händel who were slaves to Italian principles. These were Hasse (1699), Graun (1701), Naumann (1741). After the downfall of the Hamburg stage, two distinct efforts were made to establish Italian opera at Dresden. Now the Dresden orchestra is over three hundred and fifty years old, and the interest attached to the name of Hasse is due to his prominent connection with that organization and the constitution of the same under his management. This band had been noted for its excellence already in the earlier stages of its existence, and even at the time of Monteverde it enrolled no less than thirteen strings and ninety-three instruments of wood, brass, and percussion. These dimensions were of gigantic proportions for those days, indeed, they compare favorably with the present size of the Dresden orchestra. That of Hasse was but half as large, but the distribution of parts was, of course, infinitely superior, and an orchestra of even fifty instruments, of which only half were strings, could readily have overpowered singers of Italian opera, had it not been for the subservience of the accompaniment to "il bel canto," the meagre quality of tone of the wood-wind, and the "thin" scoring then in vogue. It consisted of twenty-five strings in judicious apportionment, two flutes, five oboes, five bassoons, two horns, besides trumpets, trombones, kettle-drums and two clavichords. The prominence of reed quality and the incorporation of two clavichords, from one of which Hasse conducted, was in accord with the usages which Händel accepted. Hasse stands as the most successful native exponent of extraneous ideas, and, like his method of conducting which originated in Italy, his harmonic progressions as well as his instrumentation are of the simplest kind and disclose the same influence.

Graun achieved renown first as an opera singer, next as an opera composer; but of more enduring worth are his sacred compositions. Nevertheless he and

Hasse were for a time the only *maestri* who wrote for the Berlin Opera, and the orchestral scores of Graun are considered by some to suggest a transition from the earlier symphonies to those of Haydn. One of his cantatas is scored for three flutes, three oboes, two violins, one viola, a bassoon, and a chorus in six parts. To this series of composers belongs properly the name of Naumann, even though he was born in the following generation; he displayed a fatal facility in expressing himself in conventional formulas, and his career was interrupted only by the ascendency of Gluck and Mozart.

V.

France. French musical art owes the stability of her early dramatic growth to three eminent composers: Lulli, Rameau, Gluck; and the first and the last of these were foreigners. Moreover into their hands was entrusted the moulding of French orchestration, for French orchestral music was not destined to disengage itself from bondage to the drama and assert itself as a clearly defined indigenous product until the nineteenth century. A sharp line of demarcation must be drawn between each respective career of these three pillars of the nascent stage. For Lulli had appropriated to himself all the glory attendant upon the Royal Opera, not alone as the director but as composer as well. Not until after his death did it become possible for others to reap the benefits of experience in hearing their own works produced, in consequence of which, latent talent had had no chance to expand. And the interim between Lulli and Rameau is signalized as a period of reaction during which the efforts of even the most prominent writers were but a pale reflection of those of their illustrious master.

Three composers, born in the second half of the seventeenth century, namely Campra, Destouches, Mouret, were the immediate successors of Lulli, and dedicated their services, such as they were, to the conservation of his ideals. Of these three men, Campra is popularly called the link between Lulli and Rameau. Campra possessed genuinely dramatic instincts, exercised his talents along sacred lines as well as secular, and revealed certain traits of independence and originality in that he dared to depart from Lulli's somewhat austere style by emphasizing the necessity for augmenting rhythmic effects, which was distinctly beneficial in the development of orchestration. It is interesting to note that he was the first Frenchman to employ the *cor de chasse* in opera, although Lulli introduced it into some of his ballets. The contributions of Destouches were of small intrinsic value other than the fact that the chivalrous surroundings of his earlier career as an officer had nurtured his natural temperament for the graceful and refined. And so with this æsthetic touch of a composer otherwise lacking in musical education, he added his mite to the development of daintiness in instrumentation, such as the use of two piccolo flutes in thirds in one of his ballets, and other minor though interesting details.   Of Mouret's operas little can be said; but he deserves honorable mention for his labors as a conductor of the "Concerts spirituels," which, as the name implies, had been founded in 1725 to occupy the *interregna* whenever the opera houses were closed for religious reasons.   Consequently, his name is rightfully connected with the evolution of the concert orchestra, for the "Concerts spirituels" exercised a discriminating influence at a critical time in French musical history, especially since subsequently, about the date of Beethoven's birth, it was reorganized by Gossec, with the result that it sprang into prominence equal to that of some of the foremost orchestras of Europe.

With the advent of RAMEAU (1683–1764), who was born two years before Bach, the *Opéra* was again lifted out of the lethargy into which it had fallen. Rameau, first to offer to the world a theoretical explanation of harmonic relationship built upon a logically scientific basis, was exactly fifty years old when he made his début as an operatic writer, indeed, he did not reach the summit of his success until about the time of Mozart's birth.   And since Gluck's Parisian career dates from the decade in which Beethoven was born, the chronological relationship in the labors of Rameau and Gluck can the more readily be compared.   Rameau's handling of dramatic resources was superior to that of Lulli, in fact, his methods were of sufficient merit to be subsequently absorbed by Gluck himself.   The three cardinal points of departure from traditional usage that have caused the name of Rameau, first of the genuinely French masters, to be so highly respected are his daring harmonic innovations, the important rôle assigned by him to the dramatic chorus, and what is more, the importance attached to orchestral accompaniment, together with increased independence and prominence for the orchestra itself, as well as enriched instrumentation in detail.   Since most of his operas are published in condensed form, which, with the exception of the *ritornelli*, contain but the vocal, violin, and bass parts, facilities for a satisfactory examination of his instrumentation are usually lacking.   This is a matter for regret, since many of his detached instrumental numbers are veritable little gems of descriptive writing in the miniature, not dissimilar in style to those written by his contemporary, François Couperin, who was mentioned in the previous chapter as one of the three earliest exponents of characteristic clavier music.

Though Rameau made but few changes in the constituency of the orchestra, there was assigned to each instrument an individual and appropriate rôle, and the tone-colors cross and intermingle.   He extended the range of the violins, aided the independency of accompaniment by the frequent use of arpeggios in the strings, and was the first to use *pizzicato* chord effects in the entire body of strings at once.   Although he did not employ the harp, he imitated its characteristics by means of *pizzicati* strings.   Two horns and even two clarinets are frequently to be found in his scores, and lighter touches, such as the accompaniment of the voice by two flutes and a violin, or three oboes and a bassoon, are also to be met with.

As has been already intimated, the triumphs of Rameau were followed by a second interim that lasted for nearly twenty years. But in the case of this second interim, France was not destined to remain so comparatively unproductive as during the first. For the same period that heralds the crowning point of Rameau's fame ushers in the beginnings of French comic opera, for which date Mozart's birth is again a convenient reminder. As a result of partisanship for the Italian "bouffons," the philosopher, Jean Jacques Rousseau (1712–1778), wrote both the words and music of a little French pastoral in the style of the prevailing Italian *intermezzi*, and thereby excited the interest more especially of the younger composers. Duni, Philidor, and Monsigny, who were born in approximately the same quarter century as Rousseau, were particularly happy in their efforts to evolve from this germ a lighter and more popular style, and are therefore to be regarded as the founders of *opéra comique*, which, in the next generation, was to be moulded into plasmic form by Grétry. And no style could have been more beneficial for extricating orchestral writing out of the stiff and prosaic confines within which serious opera was prone to restrict it. On the other hand, Italian orchestration was leaning more and more toward pernicious conventionalism and tawdry superficiality. Here again the early *opéra comique* appeared as a felicitous counterbalance, and infused into the orchestra that sparkle and piquancy for which French instrumentation has ever since been famed. True, none of these minor composers contributed signally to the advancement of orchestration, but each helped in little ways, and their instrumentation was more correct and finished than that of their prominent successor, Grétry. Their orchestras were still somewhat massive, but showed progress in vigor and sonority, variety and lightness of instrumentation.

And so when Gluck arrived in Paris there existed already four distinct schools for orchestral writing — the rising classic purity of his own native land; the Neapolitan traditions, fast deteriorating into triviality; the legacies of Lulli, revivified and improved upon by Rameau; and the virginal essays at phosphorescent scoring in lighter vein.

(Summary on page 68.)

CHAPTER VI.

GLUCK AND HIS CONTEMPORARIES.

I.

GLUCK (1714–1787), the third of the great drama reformers, and predecessor of Wagner in the establishment of dramatic continuity, did not appear as the champion of revivified Hellenic ideals until advanced in years. Though he had long harbored an intense antagonism to the paltry conventionalities of the existing lyric drama, his tenets awoke no sympathetic chord in his native land. And thus it came about that the arena of Lulli's scintillating pageantry witnessed the rehabilitation of genuine, legitimate, and unaffected histrionic art. This was attained by a return to a severe and truthful mode of musical declamation, by clothing the several stage characters with distinctive individuality, and by instilling into his music-dramas in their entirety, reflection, simplicity, sincerity, pathos, nobility. The chorus was raised to importance, the function of accompaniment rendered more virile, and the orchestra was made to enhance the dramatic situations. Three defects are noticeable. Gluck made no attempt to break down the barriers of stereotyped operatic forms, his melody is at times stilted, and his music is guilty of frequent grammatical errors. Despite these facts, his choruses are worthy examples of dramatic effect, and the formal structure of his overtures is more rounded than those of even Bach or Händel. But it cannot be said that his genius was conspicuously original; he was essentially a reformer, not an innovator. For as Mr. Edward Dickinson expresses it in general terms: "Gluck's success was not due to his melodic invention or mastery of musical science, for in neither of these particulars can he be ranked among the greatest composers. His ability consisted rather of producing great effects with simple means; the severe grandeur of his style was especially suited to the antique subjects which he chose, and this style was in conformity to the peculiar genius of Greek tragedy."

To independent orchestration Gluck contributed but little, but, considering the age in which he lived, none have excelled him as an interpreter, by means of the orchestra, of pathetic expression, or in the use of appropriate instrumentation, varied and rich tone-coloring. To quote from Parry's "The Art of Music," page 220: "Moreover, the expressive qualities of his admirable recitatives are very much enhanced by his way of dealing with the accompaniment. He neglected no opportunity to make use of the qualities of his orchestral instruments — as

38

far as in him lay — to enforce and accentuate the situations, and even to intensify the passing moment of feeling implied by the dialogue. Composers were successfully developing the sense of the functions and resources of instrumentation. Even Gluck's rival, Piccini, made some very appropriate effects by using his instruments consistently with the spirit of the situations. But Gluck applied himself to the matter with far more intensity, and far more genuine perception of the characters of the instruments. Indeed it would be hardly an exaggeration to say, that he was the first composer in the world who had any genuine understanding of this very modern phase of the art. Mozart was the first to show real natural gift and genuine feeling for beautiful disposition of tone, but Gluck anticipated modern procedure in adapting his colors exactly to the mood of the situation. A good deal had been attempted already in a sort of half-hearted and formal manner, but he was the first to seize firmly on the right principles and to carry out his objects with any mastery of resources." On the other hand, "his orchestration has none of the roundness or balance or maturity of Mozart's. It is unequal and uncertain, and requires humoring in performance to make it produce the effect which is intended."

Gluck relied to an excessive degree upon the string band, and his orchestral writing lacked that balance which the contemporary and sequent classicists regarded as the fundamental requirement. Notwithstanding, his instrumentation exhibits many original insignia that are worthy of record. Thus he demonstrated the dramatic power of low-written viola parts, made varied and characteristic use of the tremolo, was the first to introduce mutes into the orchestra in his "Armide," and caused the trombones to emerge from their hitherto menial subservience, and stand forth in all their dignity and tragic power of portraying peace, sorrow, fear, religion, majesty. And by proving the superior effectiveness in employing a group of three trombones, he established a precedent that has been endorsed by all subsequent composers.

But it must be confessed that in turning over page after page of his scores, one discovers the fact that in deploying his wood-wind Gluck usually laid but modest demands upon them. Their duties were more commonly restricted to the lending of comparatively simple tone-color for heightening dramatic action, or for relieving the monotony of prolonged use of strings alone. Of weird and tragic effect is his concentration of all high wood-wind *unisono*. But many of his other orchestral characteristics bear the impress of conventionalism then in vogue, which soon becomes monotonous; and his manner of writing for the deeper instruments causes much of his orchestration to sound heavy.

All things considered, the same must be said of Gluck as of his vancourier, Lulli, and of the great oratorio composers, Carissimi and Händel — neither he nor they were attracted by the kaleidoscopic potentiality of the orchestra when isolated from its kindred rivals, the opera and the oratorio. And although his name is to be revered for having opened up the resources of the orchestra, the attention he bestowed upon it was but a reflection of the greater glories that he offered up to the shrine of dramatic lustration.

THE CONTEMPORARIES OF GLUCK.

For two hundred years dramatic writing had now dominated musical art, therefore orchestration as well. The best fruits of these two centuries of experiments having culminated in the reforms of Gluck, his music dramas, with their continuity of action and dignity of subject-matter, were to be surpassed only by Mozart's splendid attainments, by reason of the latter's perfect melody, pure form and admirably adjusted orchestration.

A final glance at the dramatic situation of Europe with the date of Beethoven's birth as a consistently convenient landmark will be necessary in order to comprehend the significance of Mozart's operatic constellation as it appeared on the horizon. For the decade beginning with 1770 was replete with big events, preordained, as it were, to do homage to the future master — Beethoven. Of the generation born between 1714 and 1756, further mention has yet to be made of the Frenchman, Grétry, of the Germans, J. A. Hiller and Dittersdorf, and of the conservators of declining Italian dogmas, Jomelli, Piccini, Sacchini, Paesiello, Cimarosa, Salieri.

II.

France. After the defeat of the kindly Piccini, — who deserves more credit than is usually awarded him, not alone for his graceful melody, clear and sonorous orchestration, but especially for his judicious application of the orchestral instruments to the demands of a situation, — the stage of the French capital, now monopolized by foreign composers, patronized for a brief period the productions of the Neapolitan Sacchini, and of Salieri. The former was also a fair composer of chamber music, whereas the latter is signally notorious for his intrigues against Mozart. Both of them were pupils of Gluck, and their instrumentation was but an imitation of his. But meanwhile, after GRÉTRY (1741–1813) had fairly launched his graceful conceptions, the public soon recognized in him a worthy successor to Rameau, even though the *genre* of his offerings was of a different mould. Interest in imported art waned, and the career of the second great French composer began.

Grétry, though founding a permanent and powerful national school that was distinctly the opposite of tragedy, was an ardent disciple of Gluck's doctrines, being himself even more of a radical in his indifference for actual singing as a mode of dramatic interpretation. But in spite of his sensitive perception not alone for truthful interpretation, but as well for melodic design and novel scenic effects, his comparative neglect of the orchestra is unique in the annals of musical history. His strings were generally written in three parts, with frequent gaps between the bass and the two upper voices. His harmonies were usually too thin, and his orchestration as a whole was conventional and uninteresting. Fortunately his delicate musical thought did not require elaborate instrumentation as a means for expression, and so he rarely drew upon the resources of the orchestra for more than was absolutely necessary in simple accompaniment to the voice. Grétry is cited as having declared that the accompaniment to solo singing should be as the pedestal to the statue; but unfortunately his own orchestral accompaniments do not conform to this pretty saying, for his pedestals were feeble and lacked the essentials of ornamentation. And although Grétry towers above his contemporaries as the first great representative of *opéra comique*, he contributed practically nothing new to orchestration other than the introduction, in a few isolated cases, of some unusual instruments of percussion and other minor details of instrumentation.

III.

Italy. In 1770, Jomelli, who for fifteen years had occupied the post of Hofkapellmeister in Stuttgart, had just returned to Italy, where he found Paesiello in high favor, and Cimarosa about to begin his operatic career. Both Paesiello and Cimarosa were soon to pose as rivals to Piccini as well as to each other, but of the two, Paesiello was possessed of more scholarly attributes which found outlet in numerous independent instrumental works, including twelve symphonies and six quartets, whereas Cimarosa displayed simpler though more spontaneous fertility, and his works are better known to posterity with whom he ranks as one of the greatest Italian composers of his day. Nevertheless, the instrumentation of both Paesiello and Cimarosa was weak and non-progressive. The most prominent contemporary exponent of chamber music was Boccherini, who is credited with the authorship of no less than three hundred and sixty trios, quartets, quintets and the like, besides twenty symphonies. In antithesis to the transportation into Germany of exotic ideas, Jomelli and other Italians living in Germany showed the influence of their new surroundings by improved orchestration, though unfortunately this had but little immediate effect on their compatriots at home. For the Italians still held tenaciously to their traditions, and handled the orchestra principally as a means of support for and contrast to the human voice. Fearful lest the singer should be overpowered, they were overcautious; as a result, their scoring was thin, and decidedly weak in the bass. Jomelli's efforts are therefore especially praiseworthy. In his operas, the orchestra acquired greater importance, and, like Sammartini, he awakened also a keener interest for purely instrumental music. He was one of the first to make really effective use of the *crescendo*, increased the efficiency of the violins by adding richer and more varied ornamentation, and showed a tendency to make proper use of tone-color. In a word, his instrumentation, together with that of Pergolesi, ushered in a new epoch in Italy.

IV.

Germany. The seed of the new movement in France soon bore fruit in Germany in the form of the Singspiel, which, however, sturdily maintained its indigenous characteristics, since not the form but the spirit only of the French comic opera with spoken dialogue had been accepted. J. A. Hiller, as the prime mover in thus establishing a national form of operetta, was emulated by Dittersdorf, who learned much from the French composers, though more from Haydn, as is evidenced by the form and instrumentation of his symphonies. The climax of German operatic enterprise in the eighteenth century was reached when in 1778 the "Deutsches Nationalspiel" was founded in Vienna, bringing to that city lasting prominence in dramatic affairs. For the liberal spirit that was shown in throwing open its doors to all worthy applicants, irrespective of nationality or style of writing, attracted such composers as Gluck, Dittersdorf, Salieri, Mozart. And the eclecticism in objective, in form, in orchestration, that consequently pervaded the artistic atmosphere which Beethoven was soon to breathe, must have unconsciously struck a sympathetic chord in the insatiable longings of Beethoven's soul to find food for his selective and synthetical methods of procedure.

V.

The Concert Orchestra. Meanwhile the concert orchestra was rapidly winning wider recognition, since Haydn and his contemporaries, Sammartini, Gossec, Grétry, had already excited marked attention. In 1770 the "Concerts des Amateurs" were founded by Gossec, followed shortly by his reorganization of the "Concerts spirituels." And but a few years later the Leipzig Gewandhaus, of which Hiller was the first conductor, was placed on a permanent basis, being largely due to his untiring efforts in behalf of orchestral concerts.

Although the permanent bulwark of modern instrumentation was reared by Haydn, important experiments were successfully developed by the Milanese, Sammartini, and the Bohemian, Stamitz, both of whom were born at the same period with Gluck; further by the German, Cannabich, and the Belgian, Gossec, both born in the same decade as Haydn; finally, by the Frenchman, Grétry. Thus representatives of five nationalities were simultaneously engaged in carrying on the same work, their fields of activity being, moreover, widely dispersed. Sammartini, also noted as the teacher of Gluck, remained loyal to his own city; Gossec and Grétry were occupied in Paris; Stamitz and Cannabich, conductors rather than composers, were successively settled as directors of the Electoral band at Mannheim.[3]

It is a peculiar coincidence that Italy, which has never yet produced a great symphonic writer, should be able to point to Giovanni Sammartini as the earliest exponent of this form in the modern sense. For already in 1734 his first orchestral symphony was produced in Milan where he was conductor. At that date Haydn was but two years old. Of course Sammartini obtained no such results as did his great German successor, but he at least suggested the proper course by which clearer form and healthier orchestration might be secured, and his instrumentation abounds in new and interesting traits. In addition to having written a host of symphonies, of which twenty-four were published, his labors in other branches of composition were prodigious. Incidentally, his experience as a writer of string quartets taught him the value of the viola, in consequence of which, independent parts for that instrument as advocated by Scarlatti are likewise to be found in his orchestral scores.

The value of Gossec's persistent energy in both building up the standard of already existing orchestral organizations and in establishing a new one is twofold. For not only was the French public educated to encourage home talent to seek expression in independent orchestral language, but also by affording these same French aspirants frequent opportunity for hearing the masterpieces of foreign contemporaries was the French style of writing for the orchestra immensely strengthened and broadened. Considering the close affinity that bound Gossec's birthplace to France, he may well be regarded as a representative of the country which he had adopted as his own. As the founder of the first genuine symphonic orchestra in France, he himself set the example as a diligent composer of symphonies and string quartets, although, unfortunately, the former were at first not favorably received. Nevertheless, his perseverance eventually won the day, especially after he had been crowned with new laurels as an operatic composer; and at the time of the Gluck-Piccini controversy, some of his later symphonies finally obtained for him that recognition to which he had aspired. Lavoix avers

[3] To this list might properly be added the name of the Italian, dall' Abaco, since his scores, being now also available for study, reveal many interesting traits pointing toward originality and progress. He is to be classed among the earlier composers of this period, for he was prominently associated with the musical life of Munich during the first part of the eighteenth century.

that Gossec was the first French writer to make use of the clarinet. Again, its introduction into the Opéra in 1772 — just in time to be of service to Gluck — is apparently authenticated by Francoeur. Since, however, the clarinet was already embodied in Rameau's scoring, the present writer desires to call attention to these obvious discrepancies. At all events, we know that the resources of the clarinet were developed by both Gossec and Gluck, even though at that time only an incomplete scale in the keys of C and F could be obtained from the instrument. Gossec was not conspicuously original either in instrumental form or in orchestration, even though his Requiem, for example, does contain instances of interesting scoring. Neither does the fact that his first symphony preceded Haydn's by five years credit him with being an epoch-making orchestral composer. For his productions, like those of Sammartini, are now but of historic interest, whereas Haydn's still find ready listeners. And so his place in history is distinctly that of pioneer and promoter of independent orchestral performance, and with the organization of the "Concerts des Amateurs" his programs included the works of such foreign composers as the Belgian, van Malder, the Bohemian, Wanhal, likewise Stamitz, eventually Haydn. His career is certainly unique, since in view of the fact that he was born two years after Haydn's birth and died two years after Beethoven's death, the complete panorama of the classic era was unfolded before his eyes, and during the course of his ninety-five years it was his privilege to witness the ascendency in turn of Gluck, Haydn, Mozart and Beethoven together with their co-workers. During his lifetime, moreover, there sprang into existence also the Romantic Movement which, emerging out of the later works of Beethoven, was seized upon and elaborated by Spohr and Weber with their followers.

A striking illustration of the extent to which at this period the concert stage was already exerting its power is afforded by the biography of Grétry, who in spite of his restless dramatic disposition found time, in the enthusiasm of his productiveness, to write no less than six symphonies, not to mention a number of minor works in the form of chamber music — and this in the face of the fact that he did not know how to write for the orchestra! His saving grace in this field was his fund of humor, tuneful melody and sound musical judgment.

Notwithstanding all that has just been said, these signs of activity in France cannot be compared with contemporary achievements in Germany, henceforth to be the permanent home and supreme arbiter of cyclic form and stable instrumentation. And not the least of the inceptive stimuli leading to the discovery of the proper constituency of a perfectly balanced orchestra must be accredited to the Mannheim orchestra, which became celebrated under Stamitz and Cannabich. At the time of Mozart's birth, that organization embraced a string band of ten first violins, ten seconds, four violas, four 'cellos and four double-basses. It will be seen at a glance that excepting a paucity of violas, the value of plentiful strings and their numerical relation one to the other was keenly appreciated. The wood-wind was likewise logically represented by two flutes, two oboes, two bassoons, to which clarinets were added some ten years later. There were also four horns, twelve trumpets and trombones, kettle-drums, an organ, and a chorus of twenty-four voices. Why so many instruments of brass should have been considered neces-sary is open to question. Independent parts for not more than two horns and two trumpets was the rule among the early symphonic writers, and not one of Haydn's symphonies contains parts for more than two horns, neither did his simple demands require more than two trumpets. True, Mozart occasionally called for four horns in his earlier works, but like Haydn, he used trumpets but sparingly. It is hardly conceivable that competent conductors of so noble an organization could have been guilty of such inartistic procedure as to allow the brass, comparatively unimportant as their functions were at that time, to be reën-forced by reduplication. These supernumerary instruments must have remained silent at concert performances, being reserved rather for dramatic representations or sacred renditions for which they could be of more legitimate service.[4]

Interesting are the comparisons between the constituency of the Dresden orchestra in 1732 and that of Mannheim in 1756. It will be remembered that when referring to Hasse, the Dresden Opera was cited as harboring twenty-five strings, wood-wind instruments to the number of twelve, two horns, a number of trumpets and trombones, besides kettle-drums and two clavichords — in all some fifty instrumental performers. And, as already enumerated, the orchestra at Mannheim was comprised of thirty-two strings, six wood and sixteen brass instru-ments, as well as kettle-drums and organ, making a total of about sixty. All in all, the venerable operatic orchestras during the eighteenth century were the fuller and richer in resources, and were in possession of a larger numerical disposition of wood and brass even if inadequately supplied with strings. But the tendency to correct this deficiency in the constitution of concert orchestras resulted in the acquirement of greater elasticity and transparency, which was of all importance for the interpretation of the works of the great classicists whose servitor the orches-tra was soon to become. And subsequently in writing for specific orchestras for which a sufficient number of strings had not yet been supplied, it may be that these masters intuitively presaged that this much needed metamorphosis of internal organization would gradually take place as the direct reflex of their own

[4] Another plausible explanation is that the extra trumpeters and trombonists should be accredited to the "Hof Musik," which may have been only an adjunct to the "Hof Kapelle." Their principal duty may have been to announce the arrival of the Elector by a fanfare, and to give other signals at the many public functions of the Court. It has been pointed out to the present writer that this theory seems confirmed by an illustration in a book covering this period where is shown a boxful of trumpeters at a Court performance of opera at Dresden.

exalted demands for improved instrumentation and artistic rendition. Fortunately, sentient appreciation for careful rehearsal leading to a high standard of rendition had already found a champion in Emanuel Bach, and this objective was jealously fostered by Gossec, Stamitz and Cannabich, all of whom devoted themselves assiduously to the obtainment of purity of tone, equality of dynamic force, precision and coöperation, elasticity, phraseology, *nuance*. Naturally, the violin, by virtue of artistic merit and paramount importance, received their most careful attention, in consequence of which the standard of the strings as a whole was elevated to that proficiency which made it possible for the classicists to employ them with such freedom as had never before been essayed.

The aim of this comparative survey of orchestras and orchestration as related with the complex phases of musical progression during the careers of Bach, Händel and Gluck has been to elucidate the artistic situation as found by the three succeeding masters.

(Summary on page 68.)

CHAPTER VII.

HAYDN, MOZART, AND BEETHOVEN.

I.

IT is almost superfluous to say that [*] HAYDN (1732–1809), the true father of the modern symphony and string quartet, was, after Monteverde and Scarlatti, the most potent factor in establishing a perfectly balanced orchestra as a whole. Indeed, one might modify the eulogy previously bestowed upon Monteverde, and say that whereas *he* may be looked upon as the father of modern instrumentation, *Haydn* was the father of modern orchestration. Like Monteverde, he was constantly experimenting, being, moreover, aided by his exceptionally favorable position at the court of Prince Esterhazy. To such an extent are his achievements known to all, that it is permissible to but touch upon the vital landmarks which constitute the distinguishable features of his quasi-created cyclic forms. This term is used advisedly, for although he accepted the erudite forms of his predecessors and contemporaries, and, like them, devolved the symphony from the earlier *concerto* for several instruments, he improved upon these forms to such a degree, that they emerged from their archaic chrysalis in rejuvenated attire.

Lack of space forbids more than a passing reference to the coevolution of the string quartet, that momentous vehicle for the sonata form, whose growth was concurrent with that of the symphony. But in both these branches of art Haydn left his indelible stamp upon the creations of Mozart and Beethoven, indeed Mozart, though more emotional and impressive, did not enlarge upon Haydn's form, and even Beethoven, the tone-poet, remained to the last true to its substance. Parenthetically it should be remembered that on the other hand Haydn's quartets and symphonies were in turn influenced by Mozart, from whom, moreover, both he and Beethoven acquired a more subtle insight into the skilful handling of the wood-wind. The symphonies of Haydn and Beethoven have been felicitously compared by styling those of the former, comedies, those of the latter, tragedies. Finally, the extent to which the reputation of Haydn's symphonies travelled is discovered in the already mentioned performances thereof in Paris (at the "Concerts des Amateurs," founded by the Belgian Gossec, for which organization Haydn specifically composed several symphonies), not to speak of his triumphs in London as well as in the musical centres of his native land.

[*] See Appendix of Musical Illustrations, Examples 10 to 17.

47

These rather extended references to the rise of symphonic music are surely justifiable in that from it dates the dynasty of monarchical orchestration.[5]

Haydn's development of his formal architecture can be summed up by saying that he knit together and enlarged the cycle of complex forms, extended the separate movements individually, imparted to them order, clearness, variety, and developed free thematic treatment.

As has just been stated, the orchestra in Haydn's plasmic hands improved as a unit. He introduced no new instruments excepting later on the clarinet, indeed, his scores betray on the whole a greater reticence in the employment of numeric varieties of instruments than do those of Bach and Händel. Haydn's genius matured slowly; his earlier scoring does not exhibit any advanced degree of originality, and not until after Mozart had in turn become the greater did Haydn stand forth in the true strength of *his* greatness. The antennae of that long-lived crustacean, the Neapolitan School, had touched even Haydn as they had Händel before him, and the influence was directly beneficial, since it modified the Teutonic tendencies inoculated by his predilection for the style of Emmanuel Bach, and fostered a regard for melody. Though he used no new material, Haydn instituted a freer method of employing each instrument according to its peculiarities and powers. Despite the fact that he was addicted to the custom of three-part string writing as established by Cavalli long before, he developed the art of welding the component parts firmly together, and thereby secured vitality and elasticity.

The strings were now one complete and compact body.[a] Careful attention was bestowed both upon the manner of writing for them and upon a judicious numerical selection of each species to the end that they might not only balance, but also assist and show off to the best advantage the characteristic qualities of every part, one against the other. Only the violoncello was as yet subservient, and the harpsichord was still retained.

In the distribution of the parts for the wood-wind, he at first imitated Händel's usual methods of merely reënforcing the string parts in unison. But having benefited by repeated practical experience, and especially after the appearance of Mozart upon the arena, Haydn's writing for the wood became freer.[b] The oboe, whose functions are now largely supplanted by the more feminine and soulful clarinet, was much used as a solo instrument. And when at last the great classicists came upon the discovery that by supporting a solo instrument with held chords in the wind,[c] they could attain a more pliant mode of expression than had

---

[5] It is not intended to belittle the original and valuable efforts of the Mannheim composer, Stamitz, and of the several other representatives of various nations as referred to on pages 42 and 43, even though preëminence in the development of orchestration and form is accorded to Haydn and Mozart.

[a] Ex. 16, 17.   [b] Ex. 11, 14, 15.   [c] Ex. 13.

been possible in the earlier stiff and formal polyphonic style, — from that time on a new and poetic pathway was opened up, and the modern style of writing for the wood-wind may be said to have fairly begun.

In the use of the brass Haydn was conservative. Trombones were absent from his symphonic scheme, and the province of trumpets, if they were used at all, was exceedingly primitive, so that only the horns gained greater freedom of treatment. Thus, for example, the valuable and eventually common custom of strengthening the bass by sustained tonic and dominant horn parts was employed by Haydn in his symphony in D, No. 2 (Breitkopf & Haertel). But more than two real parts for horns are not to be found in any of his works, and the demand for four horns in the Hunting Chorus in his "Seasons" will, at a glance, be recognized as having for its purpose the reduplication of two-part writing, so as to obtain a clearer melodic delineation. And although prominence of metallic quality was thus acquired, the rich chord effect of later times is conspicuous for its absence.

When Haydn wrote his first symphony at the time when Mozart was in his infancy, he employed, in addition to strings, only two oboes and two horns. By the end of the eighteenth century, the normal symphonic orchestra had been increased so as to include strings, two flutes, two oboes, two bassoons, two horns, two trumpets and kettle-drums. To these were quite occasionally added two clarinets. The rôle of the trumpets as well as of kettle-drums was to augment the effectiveness of climaxes, to emphasize rhythm, to add virility, or to suggest martial portraiture. But the harp shared the fortunes of the trombones in that it was as yet denied admittance to the symphonic phalanx.

Of incidental interest is the characteristic deployment of bassoons in the slow movement of the symphony in D already referred to; and the introduction into the orchestra of massed short chords struck simultaneously by all the strings must also be attributed to Haydn.

Finally, his "Creation" embodies successful expedients for descriptive writing. In this masterpiece, the strings, together with a full complement of wind instruments in pairs, are further augmented by the usual kettle-drums, a double-bassoon, and three trombones, — an aggregation which, apart from the manner of using it for the purpose of tone-painting, is typical of Beethoven's enlarged orchestra as employed in his crowning graphic movements. However, this demand for so huge an apparatus as the assistant to Haydn's mightiest choral and embryo-romantic composition was exceptional, and as the corollary of his orchestration, when reviewed as a whole, one might say that he worked with simple means, and although his pages do not present delicate combinations, he obtained vigorous and fresh results.[d]

(d) Ex. 10, 12, 17.

II.

(*) MOZART (1756–1791), universal conqueror, peerless melodist, unrivalled purist, contributed equally to the development of orchestration as to all other branches of musical art. Opera, symphony, chamber and church music alike blossomed and ripened at his magic touch; and the tonal tints of his scoring assumed a mellow guise foreign to the lighter shading of Haydn's orchestration. Mozart was a cosmopolitan in so far as that he moulded his polyphony, formal structure and orchestration in accordance with the classicism of Teutonic lineage, imbibed the limpid suavity of Italian melody, and adapted the tragic energy and emotional interpretation of the text as initiated by Gluck in France. This vivid emotionalism is plainly to be seen in the dramatic scenes of "Idomeneo" and "Don Giovanni." His perfect command of contrapuntal subtleties, thematic development, and vocal composition, combined with the most precocious creative genius, enabled him not only to build upon the heirloom of Bach's church music and Haydn's symphonies and quartets, but to establish a basis for subsequent genuinely German opera. For it is beyond question that specifically the "Zauber-flöte" contains the germ of Weber's romanticism.

For the form of his independent instrumental works, Mozart followed the precepts of Haydn, but he enlarged them, and imbued their contents with a certain strategic power for evoking more serious contemplation and enduring impressive-ness. Adherence to tonality, not only in each individually complete movement, but also in successive and related complex forms, was one of the fundamental canons of Mozart's creed. This tonal consistency is to be found even in his operas, whether employed as the connecting link between the more gentle sections — suggestive of a delicate string of pearls, or as a mode of obtaining subtle continuity of thought and action in the dramatic portions.

In orchestration, Mozart combined the best characteristics of both Gluck and Haydn, and in his hands it gained counterpoise and vitality. As a natural out-come, the harpsichord was banished from the orchestra, but incidentally it should be remembered that by no means did Mozart undervalue this instrument in its proper sphere, for to him is due the ascendency of the pianoforte concerto, which he left as a direct bequest to Beethoven, who not only seized upon it with avidity, but even caused it to immortalize some of his most sublime conceptions. Mozart's writing for the orchestra is distinguishable for amalgamating as well as for contrasting the earlier polyphonic methods with the monophonic style that was being cultivated by his contemporaries. The last movement of the "Jupiter" symphony will at once be recalled as an admirable illustration of advanced orches-

(*) See Appendix of Musical Illustrations, Examples 18 to 23.

tral polyphony. [a] As has just been said, Mozart followed and elaborated Haydn's symphonic instrumentation, but he added greater freedom to the strings, [b] more variety and contrast to the wood, [c] developed the art of combining wind accompaniment and instrumental solo effects, [d] and in general illustrated the capabilities and ideal functions of each specific instrument. Furthermore, constant application to operatic writing stimulated a desire for varied rhythm, and this attainment is reflected in his symphonic compositions. Finally, it should be said with emphasis that sensitive regard for individualistic tonal tints in instrumentation was one of the most conspicuous attributes of Mozart's genius, and despite the fact that already the masters of his epoch had had recourse to the application of variated tone-color, nevertheless Mozart is universally considered as having been the first to do so in a really successful manner. By relegating the harpsichord, it became necessary to write for the strings in such a manner as to insure independent solidity and coherence. Or, to put it the other way, Mozart's scoring for the string band made further employment of the harpsichord superfluous. This he accomplished in the face of frequent three-part writing. The danger of incurring caesuras in harmonic structure or lack in volume of sound was obviated by the skilful artifice of contrapuntal motion which, so to speak, generates warmth of tonal color — heat and motion being an equivalent one for the other, and, as Gevaërt suggests, this theorem is applicable to music. But Mozart by no means neglected four-part writing, [e] and both the violoncello and the hitherto much neglected viola were advanced to a position more in keeping with their worth.

Mozart's employment of the symphonic orchestra was one of conservatism in regard to compass, as illustrated by the G minor symphony, from which even trumpets and kettle-drums are debarred. Peculiar to the scoring of his greatest symphonies is the consistent use of but one flute, whereas the remaining wind is represented in pairs. Delicacy was the key-note for the wood-wind. For example, he delighted in embellishing a melody by the combination of violins redoubled in the octave by a flute and in the sub-octave by a bassoon. Another distinguishable trait of his was the substituting of an oboe for the violins in the above combination. These are but passing exemplifications of countless dainty conceptions that the most casual perusal of his pages will divulge; and they offer an unwearying source of delectation in consequence of their naïve and guileless character. It is true that for *Tuttis*, Mozart was satisfied with certain conventional methods, such as an exaggerated use of wood-wind passages in thirds and sixths. But this practice was common likewise to Beethoven, and not until after the advent of the Romanticists did it fall into disuse, indeed, no less a modern conservative than Brahms was content to adapt classical mannerisms of this

(a) Ex. 20.   (b) Ex. 19, 20.   (c) Ex. 18, 22, 23.
          (d) Ex. 21.   (e) Ex. 19.

nature.   But only subsequent to Mozart's visit to Mannheim when he was twenty-one years of age, and not until after he had convinced himself of the indispensability of the clarinet — that sympathetic medium between high and low wood-wind — was it possible to give adequate variety of color and effect to this hitherto rather homogeneous secondary choir.   And thus, concurrent with the emancipation of the wood-wind from many stereotyped formulas, was the recognition that clarinets began to command in Mozart's orchestral scheme.   And although they were originally included only in the symphony in E flat,[f] he eventually added them to the one in G minor; and in the "Zauberflöte" the instrument received effective and original treatment.   Again, although Mozart's sunny nature would not naturally conceive such morbid and sentimental effects as elicited by Weber from the lower tones of the clarinet, he at any rate appreciated a certain value of such tones by employing them in the course of flowing passages [g] as in the first Finale of "Don Giovanni."   Mention is due, at this juncture, of the prominent appearance in the "Zauberflöte" of the obsolete basset-horn, since, as will be recalled, it belongs to the genealogy of clarinets and is now superseded by its descendant, the bass-clarinet.   The classic literature of chamber music presents no more favorable examples for profitable study than do Mozart's *divertissements*, in which various combinations of wind instruments alone are treated with rare delicacy and effectiveness.   Not being subjected, as in orchestral compositions, to comparison with the greater agility and more sensitive attributes of the strings, they are enabled to assert themselves, and to display in full measure their individual characteristics and expressive powers.

Mozart's requirements of the brass show but a slight improvement upon those of Haydn,[h] excepting that his style of writing for it betrays better judgment.   A demand for more than two horns was rare, and occurs, strange to say, in his earlier works, for some of which he employed four.   Later on he again exceptionally used this number in "Idomeneo."   But of his representative creations, the G minor symphony is scored for but two horns, the E flat and C for two horns and two trumpets.   Consistent with the usage of his predecessors, it was only in church music for redoubling the voices and in operatic works for dramatic effects that Mozart drew upon the trombones, at first sparingly, eventually, as in the "Zauberflöte," more freely; and Gluck's precedent of employing them in three-part harmony was sustained.

In so brief an outline, it is not possible to more than indicate the cardinal points of evolutionary advancement as contributed to orchestration by Mozart. But one prominent feature of his preëminent versatility reveals itself in the fact that whereas the long line of his illustrious predecessors had, with the one exception of Haydn, developed the art of writing for the orchestra more as a secondary

(f) Ex. 22, 23.   (g) Ex. 23.   (h) Ex. 20.

means to some one particular and all-absorbing primary end, Mozart's genius devoted itself with impartiality and parallel success just as much to instrumentation and orchestration as to the formal structures of his instrumental works or to the contents of his operas and masses. And the laurels that crown the herculean achievements of his brief life are symbolic of the æsthetic, the chaste, the ideal.

III.

Three prominent characteristics are associated with the name of [*] BEETHOVEN (1770–1827), the greatest universal master in the chronicles of musical history. To him must be attributed the ideal culmination of classic purity, both as to structural design and thematic development. Through him, form became subordinated to human expression. From him the Romantic Movement drew its direct inspiration. In other words, Beethoven forged the connecting link between the classicists and the romanticists, between absolute and programmatic, objective and subjective music, between the primarily formal and the essentially soulful. In the general principles of form and technical procedure, Beethoven accepted the precedents established by his immediate predecessors, and his earlier works show the influence of both Haydn and Mozart. But the impelling force of his independent and assertive genius, nurtured by the rugged characteristics peculiar to the tendencies of his Dutch and German descent, urged him to further bold and unhesitating innovations whenever novel effects could thereby be attained.

In connection with distinctively formal treatment, the most prominent feature of this amplification lies in the development even to minuteness of inner details, the unification of thematic material, the increase of proportion, and the acquisition of breadth of style and nobility of subject-matter.

But of far more momentous purport are the fruits of his spirituality and profound religiousness. Beethoven was a tone-poet to the core, and his search for emotional expression caused him to disregard fixed design whenever it interfered with freedom of thought. Thus in adapting the cyclic sonata form, he enhanced it by means of perfected monody based on the higher Folk-song, by means of richer harmonies, freer modulations, varied rhythm, greater license in the juxtaposition of tonalities, and elasticity in the application of traditional forms — Beethoven's quest for beauty of form being, moreover, only secondary in importance to its own reactionary fitness for beauty of expression. Thus Beethoven became the master of form and expression combined, reconciled, unified.

(*) See Appendix of Musical Illustrations, Examples 24 to 35.

Mozart and Beethoven share the same unique and unparalleled characteristics in that the genius of both of them was so universal in nature as to make the question of deciding in what particular branch of composition they excelled a difficult one. So Beethoven, greatest of symphonic exponents, enriched the world with string quartets and chamber music that are perfection exemplified, produced a mighty series of pianoforte concertos and sonatas that are unexcelled, and dedicated a host of his loftiest inspirations to the glorification of the Church. He wrote but one opera — it has become immortal; but one oratorio — the sincerity and depth of its pathos awaken sympathetic response at each renewed hearing; but one violin concerto — it is still the ideal, likewise the despair of every violin virtuoso. And upon riveting the attention solely upon the instrumentation of his orchestral pages, one finds that every bar of the score bears the impress of a master's touch, and of such a master as the world had never before produced. He discovered the utmost capabilities of each instrument, introduced innovations in the method of handling them, both as solo interpreters and in combination, and illustrated that even without the aid of a so-called modern orchestra, picture-painting can be attained. That is to say, impressions of the mind of insufficient distinctness to call forth verbal utterance, are nevertheless capable of tonal exposition. Hence arises the expression "musical language," and quite especially in connection with instrumentation one says that the orchestra "possesses the faculty of language." The Pastoral Symphony is a graphic exemplification of this truth.

Beethoven's instrumentation bears the unmistakable impress of his own personal individuality, and purely sensuous tone-effect is ever subordinated to the inceptive æsthetic scheme and clearness of thematic delineation. The employment of specific tonal quality of the various instruments capable of variated coloring, effectiveness, and scope, was absolutely faithful to the momentary requirements of the orchestral situation. And thus, while his predecessors had been absorbed in the contemplation and exposition of abstract musical thought, and, on the other hand, the sequent composers of the nineteenth century laid undue stress upon the portrayal of their conceptions in gorgeous orchestral raiment, Beethoven's masterpieces embody the temperate assimilation of fervent feeling, architectural structure, contrast of the various choirs, and intermixing of instrumental coloring, simultaneously and harmoniously developed, without apparent effort, all-satisfying, inseparable.

One feature of Beethoven's greatness is emphasized by the self-restraint he exercised in usually making demands for but a modest apparatus as the interpreter of his orchestral conceptions. Thus, in spite of being tremendously progressive, and betraying at every step the inclination to enlarge the scope of his creations in every way, he was content to employ Mozart's scoring for all of his symphonies excepting the Fifth, Sixth, and Ninth, — that is to say, strings, the four usual wood-instruments in pairs, two horns, two trumpets, and kettle-drums, were practically sufficient for his needs. This numerical distribution of parts differed but slightly in all but the above three excepted symphonies. Comparing this aggregation with those in Mozart's three representative symphonies, we find, as the only difference, that Beethoven's wood-wind includes two flutes in all but the Fourth Symphony, and that clarinets were now enrolled as a permanent adjunct to the orchestra. Two horns sufficed for them all excepting for the Third, "Eroica," where three are to be found, this being, moreover, the first time that more than two had been employed in symphonic writing by Beethoven.

The orchestral canvass of the Fifth, C minor, presents the coöperation of a piccolo flute, a contra-bassoon, and three trombones; all of these, however, remain silent until the victorious entrance of the Finale. To the Sixth — the Pastoral — are added a piccolo flute and two trombones instead of three, whereas in the Ninth, the usual symphonic cohort is supplemented by a piccolo, a double-bassoon, four horns, three trombones, and human voices. It is worthy of note that this new departure of employing a second couplet of horns in the symphonic scheme concludes the evolution of the classical orchestra. For the incorporation into the concert orchestra of the oboe da caccia, resuscitated in the form of the English horn, of the modern bass-clarinet, of the opheicleide and the usurper of its functions, the bass-tuba, was an outgrowth of the Romantic Movement. Likewise the harp, in spite of its venerable origin and perennial usage, was, during the eighteenth century, an adjunct to the operatic orchestra only, for histrionic effects and historic representations.

The scores of no other composer can be more profitably studied than those of Beethoven, and a high percentage of the examples set forth in all standard treatises on instrumentation are drawn from his works. Apart from the fact that his orchestration not only embodied but improved upon and matured the orthodox style of writing as bequeathed to him by Haydn and Mozart, his pages abound in daring innovations, bold and startling; in subtle combinations, delicate and pathetic; a kaleidoscope of sequent effects now contemplative and restful, now tender and languishing, impetuous and fiery, at times even jocose, weird, bizarre. And throughout is manifested the depth of his nature, the nobility of his purpose.

In writing for the strings, Beethoven attained a degree of excellence that has never been surpassed. He fulfilled every requirement, whether of solidity, sonority, flexibility, or delicacy. [a] With bold and vigorous strokes, he infused warmth and increased vitality into the inner and lower voices, and the quartet being thereby more closely knit together, the resultant effect was that of breadth and power. He was the first to carry the orchestral violins into the

[a] Ex. 30, 31, 33.

ethereal domain of their highest range in the overture to "Egmont." Incomparable is the boisterous string passage toward the close of the "Leonora" Overture, No. 3, as well as the fughetta in the Scherzo of the Fifth Symphony, where the double-basses are for the first time allowed unfettered license. [b] Finally, Beethoven elevated the violoncello once for all to its proper sphere as an emotional and heroic interpreter, of which the C minor Symphony affords a favorite example in that the 'cellos, assisted by the violas, usher in the opening theme of the slow movement. [c] The violas likewise gained in individuality, and in the last movement of the Ninth Symphony even divided viola parts are to be found.

Beethoven was especially happy in discovering the ideal potentialities of the wood-wind, and from him originated the practice of reuniting the higher species both in contrasting and amalgamating choirs. [d] No better model for successful flute writing can be cited than that in the Allegro of the "Leonora" Overture, No. 3; and the genial attributes of the oboe which, though latent, had never before been exposed, are fittingly treated in the scherzos of the Pastoral and Choral symphonies. The clarinet was now a regularly constituted member of the orchestra, and specimens of characteristic writing for it are to be found in the slow movements of the symphonies in B flat and A, and also in the Finale of the "Eroica," where a judicious introduction of clarinet arpeggios lends warmth and color to the Melos.

Perhaps no other orchestral instrument received more careful consideration from Beethoven than the bassoon, and his partiality for it resulted in detaching it from its former subservient position as bass for the wood and horns, and elevating it to the dignity of an equal associate to the remaining wood-wind, with especial regard for the quality of its tenor range. [e] Thus Beethoven evinced a peculiar predilection for redoubling a melody, assigned either to violins or to an instrument of wood, with a bassoon in the sub-octave. Again, he recognized its sustaining powers as independent bass, provided the balance of the instruments to be sustained were nicely adjusted. Gevaërt calls attention to just such a combination in "Egmont," where one bassoon acts as bass to the strings while the 'cellos and double-basses occasionally assist. And, as he further remarks, the choice was admirable, for no other instrument, as, for instance, the horn, would have been suitable. Consistent with his sentient appreciation for the bassoon, Beethoven rescued the double-bassoon [f] from comparative obscurity, and although he employed it invariably as a reduplication of the 'cellos and basses, it was awarded a more conspicuous rôle in "Fidelio" than in the C minor Symphony.

Classic conservatism in the use of the brass found no exception even when consigned to Beethoven's inspired pen other than the previously mentioned

(b) Ex. 27.   (c) Ex. 24.   (d) Ex. 25, 28, 34.
          (e) Ex. 26, 31.   (f) Ex. 30.

augmentation of horn parts and the more frequent requisition for trombones. His horn writing [g] followed that of Mozart, but his style was freer, bolder, and the results more resonant, especially in such passages as the familiar jubilant fanfare in the Scherzo of the "Eroica" and again in the Scherzo of the "Pastoral." On the other hand, the decidedly primitive functions of the trumpets [h] were in no wise ameliorated, an incident that is largely to be accounted for by the mechanical limitations of the instrument which still existed at that day. As for the trombones, to have drawn upon them merely for increase of volume, would have been contrary to the ethics of Beethoven's artistic creed. The fact that they did add sonority was therefore but a subsidiary issue, and in climaxes such as the Finale of the Fifth Symphony, their mission was primarily that of lending grandeur and richness to the final scintillating tableau. [i]

In conclusion, the kettle-drums must receive especial mention. It will be noticed that as yet but passing reference to them has been made in these pages, for it was left to Beethoven to discover their genuinely tragic resources. He not only enlarged the scope of the instruments by having them tuned to intervals other than the conventional and stereotyped fourth and fifth, but gave them expressive powers such as had never been attained before. Consequently there was added to the orchestra a practically new member, since he caused the tympani to respond to his dictates, as it were, with warm and throbbing pulse-beats, at times permeating, dominating, subduing the entire orchestral color-scheme. Striking illustrations of this latent power are to be found in the third movement of the C minor Symphony [j] and the Finale of the Pianoforte Concerto in E flat; likewise in the Finale of the Eighth and the Scherzo of the Ninth symphonies, in both of which they are tuned in octaves; and in the introduction to the second act of "Fidelio," where they are tuned to the interval of the diminished fifth. Further specimens of specifically solo writing will be recalled in the Adagio of the B flat Symphony, the beginning of the Violin Concerto, and the introduction to the "Mount of Olives."

A discussion of Beethoven's titanic achievements, even if confined to his orchestral writings, is prone to lead the student into so deep a maze of absorbing illustrations of his genius, that it becomes necessary to find an arbitrary stopping place. Therefore this review may be tersely summed up by saying that the culmination of classic purity, the subordination to human feeling of purely formal structure and sensuous tone-effect, and a systematic development of descriptive music, are the essentials of Beethoven's creations. His orchestration stands as a model for all time. He is the connecting link between the classicists and the romanticists. And in a word, the consummation of his artistic striving was freedom and spirituality.

(Summary on page 68.)

(g) Ex. 30, 32, 35.   (h) Ex. 30.   (i) Ex. 30.   (j) Ex. 29.

CHAPTER VIII.

THE CONTEMPORARIES OF BEETHOVEN.

I.

THE career of Beethoven, extending well into the nineteenth century, overlaps the rise and growth of the Romantic Movement, — a movement that embodied tendencies with which his later works show sympathetic accord. The authors of this new departure were instigated by poetic aspirations closely allied to those of Beethoven; and since his creative horizon was constantly expanding, the idealistic texture of his productions and theirs was harmoniously interwoven. But while the scope of German art was being assimilated into channels of which the objective was natural emotion so expressed as to be portrayed in tangible form, Rossini's seductive charm had hypnotized all Europe, with the result that the progress even of Beethoven was momentarily hampered and his immediate reputation eclipsed. Therefore before proceeding to a further analysis of orchestration as advanced by the exponents of the Romantic Movement with which all prominent German composers after Beethoven are to be more or less conspicuously identified, a final bird's-eye view of musical activity in other countries will properly conclude the history of the so-called classic era. To do this it will be necessary to take up again the thread of dramatic development which we have already traced as far as Grétry, in whom the first period of *opéra comique* may be said to have culminated. Moreover for the sake of continuity, this discussion may well include such of the nineteenth century composers as were not noticeably affected by the magnetism of the romanticists or of the sequent "New Movement." And the preferential arena for the reproduction of both French and Italian works was still the Parisian stage, in which was vested the dangerous power of passing conclusive judgment upon the offerings of her votaries. Consequently, the characteristics of such luminaries as were deemed worthy of her benisons can be briefly summed up without regard to nationality; and these meteor-like apparitions captivated in turn the entire musical world, to the neglect of the worthier creations of Gluck and Mozart.

The lyric *genre* as bequeathed by Grétry was ardently cultivated by a series of sturdy exponents including his contemporary of evanescent fame d'Alayrac, followed by Boieldieu, Isouard, a native of Malta, the long-lived Auber, Hérold,

Halévy, Adam. All but the last of these were born in the last quarter of the eighteenth century, being, together with the domiciliated Isouard, typical Frenchmen, devoted to national tradition, style of writing, and methods of instrumentation. And conspicuously through the collective efforts of Boieldieu, Auber and Hérold was the standard of *opéra comique* elevated to high dignity. This exclusive aggrandizement of the lyric stage by native composers affords a striking contrast to the history of opera in serious vein. For in reference to the latter, the attitude of the public was marked by illogical preferentiation, in consequence of which their vacillating plaudits were bestowed with but scant discrimination. True, French composers at first tenaciously held their own, as exemplified by the sterling achievements of Méhul (1763) and by the fleeting triumphs of his contemporaries, Lesueur, Berton, Catel. Nor did subsequently the more important representatives of the lyric style such as Boieldieu, Auber and Halévy allow undisputed sway to foreign interlopers in the field of grand opera. And the so-called "historic school" of grand opera, first introduced by the Italian, Spontini (1774), and eventually abused by the German, Meyerbeer (1791), was admirably exploited by Auber's "La Muette di Portici," which was produced the year after Beethoven's death. This work directly paved the way for "Guillaume Tell," the crowning achievement of Rossini (1797), as well as for Meyerbeer's initiatory embodiment of French romanticism, "Robert le Diable." Sequent to the baneful revival by Rossini of more or less retrogressional Italian opera appeared the mellifluous fabrications of Donizetti (1797) and of Bellini (1802), with which undramatic productions must be classed also the earlier works of Verdi (1813) in consequence of their voluptuous melodic exuberance.

In Germany, meanwhile, the standard of opera in lighter vein was upheld by Konradin Kreutzer (1780), the heir of Hiller and Dittersdorf. In England, the pianist, Field (1782), was initiating a new style of writing for the pianoforte that was to serve as a model for Chopin.

II.

It is proper that the compositions of Cherubini (1760–1842) be treated apart from those of his contemporaries, for they are in many respects distinct by themselves. The fact that he was born in Italy bears little relation to the style of his productions, for only in his earlier works are Italian methods particularly noticeable. The name of Cherubini has become immortal chiefly on account of his church music, of which he is the first truly great modern master. Nor must his permanent influence upon the form of French opera be underestimated, notwithstanding the fact that his own operas were only moderately successful. For the Gluck-Piccini controversy impressed him deeply; moreover, Mozart's operas were at that time already exciting world-wide admiration. As a result of these powerful influences, Cherubini was led to combine both the German and the French styles, as exemplified in "Lodoiska"; and henceforth the drama of France may be said to have acquired permanent and definite form.

The chief characteristics of his church music consist of a fusion of the elevated style of the sixteenth century, a severe yet masterly contrapuntal treatment, and withal a remarkable clearness in form and details. These models of sacred writing which belong, perhaps, more particularly to the French school, are convincing proof that so-called antiquated principles can be assimilated into modern methods. Lavoix calls attention to the criticism that whereas Cherubini's operas were not sufficiently dramatic, his church music was too much so. This may be true; but the purity and nobility of subject-matter, the warmth and breadth in instrumentation, counteract any possible theatrical tendencies.

The orchestra is much used in Cherubini's sacred works. The orchestration is flexible and vivid; each instrument is treated judiciously, and the tonal color is ever sonorous and varied. Prout refers to the Requiem in C minor as being a splendid piece of sombre tone-painting, and masterful in its appropriateness. The opening chorus is remarkable for its pathos, being scored for divided violas and 'cellos, double-basses, two bassoons, two horns and muffled kettle-drums. In the introduction to the "Chant sur la Mort de Joseph Haydn," an extended passage for four violoncellos *con sordini* proves that Rossini was not the first to discover the value of their independent employment. In the same work, one of Wagner's procedures in the use of the bass-tuba is anticipated in that the opheicleide is detached from its usual alliance to the trombones, and is employed alone as a reduplication of the double-basses. Cherubini was conservative in the use of the brass, although in isolated cases, where special effects were needed, larger choirs of loud-voiced instruments are, of course, to be found. As an example, the mass in A calls for four horns, three trombones, and an opheicleide. On the other hand, the instrumentation of Cherubini's operas shows greater reserve, and in one or two cases, entire acts are effectively scored without once drawing upon either trumpets or kettle-drums. It might be added that an interesting example for English horn is to be found in "Anacréon"; that the instrument was as yet but rarely heard in France is demonstrated by the fact that Cherubini felt it necessary to write "clarinet *ad libitum*" under the English horn part.

III.

MÉHUL (1763–1817) ranks among the greatest evolutionists of French instrumentation. His talents developed at an early age; his career was one of steady progress, and culminated in "Joseph," one of the loftiest dramatic works

France possesses. Following in Gluck's footsteps, he emphasized the value of declamation and made much use of melodrama. The operatic overtures also were carefully developed. Although his orchestration was somewhat heavy, and embodied the frequent repetition of certain stereotyped formulas, he proved himself a worthy successor to Gluck in the successful portrayal of dramatic personages by means of instrumental expression. Much of his music is decidedly picturesque even though his instrumentation is lacking in daintiness. The distinctive features of Méhul's orchestration are sonority, novel combinations, and at times a certain melancholy coloring. The earliest use of low string effects is attributed to him, and especial prominence was given to the viola. As is well known, his opera "Uthal" is unique in that violins are absent throughout the entire work. The harp is an important factor in both "Uthal" and "Joseph." Méhul showed considerable partiality for the brass, and more than once, four horn parts are to be found in his scores.

LESUEUR (1763) has been called the predecessor of Berlioz as an exponent of "program" music. He was fond of grand and majestic combinations, but was artistically more successful in writing for the church than for the drama. He was fortunate in having under his control a large orchestra at the Notre Dame, and his contributions to French instrumentation in detail are important. He frequently multiplied the violin parts into four, and even divided the violas. Again, the violins were at times omitted, although he did not go to the extent of leaving them out through an entire work as Méhul did in his opera "Uthal." Lesueur may have indirectly influenced Wagner's scoring of the tetralogy in that twelve harps, divided into two sections, are required for a faithful rendition of "Les Bardes," and in a footnote he specifically exacts a predominance of harp quality of tone. Like many of his subsequent compatriots, he frequently made requisition for curious instruments of percussion.

IV.

In turning to the works of BOIELDIEU (1775–1834), we find therein a refreshing example of naïveté, spontaneous originality, and flowing melody. Italian tendencies are noticeable, but the style remains pure and distinctly French. Though "La Dame Blanche" does not contain the attributes of profound scholarship, it satisfies in full the requirements of refined and poetic French comedy. Schumann regarded some of Boieldieu's creations as the representative comic operas of the world. His orchestra is not large and it is rarely used in its entire strength. The key-note is dainty scoring; the singing can always be distinctly heard, and although few novel effects of instrumentation are to be noted, variety and contrast of tone are constantly to be met with. The accompaniment is ever appropriate, and especially the clarinet and horns receive characteristic treatment. Moderation in the use of the brass was carried to such an extent that trombones are frequently omitted altogether, and even in "La Dame Blanche" only one was employed. In one opera not even trumpets and kettle-drums are to be found.

The founder of the lyric drama in the modern sense was AUBER (1782–1871). The pillars of modern lyric drama are genuine dramatic expression, varied resources, and extensive proportions. Add to these charming melody, sparkling instrumentation and piquant coloring, and we have the sum total of Auber's creations. He was, perhaps, the most typically French composer that ever lived, and yet his orchestration is not that of an innovator. He accepted the already existing French and Italian characteristics of instrumentation, but adapted them to the needs of his poetic instincts. The functions of his orchestra are essentially those of accompaniment, and the dramatic situations are lightly sketched rather than elaborately portrayed. And this lightness of touch, together with grace and elegance, is already to be found in "La Muette de Portici," as well as in the more popular "Fra Diavolo."

In spite of the fact that Auber's orchestra presents nothing actually new, the charm of his instrumentation has exerted great influence upon that art in France. When the full orchestra is employed, the effect is sonorous without being noisy, ever clear yet scintillating. For more subdued effects, Auber was especially happy in the choice of mixed tonal tints, such as the reduplication, by a piccolo flute in the octave, of a melody given to one of the wood-instruments. Moreover, he was the first to employ the piccolo in piano passages. And whether reference be made to his use of soft chords for the trombones, or to his dainty triangle effects, — these are but a suggestion of the many characteristic insignia that distinguished his sterling achievements.

The operas of HÉROLD (1791) contain strong expressive and dramatic attributes. His form and instrumentation show German rather than Italian influence, modified withal by unquestionable French coloring. The impress of "Don Juan" and of "Freischütz" is especially noticeable in the overture to "Zampa," his representative work; three principal themes from the opera itself are more or less scientifically developed, and the manner of writing for certain wind instruments like the clarinet in some ways resembles that of Weber. Although Hérold's orchestration does not embody that transparency and that grace which characterize the scores of Auber, it is more compact, and his accompaniments conform to the demands of the dramatic situation. He occupied himself also with chamber music and concert overtures, which are superior in form to many similar efforts of prominent contemporary French writers, even though they are insignificant in comparison with German models.

The works of HALÉVY (1799) present a perplexing composite of genuine art and sensational trivialities. Frequently carried away by desire for pomp and effervescent personal glory, he nevertheless gave the art of dramatic scoring a powerful impetus toward modern methods. His instrumentation is often like Meyerbeer's, and Rossinian tendencies are apparent as well. Nevertheless, his pages are imbued with his own individuality. Each instrument received characteristic treatment when not used in massed harmonic combinations. The strings were employed with much skill and variety, as exemplified, for instance, by phrases for violins alone in four parts, or for solo 'cellos in five parts. The former idea bears the germ of Wagner's subsequent ethereal string passages, whereas the latter corresponds to Rossini's familiar 'cello scoring in "Guillaume Tell." The wood-wind played an important part as dramatic interpreter, with especial attention to the expressive characteristics of the English horn and the clarinet. Above all, Halévy was an untiring advocate in behalf of improving and supplementing both the variety and functions of the brass, and was strongly in support of the newly invented instruments of Sax. As components of the orchestra proper, they were not used aggressively, although, of course, when they appeared as an independent cohort upon the stage itself, their united efforts inclined toward the bombastic. Halévy was among the first to employ a second couplet of valve horns in addition to the customary natural horns, and the manner of writing for them displays a marked departure from previous usage. Besides absorbing into the orchestra proper different varieties of sax-horns and especially the sax-tuba, he employed at times as many as eight trumpets. A part for a soprano trombone is likewise to be found in one of his scores. "La Juive" is the embodiment of Halévy's higher ideals and novel orchestral combinations, and among other interesting details of instrumentation, the employment of two English horns, the trombone solo in the fourth act, and the semi-military band on the stage will readily be recalled.

V.

Brief mention is due to the "historic school" which found its first exponent in SPONTINI (1774–1851). The tenets of this school were in sympathetic accord with the general desire for pomp attendant upon the ascendency of Napoleonic imperialism. And Spontini's masterpiece "La Vestale" entirely satisfied these demands. For in spite of many glaring defects, it is a worthy example of superb dramatic power. In this work, a new style of orchestration was inaugurated, one that has been more or less imitated by all French writers since his time. Spontini transplanted into serious opera a principle with which already Piccini and Paesiello had experimented in their lighter operas, in that, for the description of certain picturesque episodes, the orchestra appears as chief exponent, the voice as secondary.

Entirely new was the amalgamation of the whole orchestra into one mighty organism by means of doubling and redoubling each part, similar to the practice of adding the four- and two-foot stops in organ playing. Each of the three choirs is harmonically complete by itself; being absorbed into the general Melos, it is, of course, impossible for the ear to analyze the combined tone-color. Such massive tonal edifices are the embodiment of unity and sonority, but there is danger of monotony, and, as Gevaërt remarks, this method of orchestration was subsequently abused by Rossini. Spontini's style embodies much that is German, and his mastery of brilliant effects is unrivalled. And although he frequently lowered the standard of his works by a craving for ostentation, the details are carefully worked out and the orchestration is rich and manly.

With the advent of ROSSINI (1792–1868), the triumph of Italian *aria* was resumed. His operas are the embodiment of Italian emotionalism. But although much of his music must be condemned as entirely irrelevant to the demands of the dramatic situation or of the sentiment to be expressed, his orchestration was certainly an advance upon antecedent Italian methods. On the other hand, there are but few new features in his instrumentation; this consisted of certain restricted and oft-repeated formulas, of which, however, Rossini had perfect command. His crowning achievement was, of course, "Guillaume Tell." Here the orchestration plainly betrays a happy fusion of Italian and French styles. The string writing is full of life; due regard is shown to the wind instruments, and effective solos are assigned more particularly to the English horn and the French horns. The improvements that Rossini made in horn writing were probably due to the fact that his father was a horn player. Parenthetically, the same statement might be made in reference to Richard Strauss. It is also interesting to note in passing that Rossini used two batons in conducting, — a short one for *arias* and a long one for *ensemble*.

VI.

At this point it is fitting that we examine the dazzling orchestration of MEYERBEER (1791–1861), for his career is, of course, inseparably allied with the evolution of French opera. As the most famous representative of French romantic and historic grand opera, Meyerbeer would appear, at first sight, to have embraced in his operas every conceivable meretricious device for the sensational and the spectacular. He was above all an eclectic, modelling his works largely after those of Spontini, being likewise strongly influenced by Weber, combining German harmony, Italian melody, and French rhythm. His was a marked departure from the school of Gluck — so much so, that he has been accused of "playing with dynamic effects" and writing "hollow" music that cannot withstand æsthetic analysis. In a large measure such censure is merited, but it is manifestly an error in judgment to declare as one writer does that his productions are comprised of but "dazzling effects, glaring contrasts, and clever instrumental devices." True, the contents of his operas are certainly an alternating mixture of the grandiose and the paltry, but as for orchestration, none have surpassed him in judicious distribution of sonorous masses, in forceful dramatic effects, richness of details, and successful application of the individual characteristics of each instrument. Again, the consistent recurrence of a specific tone-color as the annotator to a dramatic personage contains the germ of the *Leit-motiv.* And for ever varying resource of instrumentation few can excel him! And no composer before him was his peer as a dramatic painter.

Meyerbeer of course relied primarily upon the strings as the basis of his orchestra, but they are frequently replaced by independent combinations of wind instruments. In this connection, it is worthy of especial note that complete groups of kindred instruments are employed alone, and almost invariably in complete four part harmony. Meyerbeer's scoring for full orchestra was practically identical with Spontini's; each group is again complete in four part harmony, doubled and redoubled in the octave. Though his accompaniments are heavy, it will be found that the voice is usually supported by a solo instrument. He developed great variety in string writing. The violins and violoncellos are frequently subdivided into numerous parts. The characteristics of high violins and again of low double-basses *soli* are brought into prominence. Passages are to be found in which parts of the strings are muted while the remainder are simultaneously employed without mutes. The viola d'amore is carefully treated, as, for instance, in Raoul's Romance in the first act of "Les Huguenots." The harp is used extensively, both in arpeggios and in broad chords. The English horn and bass-clarinet are constantly used as regular constituents of the secondary group, and the latent dramatic powers of the clarinet are intensified; again, every one is familiar with the earliest of bass-clarinet solos in "Les Huguenots." Apart from more common methods of employing the wood-wind group by itself, Meyerbeer was fond of peculiar combinations such as piccolo flute and English horn, or bass-clarinet and trumpet an octave apart. Further entirely novel combinations are the assignment of a melody to the English horn and bass-clarinet in unison, or the redoubling of the violoncellos by a flute two octaves above. Great variety in mixed tints is to be found. The most common is the combination in solo passages of violoncello and bassoon; more complex is the union of violins, *tremolo,* together with three flutes, all in the high range, while an English horn or a bass-clarinet produces the melody below. Or two clarinets and two bass-clarinets are united to violoncellos in three-part writing. One of Meyerbeer's chief contributions to instrumentation lay in his methods of scoring for the brass. In "Les Huguenots" a veritable military band is introduced upon the stage; the band includes both reeds and brass — likewise piccolo flutes. And the newly invented sax-horns were drawn into requisition for "Le Prophète." The kettle-drums acquired greater freedom than even Beethoven had allowed them, and "Robert le Diable" contains actual solos for the instruments. In different works, as many as three and four kettle-drums were employed. In conclusion, it is not necessary to dwell upon the realistic impression provoked by the sounding of a gong in connection with the Resurrection of the Nuns in "Robert le Diable"; nor need the reader be reminded of the deep-toned bell used for the Massacre of St. Bartholomew in "Les Huguenots." All in all, though Meyerbeer's scoring is frequently brutal, it is intensely dramatic and original.

VII.

We have now traced the wonderful growth of orchestration through the entire eighteenth century and well into the nineteenth. And the contributions thereto by the great Italian and French masters are by no means to be underestimated even though the German classicists tower above them. A final summing up of their general methods of instrumentation will properly conclude this chapter.

The classic symphony realizes its principal effects from the dialogue of instruments rather than from their collective forces. The primary object was clearness of polyphonic design, and since clearness of detail does not admit of great force, the first and second orchestral groups were rarely united other than in *forte* passages.

When examining the scores of the classics, it is important to keep in mind that in their day the numerical distribution of the string band was limited. Therefore force and volume of tone could only be obtained by keeping the intermediate and lower parts constantly in motion. Particularly the violas were inadequately represented, and it will be found that any important viola melody was almost invariably doubled by some other instrument.

The classic use of the flute for *tuttis* was generally like that of a four-foot organ stop. Many of the earlier functions of the oboe gradually passed to the more responsive clarinet. But the frequent employment of divided violas as auxiliary to the wind was due to the former absence of adequate contralto wind instruments.

The larger symphonic orchestra of Haydn, Mozart and Beethoven added two trumpets to the third group, acquiring thereby a feminine metallic diapason capable of masculine energy. In the exposition of their symphonies, the classicists usually gave the first theme to the strings, the second to the wood. The brass was reserved for climaxes, and the trumpets entered last. But the limitation of the "natural" trumpet was detrimental for employing it with invariable symmetry in the recurrence of thematic design. In employing the full orchestra, held chords were assigned to the second group as a support to the strings, whereas the third group added short rhythmic chords.

Operatic effects are obtained by contrast of collective forces rather than by detail of polyphony. The earlier Italian composers made frequent use of loud-voiced instruments. Their successors, however, learned to rely more and more upon the strings, so that not until the advent of Spontini and Rossini were the proper functions of the brass or even of the wood again sufficiently recognized in Italy.

From Philidor to Boieldieu, French orchestration was still somewhat heavy, though of dramatic effectiveness. The scoring of Méhul and Lesueur was powerful and dignified, that of Boieldieu, Berton, Grétry, supple and dramatic. Finally, in the first part of the nineteenth century French orchestration became still more varied and rich.

It is now time to turn our attention to the rise of the Romantic Movement, and with this subject the next chapter properly begins.

(Summary on page 69.)

SUMMARY OF PART II.

CHAPTER V.

BACH's orchestration was essentially polyphonic. He contrasted his differentiated groups of instruments *en masse*, and laid the foundation for effective orchestral solo writing.

HÄNDEL represents solidity and sonority, and obtained the best results when employing the orchestra for massed effects in conjunction with the chorus.

Bach's contemporaries in Italy were engaged in composing church music and in writing operas that should satisfy the existing demands for vocal virtuosity. With few exceptions, they did little to advance the standard of instrumentation, although Pergolesi's writing for string orchestra was progressive.

In Germany, regard for Italian opera was fostered by establishing a permanent home for it at Hamburg; but the evolution of orchestration was but little benefited thereby. Em. Bach did good service for the cause of independent instrumental music. Credit is due to Hasse for his efforts in behalf of the Dresden orchestra, and Graun added his mite to the development of symphonic form.

After Lulli, and before the advent of Gluck, Rameau stands as the exponent of French opera, from which French orchestration was then inseparable. Rameau's reputation rests upon his harmonic innovations, the enhanced effectiveness of his chorus, and his improved orchestration. Impelled by the enthusiasm of the philosopher, Rousseau, a number of composers paved the way for Grétry by departing from tradition and inaugurating a lighter style, since known as the *opéra comique*.

CHAPTER VI.

GLUCK, engrossed in resuscitating and furthering the principles promulgated by Peri and Lulli, used the orchestra primarily as a dramatic interpreter, and his scoring is conspicuous for the use of suitable instrumentation, and for the portrayal of genuine pathos.

At about the time that Gluck captured the Parisian stage, native French music received a powerful impulse from Grétry, who established *opéra comique* upon a permanent basis. In spite of this achievement, his contributions to orchestration are not important. Meanwhile, Italy remained true to her traditions, both as to form and contents of opera, as well as instrumentation. An exception is to be found in the scores of Jomelli. An adaptation of the *opéra comique* in the garb of the Singspiel soon sprang up in Germany.

The growth of independent orchestral music was aided by such composers and directors as Sammartini, Gossec, Grétry, Stamitz, and Cannabich, being, moreover, fostered by such organizations as the "Concerts des Amateurs," the "Concerts spirituels," the Electoral band at Mannheim, the Leipzig Gewandhaus, and the Dresden orchestra.

CHAPTER VII.

HAYDN was the third great orchestral innovator in historic evolution, and from him date the beginnings of modern orchestration, just as Bach represents organ and Protestant Church music, Händel the oratorio, and Gluck the drama. Monteverde established the precedent of a nucleus of strings, Scarlatti adjusted their tonal balance, but Haydn readjusted the equilibrium of the suppletory segments of the orchestra as a concrete entity. His symphonies were the outcome of the earlier *concerto grosso*, and thus, having remained true to the traditions of his great predecessors, he became in turn the pioneer for Mozart and Beethoven. In his scoring, the wood-wind acquired freedom and individuality as solo instruments, and, together with the brass, were led also to sustain and knit together the harmonic progressions, rather than merely to support the resonance of the strings. He emphasized the consistent use of wind instruments in pairs. Again, by exploring further their caloric capabilities, he discovered effective means for descriptive music, and his oratorios bear the seed of programmatic writing.

MOZART explored the resources of the orchestra as opened up by Gluck and Haydn. He combined and interchanged polyphonic and monophonic style of writing to a most felicitous degree. He wrote for the strings in such a manner as to insure absolute independence and stability. The wood-wind gained in freedom of solo expression, and acquired that individuality of treatment which was its own by right. Especially the clarinet owes its absorption into the orchestra to Mozart, and from him dates the genuine origin of varied and contrasted tone-coloring.

The universal genius of BEETHOVEN, prompted by the depth of his nature and the nobility of his purpose, led him to combine the legacy of his predecessors with a more sensitive regard for inner details, thematic unity, emotional expression, and greater freedom and subordination of form, leading to expansion and programmatic music. Greatest of classic orchestral masters, he brought the symphonic orchestra to its highest development, discovered the utmost capabilities of each and every instrument, increased the efficiency of both strings and wood-wind, and incidentally discerned the genuine worth of the violoncellos, bassoons, and kettle-drums. The functions of the horns likewise acquired wider significance, and the trombones were reserved for the portrayal of noble dignity and ornamentation.

CHAPTER VIII.

During the development of Beethoven's mighty conquests, Paris continued to attract aspirants to fame in operatic lines, whereas modern church music found a worthy representative in Cherubini; his orchestration is sonorous, flexible, varied and vivid. Two native composers of opera in serious vein, Méhul and Lesueur, contributed essentially to the development of French instrumentation. That of Méhul was still somewhat heavy, but embodied sonority, novel combinations, and at times a certain melancholy coloring. Lesueur was one of the pioneers in the use of grand and majestic combinations. The most prominent followers of Grétry in the lyric *genre* were Boieldieu, whose instrumentation is conspicuous for its daintiness, variety and contrast; Auber, master of clear yet effervescent scoring; Hérold, whose orchestra is compact and well balanced; finally, Halévy, an exponent of both varied and massed effects. Italian instrumentation was advanced especially by Spontini and to a certain extent by Rossini; the former inaugurated the practice of doubling and redoubling the harmonies in massed combination. French opera was also greatly influenced by Meyerbeer, who imparted to the orchestra massed effects, novel and rich detail, characteristic individuality.

Credit for the development and perfection of symphonic form and orchestration is due to the great German classicists alone; but the evolution of the genuinely dramatic resources of the orchestra rests largely in the hands of the French composers preceding the ascendency of the Romantic Movement.

PART III. — ROMANTICISM.

CHAPTER IX.

THE ROMANTIC SCHOOL.

A CONVENIENT classification of the great German composers of the nineteenth century is to be found in "Famous Composers and their Works," a classification which will be followed in these chapters. It consists of three general groups: "The Romantic School," "The Classical Romanticists," and "The New Movement." As has been already stated, the basis of the Romantic School was simply a further development of Beethoven's descriptive writing, which created a powerful impression upon the so-called founders of the school, Spohr and Weber; they in turn were followed by Schubert, Mendelssohn, Schumann, and their disciples. The Classical Romanticists accepted the substance of romanticism in music, but remained more or less true to classical form. Raff stands at the head of this classification, Brahms as its chief exponent. The New Movement dates from the tumultuous upheavals in the musical world caused by the innovations of Berlioz in France, Liszt and Wagner in Germany. The evolution of these three movements will now be reviewed in logical sequence; but it should be borne in mind that this evolution had already begun during the later development of French and Italian opera as discussed in the previous chapter.

I.

SPOHR (1784–1859). The fruits of Spohr's activity as a composer present a rather peculiar mixture of progressive zeal and conventional mannerism. He was not alive to the true greatness of Beethoven's genius, neither can he be compared with Weber as a dramatic writer. On the other hand, Spohr was instrumental in awakening a keener interest for the supernatural, and he aimed to illustrate certain definite ideas by means of musical expression. This trait is especially conspicuous in his symphonies; and these entitle him to be regarded as one of the founders of programmatic orchestral music. Again, Spohr was one of the greatest violinists of his day, and as the natural result, his writing for strings was highly effective. Consequently his double string quartets, his octets, nonets, etc., are especially valued in musical literature. Spohr contributed to the evolution of orchestration proper but little that was actually new. But here again the development of violin technique stimulated at least a freer and more elaborate manner of employing the strings. Prout suggests that his orchestration resembles to some extent that of Mendelssohn, in that the equilibrium is admirably adjusted; and the general color-scheme is further enriched by frequent use of soft harmonies for the brass. In minor details of instrumentation, Spohr made some interesting experiments similar to those of Berlioz, such as the introduction of a number of kettle-drums into the orchestra. Prout also refers to the earthquake chorus in "Calvary" where six drums are played upon by two performers, and rolls in seconds, thirds, and fifths for two drums together are to be found. But as a whole, his reputation is due chiefly to his great achievements as a violinist and to the incentive he gave to romanticism in music.

II.

(*) WEBER (1786–1826). Spohr's efforts in behalf of programmatic music are by no means to be undervalued; at the same time it must be borne in mind that even his finest works are eclipsed by those of Weber by virtue of the latter's marvellous imagination, unerring judgment in the choice of appropriate means of expression, and huge technique in orchestration. Weber began his career during what might be called the transition period in modern art. It would be here out of place to enlarge upon the general conditions attendant upon the awakening of the so-called "storm and stress" agitation in Germany. Weber's artistic development was, however, so inseparably allied with this movement that at least a brief review thereof would appear indispensable before proceeding to an examination of his orchestral works.

Langhans sums up the mental and emotional conditions of this transition period by saying that " in place of the general subject-matter with which the lyric poetry of the preceding century had been satisfied, the subjective feelings of the poet now came to the front, and the essential nature of lyric poetry, a boundless submersion into the innermost life of the soul, could under these circumstances attain full prominence." Germany was at this time greatly interested in the writings of Byron and of Jean Paul Richter. Romantic poetry in turn began to influence both dramatic and lyric music. Indications of departure from the elevated and reflective style of the great classical composers were apparent. Time-honored rules and traditions began to be neglected. Individualism asserted itself. The general tendency of the epoch embodied a certain mystical element — a return to the chivalrous atmosphere of mediæval romance. And this tendency was in harmony with the very nature of Weber's imaginative

(*) See Appendix of Musical Illustrations, Examples 36 to 47.

trend.   In turn, this unfettered realm of imagination, peopled with sylphs, nymphs, fairies, contained latent and most propitious possibilities for progressive orchestration.   Weber's instrumentation was founded upon that of Beethoven, but it was none the less distinctive and original.   It was above all dramatic.   His true greatness lay in the power of orchestral portrayal in the more vivid scenes of his operas, and in his operatic overtures.   His two symphonies are comparatively weak.   Though deficient in artistic education, Weber's romantic disposition and rare appreciation for instrumental effects enabled him to become one of the greatest modern orchestral writers, and his scoring is a model for all later composers.   He stands at the head of modern instrumentation, for with him a new period began.   Moreover, he was the creator of modern German romantic opera.   As Kapellmeister at Dresden he was instrumental in counteracting the influence of Italian music which was still in vogue at the Court, and he helped to mould the tastes of the public in favor of native dramatic and orchestral music. "Der Freischütz" is the representative of ideal national opera.   Here the orchestration is admirably adapted to depict and intensify the scenes and situations. It abounds in striking contrasts that are ever consistent with the demands of what has been called the "local" coloring.   Episodes requiring sombre and mysterious tonal tints are again offset by the purest of lyrics and by powerful dramatic climaxes.   "Oberon," on the other hand, abounds in more peaceful melodic and harmonic fancies, poetic revery, and dainty scoring.   Though the effectiveness of "Euryanthe" is marred by reason of its insipid libretto, it is nevertheless the most important of Weber's operas, considered from a musical standpoint.   Its continuous music and the interweaving of recitative and melody directly point the way to Wagner.   Weber displayed superb power in the development of his overtures.   In the second volume of his "Music and Musicians," Wagner declared that Weber might be said to have originated a novel form of overture or "dramatic fantasy," of which Wagner considered the "Oberon" overture to be the best example.

In turning to the details of Weber's instrumentation it is found that no new instruments were introduced.   Beauty and novelty were attained rather by inherent regard for suitable application of tonal color and by the discovery of new combinations.   Although Weber, like Spohr, did not venerate Beethoven as he should have done, it was not possible for him to improve upon the great master's string writing.   Of course certain novel effects are to be found, such as the subdivision of the violins *soli* into numerous parts, the viola accompaniment to Annette's ballad, [a] and the use of the same instrument as bass to "Leise, leise" [b] in "Der Freischütz."

But perhaps no other composer contributed more to the independence of the wood-wind. [c]   Weber was exceedingly modern in the use of small combinations.

[a] Ex. 47.   [b] Ex. 43.   [c] Ex. 39, 41.

In order to obtain a rare and fairy-like effect in "Oberon," the first flute and first clarinet give out the melody; the second flute plays arpeggios as does likewise the second clarinet, though in contrary motion; a solo horn is employed as bass. The opening bars of Annette's song in "Der Freischütz" may be cited as containing a good example for the oboe as does also the accompaniment to Kilian's song for the bassoon. But it was quite particularly the clarinet for which Weber showed especial predilection. Beautiful phrases for the clarinet are to be found in the Allegro of the overture to "Der Freischütz" [d] as well as in the overture to "Oberon"; and the characteristics of the instrument in its entire range are effectively displayed in the introduction to Adolar's aria in the second act of "Euryanthe." Moreover, he was the first to discover the tragic possibilities of the chalumeau range, [e] as exemplified by the held notes in the lowest part of the instrument accompanying the entries of Zamiel in "Der Freischütz."

Next to the clarinet, the horns [f] received especial consideration from Weber, and acquired greater freedom and individuality, being brought into requisition not alone for mellow *cantilene* and sustained harmonies, but also as the exponents of jubilant outbursts or of gloomy whisperings. Many admirable illustrations will readily be recalled, such as the passages for horns *soli* in the introduction of the "Freischütz" overture, [g] the trio for horns in the Romance in "Preciosa," and the horn accompaniment to the Mermaid's Song in "Oberon." With Weber, the use of four horns and three trombones became the rule, whereas with Beethoven it had been the exception.

All things considered, it is evident that modern opera and modern orchestration are immensely indebted to Weber, and his influence has made itself more or less felt upon the writings of all subsequent dramatic and orchestral composers.

III.

Two contemporaries of Weber who followed in his footsteps as composers of romantic opera were Konradin Kreutzer (1780) and Marschner (1795). Kreutzer's "Nachtlager von Granada" has become widely known, but of the two men, Marschner is by far the more important. He is popularly known as the heir of Weber, and has been called the connecting link between Weber and Wagner. Himself stimulated and influenced by his friend, Weber, he in turn helped to mould the earlier works of Wagner. His masterpiece, "Hans Heiling," abounds in natural melodic expression, truthful interpretation and dramatic energy. Neither Kreutzer nor Marschner can be cited as having contributed anything substantially new to instrumentation, but they at least helped to strengthen the foundations of modern orchestration as initiated by Weber.

d) Ex. 37.   (e) Ex. 40, 44, 46.   (f) Ex. 42, 45.   (g) Ex. 36.

IV.

The two greatest representatives of the early Romantic School were Weber and SCHUBERT (1797–1828), indeed, the latter is to be regarded as the ideal exponent of the romantic poets. He was the first to raise the Lied from comparative obscurity to such prominence as to bring the lyric element on a par with that of the dramatic and epic. His nature was contemplative rather than dramatic. Nevertheless some of his greatest masterpieces, such as the "Erlkönig," embody not only dramatic but epic characterization as well. He was above all the master of exquisite melody, and both his songs and his instrumental works are further conspicuous for their daring harmonies, animated and varied rhythm. He opened up a new pathway in the field of accompaniment which acquired not only greater importance in intensifying emotional expression, but came also to be the faithful ally of the vocal part as interpreter of the poem. The use of little motives in the accompaniment to his songs might be looked upon as an anticipation in the miniature of Wagner's thematic treatment of his "Leit-motiven."

Schubert's mode of life was in some respects similar to that of Beethoven in that he lived apart from the public. Spurred on by the example of Beethoven, he added to his series of youthful symphonies two masterpieces which are next in importance to those of his illustrious model. Both the C major and the unfinished B minor symphonies display rare skill in the handling of orchestral instruments, whether in solo passages or in combination. An intimate acquaintance with their respective characteristics was afforded him during his early training, and every bar reveals the hand of a master who without hesitation knew what effects he desired and how to obtain them. Although his orchestral works lack that depth of conception that only Beethoven possessed, Schubert nevertheless supplied the deficiency by means of beautiful melody, tender expression, forceful harmonic progressions, and, as just intimated, a perfect command of orchestral resources. Schubert enlarged the scope of practical instrumentation by discovering two exceedingly valuable and effective modes of expression that were entirely new so far as manner of treatment is concerned. No composer before him had elicited from the trombones such impressive utterance as is to be found, for instance, in the first movement of the symphony in C where the trombones *pianissimo* intone the melody. The first innovation consisted, therefore, of employing the trombones freely as solo instruments, or again as independent factors in three-part harmony, *pianissimo*, or in unison, *forte*. The second innovation was the felicitous manner in which he contrasted solo instruments of the wood-wind group, or what Prout calls "a kind of dialogue between them."

As an admirable illustration well-known to all, he calls attention to the charming dialogue between the flute, oboe, and clarinet in the two Ballet airs and in the Entr'-act in B flat of the music to "Rosamunde." Many other interesting details of instrumentation could be cited such as the effective use of the trumpet in the slow movement of the symphony in G; his chamber music, also, furnishes admirable examples of string writing. Among the most prominent are the trio in E flat, the quartet in D minor, and the quintet in C.

Only in recent years has the influence of Schubert's orchestral works made itself prominently felt, for until the middle of the last century most of them had remained in manuscript. Moreover as recently as fifty odd years ago one of his symphonies was considered excessively difficult by the principal orchestra of Vienna. Grove says that "though the whole work was announced, such had been the difficulties at rehearsal that only the first two movements were given, and they were carried off by an interpolation of an air from 'Lucia' between them."

V.

(*) MENDELSSOHN (1809–1847). Concurrent with the advent of Mendelssohn and Schumann, the fascination that Rossini had exercised in Germany lost its hold, and the public learned to appreciate more and more the sterling qualities of its own native music. But not only did the efforts of the German composers of the nineteenth century begin to win due recognition, but also there was rekindled a veneration for the creations of the great classicists. This was in a large manner due to Mendelssohn's untiring efforts. Possessed of broad culture, wealth, and attractive personality, he combined the spirit of romanticism with the structural forms of classicism; this conservatism helped to balance the restless tendencies that were at that time dominating music and poetry. His compositions are imbued with beauty and sweetness of melody, with varied harmonies, buoyant orchestration; his choral writing is the most fluent since Bach's and surpasses in this respect that of Händel. Melody is emphasized; tragic depth is lacking. He excelled as a writer of "representative" music, but even here his refined sense for euphony never deserted him. He was successful in all forms excepting opera. "St. Paul" and "Elijah" are the most important oratorios since those of Haydn; his violin concerto comes next to Beethoven's as a favorite; his symphonies are characteristic, romantic, and abound in "local" coloring. His style may be divided into two distinct classes: the lyric, as typified in the "Songs without Words," and the fantastic and imaginative as exposed in the Scherzo of the "Midsummer Night's Dream."

Mendelssohn's contributions to the details of instrumentation were both

(*) See Appendix of Musical Illustrations, Examples 58 to 66.

original and varied. Already in "Midsummer Night's Dream," of which the Overture was written when he was but seventeen years old, are to be found marvellous effects that are indeed fairy-like in their daintiness.[a]   In fact it might be justly claimed that this is Mendelssohn's best orchestral work, taking into consideration its polished form, transparent and perfectly balanced instrumentation. Noteworthy for their novelty are the rapid staccato passages for the wood-wind in the Scherzo.[b]   In none other of his works has the flute been treated in a more charming manner.[c]   Familiar to all is the romantic and extended employment of the horns in the Notturno,[d] as well as the ludicrous utterances of the opheicleide in the Overture.

As a composer of oratorio, Mendelssohn's choruses, recitatives and German chorale melodies plainly show the influence of Bach's "Passion Music." This is particularly noticeable in "St. Paul." Mendelssohn's mightiest creation is undoubtedly "Elijah."   It satisfies every demand by reason of its expressive recitative, its dramatic and descriptive choruses, its beauty of lyric episodes and the appropriateness of its structural form. The orchestral score of "Elijah" is one of Mendelssohn's best. Among minor details, the violas are brought into prominence as in the accompaniment to "Lord God of Abraham" where they are given the highest part. A well-known phrase is the 'cello accompaniment in thirds to the baritone solo. The brass is again reënforced by an opheicleide. The opening of the chorus, "O be gracious, ye immortals," in "St. Paul" is accompanied by divided violas and 'cellos, and parts for the serpent are to be found in the same work.

Both the subject-matter and the orchestration of Mendelssohn's symphonies show exceptional originality, and the "Scotch," No. 2 in A minor, as well as the "Italian," No. 3 in A major, are worthy companions to the "Midsummer Night's Dream." His symphonies are full of freshness and vigor. Though classic purity of form is strictly adhered to, Beethoven's polyphony and Weber's picturesque portrayal are skilfully combined. Like Beethoven, he embodied in his symphonies certain dramatic characteristics. Rapid passages for the wood-wind, similar to those in the "Midsummer Night's Dream," are again to be met with in the Scherzo of the "Scotch" symphony. Mendelssohn was conservative in employing the brass; of all the early romanticists he remained the most faithful to traditional usage of the third group, although trombones were now incorporated as habitual members thereof. Among other novel combinations, divided violas, reënforced by clarinets, intone the second subject in the first movement of the "Lobgesang" symphony. In connection with Mendelssohn it is interesting to recall the fact that as late as 1829 the pianoforte was still sometimes employed

(a) Ex. 58, 62.   (b) Ex. 59.
(c) Ex. 60, 66.   (d) Ex. 65.

as a means for conducting, since in that year he directed his C minor symphony in that way in London.

Mendelssohn's overtures are more pronounced in their modern romantic tendencies than his symphonies. They are distinctly programmatic, even though in structure they are moulded on classic forms. From them dates the development of the modern romantic concert overture. Mendelssohn's merits and defects have led to much violent discussion, but the suavity of his melody, the purity of his form and the delicacy of his orchestration have been excelled by none.

VI.

The most prominent associates and disciples of Mendelssohn were F. Hiller, Rietz, the Englishman, Bennett, and the Dane, Gade.

Ferdinand Hiller (1811) was a celebrated and prolific composer, being in his day considered the most notable musician in West Germany. It was his rare privilege to be personally acquainted with no less than seven of the greatest composers the world has ever produced — Cherubini, Beethoven, Meyerbeer, Rossini, Berlioz, Chopin and Liszt. He was, moreover, a fine pianist and conductor, and was particularly happy as an interpreter of Beethoven. His compositions are pleasing and well-rounded in form; but they were modelled after those of Mendelssohn and are now comparatively forgotten in consequence of their lack of individuality.

Julius Rietz (1812) was closely associated with Mendelssohn whom he eventually succeeded as conductor of the Gewandhaus Concerts. He is primarily to be remembered for having edited Beethoven's symphonies as well as the entire works of Mendelssohn.

Sterndale Bennett (1816) was one of England's greatest composers, the most gifted, in fact, after Purcell. He was a friend both of Mendelssohn and of Schumann, and their enthusiasm encouraged and stimulated him to further develop his own talents. Although the influence more particularly of Mendelssohn is plainly to be found in his works, he retained his individuality and displayed numerous traits that are undeniably original. His most important works are an oratorio "The Woman of Samaria"; a cantata "The May Queen"; a symphony in G minor; four overtures, and four pianoforte concertos. He has been called the founder of a new "English School."

Since the substance of Gade's music is nominally Scandinavian in character, it will again be referred to later on in connection with the Northern countries.

VII.

SCHUMANN (1810–1856). In spite of the depth of thought and feeling, the brilliancy of ideas, and the programmatic tendencies that signalize Schumann's monumental productions, he unfortunately holds the unique position of being one of the few great masters who did not excel in orchestration. Nevertheless, such is the importance of his orchestral works that they have won for themselves an exalted and permanent place in musical literature. Schumann's relation to the Romantic Movement may be tersely stated as in one of Dickinson's condensed reviews: "The romantic ideal attains self-consciousness in Schumann. Weber and Schubert never called themselves romanticists and were not wholly aware of the tendencies of their work. Schumann, a critical thinker and self-analyst, not only moulded and colored his music in accord with certain definite poetic conceptions imbibed from the romantic writers, but also became the literary champion of romanticism in music, and aimed directly at fixed radical principles in the critical and creative thought of his time. He, therefore, not only marks the beginning of a new era in musical art, but is also the type of the modern liberally cultured and reflective musician." With Schumann, the subject-matter and treatment of design are of all importance. His compositions contain the quintessence of the poetic and romantic. Every little melody is a miniature poem in tones, tinged by a certain melancholy and even gloomy coloring. He was, like Mendelssohn, an ardent disciple of Bach, but his harmonies are freer and bolder than Mendelssohn's, and his pianoforte compositions show the influence more especially of Chopin. The chief characteristics of these works are *cantabile* expression, intricacy, and the predominance of harmony and rhythm over melody. A multitude of ideas are frequently crowded into the space of a few bars. As a song writer Schumann rivalled and perhaps even excelled Schubert. The songs of these two peers, together with those of Franz (1815), represent the highest ideal of the German Lied, for the exquisite taste and sentiment of Franz appeal strongly to the cultivated musician. Although Schubert's influence upon Schumann's songs is plainly to be seen, Schumann enhanced the functions of the accompaniment and frequently assigned but a secondary rôle to the vocal part. Novelty of form and style characterize his works for soli, chorus and orchestra; portions of "Scenes from Faust," "Paradise and the Peri," "Manfred," represent his highest attainment and contain also some effective scoring. The instrumentation of his chamber music betrays more regard for sonority than for classic counterpoint. Of surpassing beauty are the quartets in A and in A minor, and the greatest of all, the quintet in E flat.

Schumann's four symphonies rank next in importance to those of Beethoven and Schubert, and in depth of sentiment and emotional power he proved himself a worthy successor to Beethoven. His symphonies are stamped with distinctive individuality, traditional form being subjected to certain modifications that were in keeping with the progressive tendencies of his nature. Thus the D minor symphony is intended to be played entire without a pause, and subject-matter from one movement reasserts itself in another. It would be a waste of time to analyze Schumann's instrumentation too closely. He followed but could not equal that of Mendelssohn. Artistic feeling for orchestral effects and occasional good scoring are to be found, but much of the latter is thick and heavy. He was apt to follow Rossini's more or less trivial methods of employing the third enlarged orchestral group. Even Schubert was not entirely exempt from this mannerism. Such incongruities as the employment of a bassoon as a bass to trombones could also be cited. Of material advantage, however, was his introduction into German orchestras of valve-horns and valve-trumpets. But in a word, it is the substantial worth of the music itself, not the instrumentation, that has made Schumann's orchestral works immortal.

VIII.

Among the prominent associates and disciples of Schumann should be mentioned Volkmann, Reinecke, Bargiel, and Jensen.

The compositions of Volkmann (1815) show affinity to Schumann's. His pianoforte works bear fanciful titles, and his symphonies and quartets are massive and musicianly. But like most satellites, he was not possessed of sufficient spontaneity to acquire wide-spread or enduring recognition. The compositions of Carl Reinecke (1824), who held the honorable position of director of the Gewandhaus Concerts from 1860 until 1895, show the influence more especially of Schumann, although that of Mendelssohn as well as of Wagner and Brahms is also apparent. He owes his reputation as a composer largely to his smaller works, in which the tastes of a refined pianist are much in evidence. Few could be compared with him as an interpreter of Mozart, and his activity not alone as a composer of merit but also as a prominent pianist and distinguished conductor has won him universal fame. Bargiel (1828) was one of the foremost disciples of Schumann whose principles he zealously disseminated, both in his capacity as a fine teacher and as composer. His symphonies, chamber music and quite especially his psalms for chorus and orchestra show considerable originality and fine musicianship. Likewise Jensen (1837) took Schumann unreservedly as his model in spite of being in sympathetic accord with Gade. His songs and pianoforte pieces in the lyric *genre* are imbued with true feeling and rare sensuous charm.

IX.

In a general sense, all modern composers belong to the Romantic School, but for the sake of consistency in this general classification, Lachner, Jadassohn and Moszkowski should be mentioned as direct followers of both Mendelssohn and Schumann.

Franz Lachner (1803) was prominently connected with the musical life of Munich prior to the rise of Wagner worship in 1865. In spite of his untiring activity as a conductor, he was one of the most prolific and at the same time most popular composers of South Germany. His style betrays the mind of a learned man. The harmonies are modern, but his works are none the less imbued with a certain tinge of classicism. Lachner wrote several operas and oratorios, eight symphonies, and much chamber and church music; but of greatest importance are the suites for grand orchestra of which he wrote eight. They are magnificent specimens of contrapuntal knowledge. Some condemn his writings as being "Kapellmeistermusik" and as containing nothing truly original or great. Riemann's views are radically different: — "Lachner is at his best in his orchestral suites, which, as a kind of modern continuation of Bach-Händel orchestral movements, occupy a distinctive place in musical literature. Sovereign command of contrapuntal devices combined with nobility of invention will secure for them in the future greater appreciation than is accorded them at the present day."

Jadassohn (1831) holds an important position in the history of instrumentation, not so much, perhaps, as a result of his own composition as for the excellence of his teaching and of his theoretical works, which include the valuable "Lehrbuch der Instrumentation." A prominent feature of many of his works is the facility with which canonic writing is applied. Among the best-known and most popular of his orchestral compositions is the Serenade, opus 35.

Moszkowski (1854) is one of the younger composers whose writings are imbued with the spirit of Mendelssohn and Schumann rather than with the local coloring of Poland as might have been expected since his father was a native of that country. The most popular of his works are the "Spanische Tänze" for pianoforte, whereas the most important in orchestral form is the symphonic poem "Jeanne d'Arc." The style is dignified and musicianly, but lacks the true greatness of originality.

The list of faithful adherents to the pure romanticism of the early school is herewith properly concluded. Only an imaginary line, however, separates Spohr and Weber from Raff and Brahms; so the following chapter is nothing more than a continuation of the present discussion.

(Summary on page 175.)

CHAPTER X.

THE CLASSICAL ROMANTICISTS.

THE representatives of classical romanticism are Raff, Rubinstein, Goldmark, Brahms, Bruch, Rheinberger. The influence that Raff and Brahms had upon orchestration requires especial consideration. Rubinstein will be referred to again in connection with Russian composers. And a brief analysis will be sufficient to discover the respective characteristics that distinguish Goldmark's highly colored orchestration, that of Bruch in accompaniment to noble choral works, and Rheinberger's conservative yet finished instrumentation for sacred composition.

I.

RAFF (1822–1882). To begin with Raff, it is by no means easy to determine the precise value of his compositions. Masterpieces must be arraigned side by side with works of decided inferiority. He adapted Beethoven's calorific polyphony together with the charmingly picturesque style of Weber, but did not approach his eminent contemporary, Brahms, either in depth of thought or in originality of ideas. He was, however, superior to Brahms as an orchestral colorist. Encouraged by the sympathy and practical help of such men as Mendelssohn, Liszt, von Bülow, he became in his younger days a sturdy advocate of the modern German tendencies, and even wrote a pamphlet entitled "Die Wagnerfrage"; but in spite of his affiliation with the Weimar coterie, Raff eventually developed into a composer more especially of chamber music and symphonies. "Im Walde" and "Lenore" are the best known of the orchestral works, — indeed, the first named is without doubt his most important production. Raff was essentially a romanticist; what is more, he went so far as to write descriptive program music. Nevertheless, his style bears but little relation to that of Wagner or Liszt; it displays, in fact, a decided reserve in that he employed traditional forms and Beethoven's symphonic orchestra. Notwithstanding Raff's descriptive faculties, his works betray unquestionable lyric tendencies. Occasional approach to the *salon* style is also in evidence, nor do the larger works reveal that breadth of style and invariable loftiness of purpose that signalize those of Beethoven and Brahms. He possessed great facility, but this very attribute endangered the quality of his conceptions and was conducive to carelessness and loss of fine feeling.

Striking insignia of absolutely original scoring are not conspicuous, although the entire character of the orchestration gives evidence of fertile imagination and sound judgment. Some of Wagner's full and rich effects found their way also into Raff's symphonic pages. The latter was particularly happy in the use of horns, wrote almost exclusively for valve-horns and valve-trumpets, and established a precedent by selecting those in F for regular practice.

In view of the fact that Raff's style is a compound of classicism and romanticism, together with yet more advanced tendencies so far as the "program" element is concerned, his title as pioneer of the classical-romanticists has been applied with good judgment. The succeeding luminaries of this school revealed similar tendencies. Rubinstein, Goldmark and Bruch are all to a more or less degree exponents of the programmatic idea. Even so conservative a composer as Rheinberger, whom some are tempted to call even a reactionist, was at times subjugated by its fascination. This is borne out by his "Wallenstein" symphony. Brahms stands forth in his solitary grandeur as the one exception to the rule. Towering above his fellow classical-romanticists, he attained the exaltation of his fame by a path they could not tread. It is to him that we now must turn.

II.

BRAHMS (1833–1897). In the April number, 1895, of the magazine entitled "Music" are to be found the following remarkable assertions in an otherwise admirable article by Mr. W. S. B. Matthews: — "Händel is antiquated; Bach still lives, but we can enjoy his works only as exceptions to our current diet; Haydn symphonies sound like string quartets played a trifle large and seasoned with a few notes of trumpets and wood-wind. Mozart in feminine phrase is 'too sweet for any use,' and Mendelssohn has departed to the place where good boys go. We have left to us the over-worked immortal nine of Beethoven (now rather shrunk to five) and two of Schubert; we tolerate Schumann for the sake of his ideas. We hear Tschaikowsky because he is a master in his way. But the greatest of tone-poets now living, and the greatest since Beethoven, appears to be Brahms."

These broad assertions may be looked upon as revealing in all good faith the convictions of the author himself; again, Mr. Matthews may have aimed to be facetious; or else these assertions were intended merely to expose the tenets of the ultra-enthusiasts for one of the latest phases of art. It would appear to the present writer that, irrespective of motives, *such* comparisons are entirely superfluous. Brahms occupies an isolated and lofty pinnacle by himself. Calm and self-contained in the midst of the restless and feverish impetuosity that characterizes the "Sturm und Drang" period, he preferred the seclusion and intellectuality of a reflective student's life, and moulded his creations in accordance therewith. The only comparison that would appear at all relevant is the unshaken faith in an ideal that he shared with Wagner. Beyond this their views diverged when it came to the question of what this ideal should be or how it should be attained. Brahms was a strenuous opponent of the "New German School." The intellectual and tragic aspect of modern absolute music was *his* ideal. The leading theme was the germ for synthetical treatment. Orchestral coloring or dramatic effect was of secondary consideration. Brahms accepted as his model Bach's austerely noble methods and strict logical process of thematic development, whereas the exterior forms of Beethoven and Schumann were virtually sufficient for his needs. Nevertheless, it cannot be said that his conservative formal structure was but a slavish imitation of theirs. Many of his works, such as the Rhapsodies and Klavierstücke, are certainly not in strict sonata form, nor are they lacking in distinctive individuality. Brahms is the ideal exponent of purity, strength, profundity, nobility, greatness of expression and novelty of treatment. His aims differed from those of the earlier classicists in that his subject-matter embodies beauty of thought rather than external beauty in music. The prevalence in many of his works of a certain heaviness of spirit and the reflex even of asceticism have been pointed out by more than one of his biographers.

It is not surprising to find that in the terms in which Rheinberger once expressed himself to the present writer, the background of Brahms' orchestral canvass is of a grayish hue. Nor can his scoring be cited as a model for felicitous instrumentation or glowing orchestral colors. In listening to his symphonies, one is occasionally disturbed by a certain heaviness or what can be better expressed as "muddiness." This defect is primarily due to the low distribution of parts for violas as well as for basses. Vagueness of detail in melodic delineation of inner voices is the more conspicuous since Brahms attached great importance to the functions of the viola, in addition to which he frequently divided them. Certain conventionalities in writing for the wood-wind are also apparent. Passages in thirds and sixths are analogous to those in Beethoven's earlier works; other passages recall certain ones of Schubert. But we can verily afford to overlook such minor details. Let us rather turn to a consideration of those essentials of Brahms' symphonic and other orchestral writings that have caused him to be justly regarded as the worthy apostle of Beethoven and direct successor to Schumann.

The most striking feature of his symphonies is their colossal structure. They are evolved without apparent effort. There is no retrogression, no episodic mediocrity. Brahms had no theories to promulgate, no gorgeous tableaux to portray. Nevertheless, his orchestration, though conservative, bears the impress of distinctive individuality, is replete with variety and characteristic tone-color, and abounds in peculiar and interesting combinations. A few examples, drawn from four distinctive types of composition, will be sufficient to illustrate the fertility of his imagination. Prout calls special attention in one of his articles on the orchestra to the second Serenade in A, the Symphony in D, and the "Deutsches Requiem." We will add to these the "Variations on a theme by Haydn." The Serenade, opus 16, is one of the earlier works. It is scored for the usual wood-wind in pairs, besides horns and strings, but there are no violins throughout the entire piece. It presents a phase of instrumentation foreign to the usually heavy style of Brahms, and abounds in variated shades of coloring. The symphony embodies the highest attainment of orchestral development and "solid" instrumentation. The nine variations suggest novel aspects in the field of independent orchestral music. But on the whole, perhaps the finest orchestral effects are to be found in the "Deutsches Requiem," and it is possible that some of the tonal tints employed therein were suggested by Cherubini's Requiem in C minor. The reader may recall the citation on page 60 of Cherubini's choice of instruments for the purpose of accompanying the opening chorus. There the required sombre tone-color is obtained by employing divided violas and violoncellos with double-basses, bassoons, horns, and muffled kettle-drums. The solemn and appropriate color that pervades the opening chorus of the German Requiem — "Blessed are they that mourn" — is due to the expressive powers of the string band without violins. The violas and violoncellos are again divided, and the general subdued effect is further enhanced by means of sustained notes for the horns. It is not intended to convey the idea that these two requiems could in any way be suggestive one of the other beyond a certain similarity of tonal color in the opening choruses of both. In all other respects they are radically different. The treatment of musical subject-matter proper as well as the exposition of sacred words show diametrically opposed points of view. The funeral march which ushers in the following chorus "For all flesh is as grass" affords another proof of Brahm's versatility when searching for further religious effects that shall nevertheless embody sufficient contrast so as to avoid monotony in two consecutive movements. The violins and violas are not only divided into six parts, but are muted as well. The string parts are redoubled by the wood-wind, while the kettle-drums lend distinctive character to the passage by means of a prominent though subdued rhythmic figure.

The question may well be asked why Brahms should not be regarded as the seventh of the great classicists rather than as a classical-romanticist. The answer is not hard to find. His treatment of form and instrumentation is distinctly classic. His method of harmonization contains modern characteristics. The complex rhythms that are conspicuous in many of his earlier works together with their rather obtrusive syncopations and cross accents are suggestive of Schumann; but whereas Schumann adhered to some marked rhythm that was consistently carried out in order to acquire variety and to knit together the organic structure as a whole, Brahms gradually branched out into broader fields, so that eventually the relegation of rhythm to a comparatively subordinate relationship to the general architectural scheme reverts once more to Beethoven's methods of procedure. Thus Brahms displayed a progressive spirit when employing doctrines of the classic school, which was tempered withal by extreme caution in the acceptance of modern tendencies. The amalgamation is felicitous to a high degree, and has had a most salutary effect upon the ever increasing inclination of the ultra-modern school to enslave music in the throes of what has been called "a thrice-intensified *Weltschmerz.*" Even as Wagner stands supreme as the representative dramatic and orchestral writer of the nineteenth century, so Brahms may be regarded as a peer without rival in the art of thematic development, as the noblest exponent since Beethoven of large proportions and great breadth, and as the most prominent symphonic writer since Schumann, whose superior he was in the technics of orchestration.

III.

The fact that GOLDMARK (1830) was born in Hungary does not entitle him to recognition as a composer of decisively indigenous characteristics, — indeed, the scenes of three of his most important works are all laid in the Far East. Neither can it be said that his strength lies in spontaneity of musical thought or freedom of thematic treatment. He owes his reputation primarily to his gifts as an orchestral writer. Like Berlioz, he lacks the geniality of musical inspiration, but atones for this by vivid orchestral color and mastery of material effects. The fortunes of divers Oriental queens have evidently aroused Goldmark's most lively sympathy! But this peculiar circumstance is felicitous to a high degree, for what a wealth of glowing color surrounds his dramatization of the queen of Sheba, how picturesque is the presentation of the Amazon queen in the overture "Penthesilea," what power of imagination is revealed in the unfolding of Kalidasa's poetic love story! Goldmark could have found no finer opportunity for rare contrasts and telling effects than in this portrayal of Dushyanta, the Rajah — chivalrous, though unfaithful, of Śakuntalá — tender and guileless, yet queenly. Goldmark succeeded admirably, and this world-renowned overture is, by virtue of its orchestration, a faithful interpretation of Dushyanta's wooing, the secret marriage, his forgetfulness of Śakuntalá and her womanly fortitude during the years of unrecognition, her solicitous watchfulness over the welfare of Sarva-

Damana, their child, and the final touching reunion and retribution. Although "Die Königin von Saba" has won wide-spread popularity, Goldmark is, on the whole, at his best in purely instrumental forms. The opening up of his career is largely due to "Śakuntalá" and to a Scherzo for orchestra, opus 19, both of which precede the above-named opera. His pleasing symphony "Die ländliche Hochzeit" may not embody the warmth and passion that characterize the Oriental subjects, but it is orchestrated with rare skill, contains some daring harmonic progressions, and reveals sentient appreciation for rich and glowing colors. But this symphony and that in E flat again prove that Goldmark holds the attention of his audience not so much by originality of themes and elaborate development as by the sterling qualities of his instrumentation.

IV.

Antithetical to Goldmark's dependency upon the orchestra for effect is the euphonious choral style of BRUCH (1838). Here are to be found naturalness of invention, graceful and flowing melody, simplicity, and above all beauty of harmonic structure. Bruch exhibits extraordinary power in handling large vocal forces, and displays, moreover, marked predilection for Greek and Scandinavian subjects. The cantatas "Odysseus" and "Arminius," for soli, mixed chorus and orchestra, are counted among his most important works and embody the most favorable phase of his orchestration. "Salamis," a cantata for male chorus, is an inspiring song of victory, and "Frithjof," likewise written for men's voices, is an intensely dramatic exposition of six scenes chosen from the Frithjof Saga of Tegner. Best known is perhaps the "Lied von der Glocke," whereas the grave and earnest accents of the Hebraic "Kol Nidrei," together with the tragic intensity and passionate nature of the violin concerto in G minor, opus 26, show what Bruch could do when employing the orchestra to throw a solo instrument into relief. His independent orchestral works are not sufficiently spontaneous, whereas his accompaniments embody perfect taste, genuine expression and an abundance of energetic force. The very nature of his themes is such as to require either vocal forces or a solo stringed instrument to present them in the most favorable light. Bruch possesses supreme mastery of modern orchestral resources, but is at his best in the art of accompaniment.

V.

No composer has ever taken his art more to heart than RHEINBERGER (1839). Composition was for him a serious, even sacred avocation. It was not to be approached in a spirit of levity, nor could it assume for him so humble a mission as merely to amuse and entertain. This loftiness of purpose is visible even in his rather infrequent efforts in lighter vein. Although he was, to a degree, unconsciously swept along on the irresistible tidal wave of the epoch, nevertheless his conceptions found utterance in a but mild form of romanticism, and his works are seasoned with a certain spice of classic severity. It may be fearlessly asserted that Rheinberger is the greatest of all composers for the organ after Bach and Mendelssohn. His organ works are rich in color and of masterful effect. They combine free harmonic treatment, freely developed counterpoint and freedom of form. These attributes are particularly noticeable in the first organ concerto. His genius further reveals itself in the religious fervor that pervades his mighty series of sacred works. These two forms of composition — organ and church music, together with part-songs of rare beauty, are the most notable accomplishments of this versatile master. On the other hand, neither his operas nor his orchestral works can be regarded in the light of important contributions to musical literature. Strange, therefore, that Rheinberger should have first won general recognition through his "Symphonische Tongemälde Wallenstein." What is more, this is the work for which its author was led to essay the programmatic style of writing. Had he continued to develop his talents along similar lines, the world might have been impoverished to the extent of divers organ and sacred works, but Rheinberger himself must have risen to far greater eminence. It is to be admitted that his subsequent Florentine symphony, as also the oratorio "Christoforus" and the opera "Thürmers Töchterlein," are none of them equal to the Wallenstein symphony, but according to Rheinberger's own confession he became disheartened by neglect at the time when Wagner stormed the portals of the Munich Opera House. Thenceforth he turned for relief to other fields of composition and became, as he grew older, more and more conservative — one is almost obliged to say bigoted.

The instrumentation of his purely orchestral works is pointedly restricted to Beethovian procedure and reverts even to that of Mozart in the use of trumpets and kettle-drums. Its general effect is one of great refinement; it is marvellously smooth and perfectly rounded in every detail; but the essential elements of individuality and novelty do not enter into the orchestral scheme to any appreciable extent.

Rheinberger's last years were saddened by family affliction and embittered by physical suffering. He displayed an heroic fortitude, but his assumed cheerfulness concealed the loneliness, the sadness, the melancholy even to morbidness that were constantly preying upon his soul. His life became more and more that of a recluse and an ascetic. Meanwhile his compositions continued even to the end to reflect unswerving faith, serenity, loyalty of heart and nobility of mind. The greater his honor for thus excluding the "ego" from his final offerings to the world! A certain melancholy coloring does assert itself in his unfinished mass in A minor, but unaffected simplicity and touching pathos were wonderfully appropriate for what proved to be his "Schwanengesang." †

It is now time to leave the peaceful haven of the classical-romanticists, and embark upon the restless seas of advanced thought as set forth in the next chapter.

(Summary on page 175.)

† The present writer has developed and edited this mass as a posthumous work, opus 147, in the hope of presenting it in a form suitable for performance.

CHAPTER XI.

THE NEW MOVEMENT.

THREE countries, France, Hungary and Germany, share the honors in having brought forth three of the greatest orchestral composers, Berlioz, Liszt and Wagner, who together founded the so-called "New Movement."

I.

(*) BERLIOZ (1803–1869). The contributions of Berlioz to the development of "program" music and to modern science of orchestration loom up in gigantic proportions. He was practically the first representative of the New Movement, but contrary to the natural course of evolution, he was not only its founder but at once its most radical exponent as well. Liszt in his younger days heard some of Berlioz's compositions in Paris, and it was thus that the new seed was transplanted into Germany where it was cultivated in concert music by Liszt himself, who thereby in turn influenced Wagner's music dramas. The difference in objective between the principles laid down by Schumann and Berlioz was that the former aimed to portray a single independent thought or image, whereas Berlioz's music was connected with a series of events or ideas. His objective was to make the music symbolic of images and conceptions that should be capable of being expressed in words, and his pseudo-symphonies were accompanied by an elaborate word exposition as a running commentary on the music. As the result of his activity, the dawn of a new era in concert music appeared in France. As the chief representative of her romantic musical art, he combined dramatic and symphonic effects. As an opera composer he was not successful, but he seized upon the orchestral experiments of the contemporary operatic composers, and endeavored to express theatrical ideas by means of the orchestra alone. Henceforth the power of description was to be entrusted to music itself and not to the accessories of the stage.

Berlioz represents the ultra-realistic school of instrumental music. His works are the reflection of his own temperament and individuality. His somewhat eccentric genius displayed itself in grandiose, weird and picturesque effects, in exaggeration, morbidness, vivid portrayal, and in extravagant orchestral demands.

(*) See Appendix of Musical Illustrations, Examples 48 to 57.

The primary object was tone-color in its own right, an object that was foreign to the more æsthetic ideals of the classicists. He was the most daring orchestral writer that has ever lived, but his originality was confined to the scoring rather than to the musical substance of his works. When transcribed for pianoforte they lose their fascination. He was a veritable poet in sound, and he sought in every possible way to intensify characteristic expression.

To enlarge upon the details of Berlioz's instrumentation would be futile, for his standard treatise is a familiar book of reference to all music lovers. It is therefore permissible to make mention of only the most important of his innovations. Moreover, in order to realize the magnitude of Berlioz's achievements, one should keep clearly in mind the exact extent to which orchestral evolution had advanced before his day; for many effects that were then strikingly new are now the property of all and excite no comment. The distinctive features of his orchestration are power of musical description; new combinations, new effects, new treatment; insight into the characteristics of the instruments whereby their possibilities both individual and collective are demonstrated; excessive polyphony and complicated rhythm. He removed many prejudices even though many of his experiments are impracticable.

The "Symphonie fantastique — An Episode in the Life of an Artist" offers the best illustrations for studying his programmatic methods. The dimensions of the orchestra are kept within bounds, being augmented by but a few additional instruments such as two opheicleides and two pair of kettle-drums. [a] No more poetic duet or instrumental dialogue can be found than that between the oboe and English horn in the third movement — "In the Fields" [b] — where they represent two lovers in the guise of a shepherd and shepherdess. The March to Execution, [c] and the Witches' Revel are fine examples of dramatic intensity and accentuated volume of sound. "Lélio," a symphonic poem with vocal music, which was intended as a sequel to the "Symphonie fantastique," contains parts for four clarinets. This was consistent with Berlioz's tendency to employ homogeneous tone-color in full four-part harmony. The pianoforte is also introduced into the Finale of the same work. The huge dimensions of the Requiem or "Messe des Morts" are exceptional and should not be cited as being typical of Berlioz's usual methods of scoring. Tremendous combinations are brought into use for the Sanctus, the Tuba mirum, and the Agnus Dei. They include twelve horns, sixteen trombones, and eight pair of kettle-drums. Of uttermost impressiveness is the Tuba mirum with its four separate orchestras of brass instruments stationed at the four corners of the stage or of the auditorium itself. The various types of instruments of percussion received the most careful consideration even to minuteness of detail. The Requiem presents one of the earliest examples

(a) Ex. 51.   (b) Ex. 49.   (c) Ex. 52, 53, 54.

of employing three flutes. Berlioz selected the viola as the central figure for his symphony "Harold en Italie." [d] Its functions are to impersonate Childe Harold himself, to portray his impressions and emotions, to supply the rôle, so to speak, of a vocal interpreter. The ravishing effects elicited from the harmonics of divided violins combined with those of the harp will be recalled in the Queen Mab scherzo of "Roméo et Juliette." The score of the Biblical trilogy "L'Enfance du Christ" contains some curious passages of interwoven viola and 'cello parts. The charming ballet is performed by three flutes and a harp. Berlioz's greatest work is unquestionably the dramatic legend "La Damnation de Faust." Nothing can be daintier than the Dance of the Sylphs; nothing sadder than the portrayal of Marguerite's remorse by an English horn; nothing more brutal than the Chorus of Students, accompanied by viola, double-bass, bassoon, horn and tuba — all in unison.

In conclusion, Berlioz must be accredited with having anticipated many effects that were subsequently elaborated upon by Wagner. Unfortunately the potency of Berlioz's music depends almost entirely upon orchestral tone-color; on the other hand, the unadorned substance of Wagner's music will withstand the closest scrutiny. Berlioz frequently assigned to the orchestra and specially to the strings a large number of independent parts which were further enhanced by simultaneously contrasted rhythm. This contrast was, moreover, applied to instruments of the same group, such as first and second violins. The violins are divided at times into as many as six and eight parts, the 'cellos into four, whereas in "Cinq mai" he wrote five actual parts for the double-basses. He appreciated the true value of the viola, and was the first to introduce the harp into the symphonic orchestra. The wind-instruments are often split up into what might be called separate little orchestras. Families of affiliated tone-color are represented by three and frequently four members. It was Berlioz that discovered the richness of pianissimo brass effects, and the substitution of the tuba for the opheicleide is due largely to him. He made divers experiments with many varieties of instruments of percussion apart from those with kettle-drums. In the Te Deum for three choirs, orchestra and organ, no less than five pair of cymbals are required. His occasional demands for an enormous apparatus were certainly extravagant; nevertheless he rarely used the full force of their combined strength excepting in isolated cases.

(d) Ex. 56, 57.

II.

LISZT (1811–1886).   It is not proposed to analyze Liszt's rich and heavy orchestration, for the importance of his orchestral works consists rather of the bearing they have upon the unfettered form, the freedom of tonality and the novelty of treatment that characterize the New German School.   The scoring of his symphonic poems is masterful, highly colored and ingenious.   But although it bears the unmistakable stamp of his own personality, the orchestration embodies nothing conspicuously new.   Beethoven and the early romanticists, Berlioz, and above all Wagner were his models in instrumentation.   Favored by the opportunities afforded him in consequence of his precocious genius when but a mere child, Liszt's impressionable temperament seized upon the progressive tendencies of the times, thereby strengthening the already half-formed conviction that music should be descriptive, representative, reproductive, realistic.   After hearing Berlioz's "Episode de la vie d'un artiste" he proceeded to develop his own talent along similar though individual lines, and thus became the champion of German "program" music.   As has been previously stated, these doctrines of Berlioz and of Liszt were destined to be reflected in Wagner's works, for though the latter at first condemned such doctrines in no uncertain terms, his opinions subsequently underwent a radical change.   In his monograph on Liszt's symphonic poems he says:— "Program-music does not aim to override speech or the plastic arts and represent things accessible to them only, but rather forms a special kind of union of two independent factors: poetry and music."

Now although Beethoven's "Pastoral" symphony, Mendelssohn's "Fingal's Cave" and Raff's "Lenore" were all in the direct evolutionary line of descriptive music, Liszt soon perceived that classic forms were indeed the ideal vehicle for abstract and purely æsthetic music, but could not be successfully applied to portray a series of emotions, events or ideas.   This discovery led him to modify the cyclic form of the symphony which became transformed into the symphonic poem with its continuity of music, monothematic principle and absence of conventional formulas.   He retained all the symphonic expedients of thematic development, but form was now subjective to the program.   His methods were simpler and can be more readily grasped than those of Berlioz.   The range of subject was cosmopolitan, and the introduction of national traits, such as the Hungarian element, resulted in what Dickinson calls "shaping and coloring the work through imagined correspondences."   Liszt's symphonic poem "Les Préludes" affords the best illustration of his aims and ideals.   "Eine Faust Symphonie" embodies the suggestion of personal qualities by means of music.   The oratorios "Christus" and "Die Legende der heiligen Elizabeth" display novel treatment as well as a departure from traditional forms.

III.

(*) WAGNER (1813–1883). The recorder of the history of music and of orchestration can find no more inexhaustive topic than when he approaches that of Richard Wagner's epoch-making innovations. What is more, the literature in connection therewith is so voluminous, that opportunity for even the slightest original deduction is denied him. No alternative is left him other than to restate in condensed form what the cardinal features of Wagner's ideals and reforms were. Such a review is indeed indispensable if these pages are to be complete.

At the time that Wagner entered upon his career, German dramatic art was largely under the subjection of Meyerbeer, for Weber had not yet won universal popularity. The singer still reigned supreme; dramatic orchestration was primarily realistic and bombastic. Wagner himself betrayed in his earlier works how tempting and insidious the influence of Meyerbeer's dazzling mannerisms and idiosyncrasies could be. Moreover, in order to realize the full significance of Wagner's artistic growth, one should not lose sight of his youthful enthusiasm for Italian melody, even though his subsequent creations proved him to be a Teuton through and through, both in sentiment and in art.

The highest ideals of German opera culminated in the music dramas of Wagner. As musician, poet, dramatist, and master of scenic effects and theatrical requirements, he grew to be the champion of national art, a self-appointed reformer not alone of opera as an end to itself, but as a means whereby the conditions of social life might be inspired and uplifted. And the remarkable concentration of his musical thought, his rare gifts as a poet, and his noble histrionic conceptions proved him worthy of the task. The philosophical aspect of this attainment embodies intimate connection between drama and music; merging of voice and orchestra; intensification and completion of the singer's thought by means of the orchestra; finally, dramatic illusion whereby conditions of mind rather than dramatic situations are portrayed. By developing the so-called *Leit-motiv*, Wagner discovered a most potent factor for recalling past events, for emphasizing those present, and for anticipating those of the future. The *Leit-motiv* was, moreover, particularly well adapted to reveal the true conceptions of the composer himself. Vividness of portrayal was enhanced by means of intricate combinations of melodies and figures, free chromatic harmony, unfettered modulation, and elaborately conceived dramatic as well as thematic development toward some supreme climax. The application of the *Leit-motiv* theorem was conducive to greater license in the treatment of vocal interpretation.

(*) See Appendix of Musical Illustrations, Examples 67 to 75.

A fusion of *parlante* and the *arioso* was the result, and in later works the comparatively unintelligible enunciation of combined vocal forces was obviated by discarding the chorus almost altogether.

Retrospection shows us that there were originally three distinct divisions in opera: the *recitativo*, the *aria*, and the *ritornello*.   At first the *ritornello* was but the repetition of the cadence, but developed subsequently into a transitory period intended to complete an unfinished vocal phrase or to describe the action on the stage.   Later, a union of these three distinct divisions resulted in the *arioso*, or fragmentary *cantilena* joined to *recitativo*.   The *parlante* or musical declamation over a melodic phrase in the orchestra originated in opera-buffa as developed by Piccini and Paesiello; subsequently Spontini transplanted it into serious opera. It is equivalent in spoken drama to melodramatic recitation.   Wagner's style is therefore nothing more than an additional link in the chain of natural evolution.

The pith of Wagner's ideals may be summed up by saying that he aimed to substitute a noble form of art in the place of mere pleasure-giving and sensational fabrications.   Music, poetic ideas, action and stage setting were all to be worthy of the subject intended for presentation.   His choice of subject for dramatization was restricted to such as could embody characters capable of being treated morally and intellectually as well as æsthetically.   Wagner above all others defined the true mission of German national art and guided her to a tangible realization of that mission.

IV.

Wagner's operas and music dramas may be divided into either of two general classifications.   The first treats of the musical contents and structural form of his dramas, and of the evolution of his philosophical ideas.   The second relates solely to differentiated style of orchestration and numerical distribution of instruments.

The first classification embodies three distinct groups.   The first of these groups contains all of Wagner's earlier attempts including "Rienzi," which is modelled according to the French and Italian "historic" school. With the exception of "Eine Faust Ouvertüre" which belongs also to this category, only occasional indications of marked genius are to be found in these works.   The second group includes "Der Fliegende Holländer," "Tannhäuser" and "Lohengrin."   These display a radical change in style, form and treatment, pronounced originality, continuity of music and a fusion of recitative and aria.   The topics chosen for dramatization treat of German myths, mediæval legends, and chivalrous ideals.   Indications of the *Leit-motiv* principle, though used in an unobtrusive manner, are in evidence.   The musical forms are not yet influenced by the profundity of thought and reflection that characterizes the works belonging to the third group. The third and last group includes "Tristan und Isolde," "Die Meistersinger von Nürnberg," "Der Ring des Nibelungen," and "Parsifal." The complete fulfilment of Wagner's philosophical theories are here exposed. Wealth of harmony, characteristic rhythm and intensity of expression are combined with poetic reasoning, depth of thought and vivid dramatization. The centre of gravity, so to speak, is transferred to the orchestra. *Sprech-singen* is emphasized, whereas the *Leit-motiv* principle reaches its full development.

V.

The second classification, relating to differentiated style of orchestration, is popularly divided into three groups, but a division into four groups would seem more appropriate to the present writer. Wagner's earliest orchestral attempts need not be taken into consideration, and so the first group may include only "Rienzi," "Der Fliegende Holländer" and "Tannhäuser." The scores of these works do not display radical departure from contemporary methods excepting in polyphonic treatment and individualistic coloring. The instruments of wood are as yet represented only in pairs, although already a cor anglais and a bass-clarinet are regularly employed. The addition of a second piccolo flute, a second English horn and a third bassoon is but exceptional. The numerical distribution of strings and the constituency of the brass are normal. Entirely new tendencies are discovered in "Lohengrin" and "Tristan und Isolde" which comprise the second group, since each wood-wind family is now represented by three instruments. The number of strings are augmented so as to balance the wood-wind, as well as in consequence of their own frequent sub-division; but the brass is the same as in Group I. The magnitude of the Nibelungen Tetralogy gave rise to the adaptation of the exceptional third group. The augmentation affects both the wood and the brass. The wood-winds are divided into families of four each, and the same principle is applied to the brass. Strings, harps and battery are augmented in proportion. The reason for regarding "Die Meistersinger" and "Parsifal" as representatives of a separate fourth group is that in the former, Wagner reverted to the orchestra of Groups I and II, whereas the number of instruments used in "Parsifal" correspond to those in "Tristan." Notwithstanding, the orchestration and the treatment of instruments for both "Die Meistersinger" and "Parsifal" embody a composite style that frequently suggests certain traits peculiar to the Tetralogy. They may, therefore, be rightfully regarded as belonging to a distinct group by themselves.

We need not here concern ourselves again with the first mentioned philosophical and æsthetic classification. On the other hand, the purpose of these pages certainly demands some further analysis of the second orchestral classification.

GROUP I.   RIENZI; DER FLIEGENDE HOLLÄNDER; TANNHÄUSER.

Strings; 1 or 2 harps.

1 piccolo flute (sometimes 2); 2 flutes; 2 oboes; 1 English horn (rarely 2); 2 clarinets; 1 bass-clarinet; 2 bassoons (sometimes 3 bassoons or an additional contra-bassoon).

4 horns (of which at least 2 are chromatic); 2 chromatic trumpets (often 3); 3 trombones (2 tenor, 1 bass); 1 bass-tuba.

2 kettle-drums (sometimes 3); further instruments of percussion.

"Rienzi" was first given at Dresden in 1842. Of its orchestration little need be said. Being influenced by Meyerbeer and the French dramatic traditions, the scoring embodies much that is extravagant and bombastic, though many instrumental passages of surprising beauty are by no means absent. What might be called the composite of rich, velvet tone-color peculiar to Wagner's orchestral palette is already noticeable — a coloring that was not attained even by Spontini, Meyerbeer or Halévy. "Der Fliegende Holländer" (Dresden, 1843) revolutionized at one stroke the dramatic functions of orchestration as well as the treatment of instruments, even if the combinations themselves are not radically different from contemporary procedure. In this transition work Wagner revealed the future path he was destined to pursue. The innovation of continuity and alliance of music, poetry, scenes and action proved that his latent powers had already begun to unfold themselves. "Der Fliegende Holländer" is the direct successor to Weber's romantic operas, and in detail and color it resembles Marschner's "Hans Heiling." For the first time he made use of the German myth. He drew freely upon a naturalistic use of chromatics and of astounding brass effects for portraying the tempest, called into requisition the most characteristic accents of the wood-wind to depict the gloomy atmosphere of the Northern seas, and elaborated upon Weber's use of the horns for romantic episodes. His subsequent predilection for divided strings is already to be found in a modified form. In a word, the entire work is imbued with virile force and truthful expression. Its successor, "Tannhäuser" (Dresden, 1845 — Paris, 1861), follows along similar lines but displays greater advance both in the handling of the mediæval legend itself and in style of orchestration. Of decidedly modern effect is the condensed declamatory style of Tannhäuser in the last act, as well as the powerful sweep of the violins in the Overture, the passage for 4-part violas in the March, and the important rôle assigned to the harp throughout the opera. An admirable illustration of writing for unsupported wood-wind accompanies the exit of Elizabeth in the third act. Her grief and resignation could have found no more faithful interpreter than that solo for bass-clarinet beneath syncopated chords of gentle and tender-voiced flutes. The 12 horns on the stage in the first act, and the 12 trumpets for the March in the second act are treated in a novel and interesting manner that bears but slight resemblance to the previous experiments of the " historic " school.

In thus briefly analyzing the general characteristics of this first group, it is seen that in relation to practical instrumentation, only the brass was especially affected. The incorporation of regularly employed chromatic horns and trumpets afforded completeness and freedom. The use of three trumpets, which is also to be found in the scores of Mendelssohn and Schumann, balanced the trombones; and the substitution of the tuba for the opheicleide yielded greater sonority as well as a closer affinity in tone-color to that of the trombones themselves.

GROUP II. LOHENGRIN; TRISTAN UND ISOLDE.
Strings; 1 or 2 harps (frequently 2 individual parts).
1 or 2 piccolo flutes; 3 flutes; 2 oboes and 1 English horn (or 3 oboes); 2 clarinets and 1 bass-clarinet (or 3 clarinets); 3 bassoons.
4 chromatic horns; 3 trumpets; 3 trombones; 1 bass-tuba.
2 or 3 kettle-drums; instruments of percussion.

"Lohengrin" was first performed at Weimar in 1850 under the direction of Liszt. It bears a striking relation to Weber's "Euryanthe," but exhibits, nevertheless, entirely new tendencies. It breathes the very atmosphere of chivalrous splendor, embodies ideal purity of sentiment and expression, and supplants traditional form by means of continuous and absolutely flexible melody. Conspicuous is the reconstruction of the orchestra in that the strings are much divided, and the wood-winds are represented by families of three instead of two instruments. Both Meyerbeer and Berlioz had made use of such triplets of uniform tone-color, but Wagner was the first to do so consistently. Not only were the resources for obtaining variety of individual and also of combined tonal effect thereby increased, but the *ensemble* of the full orchestra acquired greater firmness and sonority as well. Striking and entirely new effects confront us on every hand. The string writing is of surpassing beauty, whether illustrated by the division of violins in their ethereal range, or by passages assigned to divided violas and 'cellos combined with the harp. It is, however, primarily the wood-wind that is treated in a particularly novel manner. Familiar examples containing rare tonal tints and intense depth of sentiment are those associated with Elsa's first entry, or with the dramatic situation in the earlier part of the second act, where the English horn, clarinet, bass-clarinet, bassoons and 'cellos are most effectively combined. The cathedral scene in the second act presents another complete exposition of unsupported wood-wind. Not until 1859 was the score of "Tristan und Isolde" completed, for Wagner was simultaneously at work on the "Meistersinger" and the "Ring"; moreover, after the first performance of "Lohengrin," fifteen dreary years elapsed before "Tristan" was first presented, which finally took place in Munich in 1865. The exposition of this Keltic legend is marked by splendor of color and musical intricacy. Although it ushers in the beginning of Wagner's third creative period whereby the logical unfolding of his ideas of reform is carried out, the work is properly included in the second group of the "orchestral" classification, since the numerical distribution of instrumental parts is practically identical with that in "Lohengrin." However, the scoring is of a far higher degree of intensity. It abounds in every conceivable shade of composite tone-color, of striking contrasts, of inspiring outbursts. One of the most magnetic features is the impassioned yet melancholy tint that envelops the entire work as it were in its veiled embrace. The attainment of this objective colors much of the orchestration, as exemplified, for instance, by the predominance of violoncellos in four parts as well as by the combination of oboe, English horn, horn and bassoon *soli* in the Vorspiel. Again, a subdued yet intense impression is caused by the union of English horn, bassoon and trombones in the first act during the scene between Tristan and Isolde. Astounding skill is displayed in the development of thematic treatment leading to ever alternating climaxes, anticlimaxes, and monumental finales.

In the above second group, the orchestra is enlarged chiefly by the introduction of triplets of wood-wind instruments. The English horn and the bass-clarinet are employed as components of their respective families rather than as solo interpreters. They are replaced by a third oboe and a third clarinet in concerted *forte* numbers of extended length. No further purely practical innovations are to be noted other than a logical augmentation of the string band and progressive treatment of the brass.

(If the topics of this review were subject to despotic chronological sequence, it would be necessary, at this point, to touch upon the characteristics of "Die Meistersinger," for that work was first performed at Munich in 1868, three years after "Tristan" and one year before "Das Rheingold." As already suggested, however, the scoring of "Die Meistersinger" is such as to make it advisable to include it in a separate fourth group together with "Parsifal.")

GROUP III.   DER RING DES NIBELUNGEN.

16 first violins; 16 seconds; 12 violas; 12 violoncellos; 8 double-basses.

6 harps (exceptionally in 6 individual parts).

1 or 2 piccolo flutes; 3 flutes; 3 oboes; 1 English horn; 3 clarinets (at times a small clarinet); 1 bass-clarinet; 3 bassoons; 1 contra-bassoon.

4 horns (often 8); 3 trumpets; 1 bass-trumpet; 3 trombones; 1 contrabass-trombone; 4 tubas (tenor and bass); 1 contrabass-tuba.

2 pair of kettle-drums; instruments of percussion.

The Tetralogy presents not only the culmination of Wagner's poetic ideas and philosophical aspirations, but the final transformation in orchestral resources as well. The première of "Das Rheingold" took place in 1869 in Munich, followed in 1876 by the first performance of the entire "Ring" at Bayreuth. The music of the "Ring" is so inseparably welded to the drama that, apart from certain striking exceptions, much of it loses its significance when performed as "absolute music" away from the stage. At first sight the requisition made for so mighty an aggregation of instruments must have been indeed terrifying to a "Herrn Kapellmeister" of the old operatic school, but closer inspection of the orchestration reveals the fact that the glories of this noble tableau are obtained by masterful contrasts of detached little groups of uniform tone-color, rather than by cumulative tone quality and quantity. Space forbids more than a cursory glance at a very few of these novel characteristics in details of instrumentation. "Das Rheingold" shows, on the whole, great reserve in the simultaneous employment of large forces. For instance, the scene of the Rhine maidens is accompanied by the most transparent orchestration. Many variations in the use of unmixed tone-color could be cited, such as three oboes and English horn by themselves; English horn with three bassoons; horns alone, or with bassoons, or with bass-tuba. One of the most striking examples is to be found in the fourth scene where the chord of the diminished seventh is assigned to the lower notes of three clarinets and a bass-clarinet. The same consistent use of homogeneous quartets marks the deployment of the brass. The tubas appear entirely alone, as do also the four trumpets in combination with the four trombones. The final scene presents one of the exceptional instances of six independent parts for harps. The first act of "Die Walküre" is, in the opinion of the present writer, the most perfect specimen of dramatic writing in the literature of music. [a] Here again, the avoidance of massive scoring is particularly to be noted throughout almost the entire act. And what other instruments could have attained that maximum intensity of expression that characterizes the deployment of five solo violoncellos [b] as interpreters of tender longing and suppressed emotion? Some of the most impressive effects are obtained by means of such comparatively simple combinations as one solo oboe supported by two flutes, a clarinet and a bassoon, further assisted by a second fragmentary melodic theme in the 'cellos. Instances of independent phrases for three clarinets and bass-clarinet are again to be found, and in the third act, the horns are employed in six real parts. A large majority of effects and combinations that are conspicuous in "Das Rheingold" and "Die Walküre" naturally reappear in "Siegfried" and "Götterdämmerung." Further distinctive traits in "Siegfried" are the manifold division of violins and violoncellos, the extensive arpeggio passages for violas, the employment of viola harmonics, the important rôle assigned

[a] Ex. 67 to 75.   [b] Ex. 67.

288 41

to the double-basses, the composite tonal tint resulting from a reunion of the clarinet quartet and four solo 'cellos, and the use of bass- and double-bass tubas for impersonating the dragon. Another prominent illustration of sonorous yet transparent scoring is seen in the scintillating Forest Music in the second act and again in "Götterdämmerung," to which a striking contrast is subsequently afforded by the solemn and massive harmonies of the tubas in Siegfried's Funeral March. Nor should the prominent function of kettle-drums throughout the entire Tetralogy be overlooked.

In comparing the distribution of parts in the first, second, and third groups, we have seen that in the first of these the orchestra is normal, though the balance of the brass is improved. The augmentation of the second group is effected by employing three instruments in each family of the wood-wind. The third group, however, embodies a readjustment of both wood and brass into families of four. This requires a strong body of strings; incidentally, more harps are employed, whereas both the number and variety of instruments of percussion are increased. In addition to four trumpets and four trombones there are as many as eight horns and five tubas. Not only are these massed instruments never used simultaneously, but their latent powers are further intended to be modified by Wagner's plan for a partially concealed orchestra as at Bayreuth. To the brass is primarily entrusted the important function of contrasting three fundamental conceptions in the Tetralogy. Horns are symbolic of the poetic, of distant visions, of reminiscences, of imagination, of conscience. Trumpets and trombones represent a world of light midst the gods and heroes. Tubas portray material force, human suffering, fate.

GROUP IV. DIE MEISTERSINGER VON NÜRNBERG; PARSIFAL.

To classify these two works under one heading might at first sight appear incongruous, for apart from the fact that some dozen years separate the respective periods of their creation, the difference between them in style and objective is as that of the antipodes. The comic features and satirical purpose of the one bear absolutely no relation to the mystical and devotional tone of the other. In two respects, however, they have some points of affinity. The orchestration of both is more like that of "Tristan" than of the "Ring," and the harmonies are, to a certain extent, the adventitious corollary of intricate polyphonic voice-leading. This is, of course, particularly pronounced in "Parsifal," but it is in evidence in "Die Meistersinger" as well. Both works prove that the exceptional orchestral forces required for "Der Ring des Nibelungen" are by no means necessary to obtain sonority, richness, exhaustless variety and supreme dramatic intensity. Again, none of Wagner's dramas can rival "Die Meistersinger" in musical power, whereas "Parsifal," as the exponent of Wagner's religious views and his attitude toward Christianity, is unsurpassed for nobility of subject and dignity of treatment. With the performance of "Parsifal" at Bayreuth in 1882, Wagner ended his stupendous lifework. His death followed barely seven months later, but he had lived long enough to witness the attainment of his ambitions and ideals.

VI.

It is needless to enlarge upon the hostile criticism evoked by Wagner's theories, for his titanic achievements have remained unscathed in the very face of even such violent attacks as were hurled forth by Nordau and Nietzsche. Nevertheless, the present writer cannot refrain from referring to the petty antagonism Wagner had to endure as a consequence of the narrow-mindedness and non-progressive spirit of many of his most distinguished contemporaries. Even Rheinberger was not exempt from this defect, and his attitude toward Wagner must be regarded as being the more unaccountable since the memory of the Munich master is to be revered not alone for the profound knowledge, the depth of feeling, and the refinement that revealed themselves in his teaching and composition, but for the nobility of his soul and the loftiness of his purpose as well. And the close of Lobe's otherwise unprejudiced treatise on instrumentation displays a glaring inconsistency in its strictures upon Wagner's so-called overloaded orchestration. In his anxiety to decry overzealous Wagner worship, Lobe made laborious efforts to select examples that should support his adverse criticisms. This he openly acknowledges, although he admits that not all of Wagner's "Kraftbilder" are scored in so unfelicitous a manner. One of the two such illustrations cited by him embodies the episodic climax in "Lohengrin" where Elsa's ecstasy is portrayed in

Fänd—— ich Ju - bel - wei - sen

Lobe claims that the initial tones of Elsa's outburst are overpowered and that further, her succeeding phrases are marred rather than supported by reduplication of oboe and clarinet! No author can convince his readers with such biased and absurd arguments. To deliberately confine one's-self to such trivial points in demonstration of Wagner's scoring is not in keeping with the dignity of what is still a standard treatise. Even though it was published as early as 1864, that was the very year in which Wagner was called to Munich by King Ludwig II. By that time his works had already received sufficient recognition to command the most careful consideration even from pedants. Lobe's entire paragraph will bear repeating in consequence of its very incongruity: —

"In diesem Beispiel *sehen* wir als Hauptzeichnung die Melodie Elsa's. Ihr Entzücken ist herrlich deklamirt, aber für wen? Kann irgend ein Zuhörer von dem Eintritt *dieser Singstimme,* und sie ist die wesentliche oder sollte es doch sein, auch nur eine Ahnung bekommen? *Drei* Flöten, *drei* Oboen, *drei* Klarinetten, *vier* Hörner, *drei* Fagotte, *drei* Trompeten, *drei* Posaunen, *Tuba, Pauke,* das Streichquartett, der König und der ganze Frauen- und Männerchor schreien *fortissimo* gegen die einzelne Stimme des zarten Wesens Elsa! Dieser Riesen-accent aller vereinten Orchester- und Chorstimmen verstummt nun zwar und die Folge der Singmelodie Elsa's wird *etwas* hörbar, aber von einem rein und deutlich hervorglänzenden *Gesang* kann nicht die Rede sein; den die Mitsprache der ersten Oboe und ersten Klarinette im Einklang — beiläufig bemerkt eine der fatalsten Verbindungen dieser beiden Instrumente — sowie der andern Blasin-strumente verwischen und verzehren den Klang der Singstimme und lassen gleichsam nur einen Schatten derselben vernehmen.''

VII.

In summing up the chief characteristics of Wagner's perfect orchestration it is seen that although he was at first susceptible to tone-color as an end to itself, he learned to subordinate it to the demands of the musical and poetic ideas of the immediate dramatic situation. Greatest of masters for the orchestra, Wagner brought that organization to its highest point of evolution. Even though the scores of "Lohengrin" and "Tristan" contain, with the exception of bass-clarinet and bass-tuba, no instruments that had not been employed by Haydn and Mozart, it was Wagner that emphasized solidity, that made the orchestra firm and supple, that increased its melodic as well as harmonic force, and used it for two definite purposes: to render emotion and to portray action and situations. He was for-tunate in being aided by the rapid improvements that were taking place in his day in the mechanism of instruments, as well as in the advance in musical educa-tion and technical skill of orchestral performers. His orchestration does not deviate from well-established and approved traditions, but the grouping and treatment of instruments are entirely new. The use of deep, sonorous basses never interferes with harmonic clearness or with the outline of melodic and rhythmic movement. The modern extreme development of unsupported wood-wind [c] is entirely due to Wagner. When his predecessors had had occasion to employ an English horn or a bass-clarinet, one of the oboe or clarinet players usually undertook the part, thus depriving the orchestra of possible effects for two oboes and English horn, or two clarinets and bass-clarinet. This defect was remedied by both Berlioz and Wagner in augmenting the wood-wind for the pur-pose of obtaining harmonies of uniform tone-color. The addition of horns as regular constituents of the second orchestral group [d] lent smoothness and cohe-

(c) Ex. 70, 71.   (d) Ex. 71.

sion to the former somewhat thin and uneven quality of the combined wood-wind. Scme of the most mournful accents in Wagner's orchestra are those obtained from the velvet harmonies of three flutes in their lowest range. He regarded the clarinet [e] as the most expressive solo wind instrument in the orchestra, and recognized the latent efficiency of the bassoons whether as solo interpreters or in independent harmonies, whether as bass to the wood-wind or together with the horns alone.[f] The most radical changes are those affecting the brass. Nevertheless, the principle of using three or four instruments of the same family is in reality based upon Gluck's and Mozart's euphonious distribution of three-part harmony for trombones. Of incalculable value was the permanent employment of valve-horns and valve-trumpets, the immense development in horn writing, and the discarding of opheicleides. A world of majestic light, as exposed by the homogeneity of trumpets and trombones, is made to stand out in strong relief against the tubas' luxuriant wealth of harmony, or the veiled yet picturesque tonal tints of horns. The introduction of a complete group of tubas was certainly an entirely new idea. Much of Wagner's warm and rich orchestration is due to a substratum of soft brass harmonies that are apparently not audible at all. No composer knew better than he how to obtain the best effects from instruments of percussion without overstepping the bounds of artistic refinement. His use of kettle-drums was more practical than that of Berlioz; but it should not be forgotten that when Meyerbeer or Berlioz needed a numerical variety of tones or rapid changes in pitch, it was necessary to employ a number of drums and several performers, whereas Wagner was able in later years to attain the same object with fewer drums, in consequence of the perfecting of the "machine-drum" which allows of almost instantaneous change of pitch. The art of conducting received also a powerful impetus from Wagner, and his untiring efforts to raise the standard of the dramatic and concert stage were ably seconded by Liszt and subsequently by von Bülow. When exercising the functions of a conductor, one of Wagner's strong principles of interpretation consisted in modifying a tempo in accordance with the momentary character of the dominating melodic themes.

The bitterness of conflict over Wagner's works has expended itself; hostile criticism is now exceptional. To-day Wagner stands forth as the accepted champion of dramatic reforms, as the most eminent composer of the nineteenth century, and as the greatest master of orchestration in the annals of the world.

VIII.

In these days the "New Movement" is no longer new, for the trend of modern music is ever progressive. For convenience, however, this classification may

[e] Ex. 73.   [f] Ex. 69, 72.

include Cornelius, Bruckner, Lassen, A. Ritter, Draeseke, Weingartner, Nicodé, finally Richard Strauss.

Cornelius (1824) would appear to be thus far the only writer for the German stage since Wagner who has had something decidedly original and lasting to say. [6]   Being a protégé of Liszt, he became an ardent partisan for Wagnerism. The cool reception of his "Barbier von Bagdad" when first performed at Weimar in 1858 was the immediate reason for causing Liszt to withdraw from that city in disgust.   This lack of appreciation is the more unaccountable in that but eight years had elapsed since the residents of Weimar had welcomed Wagner's "Lohengrin" with enthusiasm.   "Der Barbier" was a worthy successor to "Lohengrin"; not that the styles of these two operas have even the remotest affinity to each other, but rather the very originality of the "Barbier" should have commanded unquestionable approval.   However, the succeeding generation of theatre-goers has been pleased to commend the work after a fashion, though it is to be regretted that this appreciation has not become whole-souled and universal.   Not only is the music itself charming and vivacious, and the plot highly ingenious, but the orchestration is brimming over with mirth and good humor, portrays in the most subtle manner the amorous as well as the sentimental situations, and brings into requisition some very ludicrous traits of instrumentation.   Moreover the Finale, "Salamaleikum," is a most magnificent piece of *ensemble* writing.   Cornelius followed Wagner in writing all of his texts himself.   "Der Cid" is less spontaneous than its predecessor, but the orchestration is that of a master, being imbued with genuine local coloring together with profound melancholy, suppressed emotion and heroic outbursts.   It is interesting to conjecture what the outcome of Cornelius' setting of "Gunlöd" would have been, for he left behind him an unfinished text based upon the elder Scandinavian Edda.

Anton Bruckner (1824) is commonly identified with the New Movement, but he might with equal propriety be rated as a classical-romanticist.   Although he possesses many warm admirers, the permanent value of his writings is open to question.   His formal structure, contrapuntal treatment, and thematic development bear the impress of a scholarly touch, but in spite of certain leanings toward Wagnerian principles, his heavy style and rather precise music have a chilling effect upon the majority of listeners.   The melodies are not flowing, the rhythm is monotonous, and the orchestration, though clever, lacks buoyancy and warmth.

The next four composers of this somewhat arbitrary list can be summarily disposed of, since they have advanced the evolution of orchestration to no perceptible degree.   This statement is by no means intended to belittle the sterling qualities of their musicianship.   All of them have won renown in their respective

[6] See footnote on page 118 in reference to the sensation recently created by Richard Strauss' opera "Salome."

fields of activity, and their creative efforts disclose broad culture, wide experience, and a facile pen. Their instrumentation is invariably effective. Eduard Lassen (1830) and Felix Draeseke (1835) took a prominent part in propagating the tenets of Liszt and Wagner. Draeseke frankly declared himself for Wagner, and assisted him by means of his literary skill. Lassen succeeded Liszt as Generalmusik-director of the Weimar Opera. Similar to that of many another talented though at first obscure aspirant, the success of his operas was due to the enterprise of Liszt himself. During his later years Lassen devoted himself almost exclusively to song-writing. As recently as two years before his death, which occurred in 1903, he remarked to the present writer that after having studied and conducted Wagner's works as far back as forty odd years ago, he had come to the conclusion that he himself had no further message to give to the dramatic world; consequently he withdrew from the arduous contest. Alexander Ritter (1833) was an able and painstaking composer, and wrote for the opera as well as for the orchestra alone. His scoring was consistent with his scholarship, but the substance of his productions embodies little that is new. Weingartner (1853) is best known as a concert con-ductor. His directing exercises a peculiarly magnetic fascination, and that quite especially upon the ladies! His movements are wonderfully graceful, and suggest, at times, a subtle hypnotic power flavoring of Orientalism.

In turning to the magnum opus of Nicodé (1853), we find ourselves face to face with one of the most interesting specimens of modern orchestration — which is saying a great deal in this age when the art of scoring has reached such stu-pendous virtuosity. "Das Meer," symphonic ode for solo voices, male chorus, orchestra, and organ, may not reveal striking originality of subject-matter, but it is a magnificent exposition of realism and discloses the author's keen appreciation for the imaginative, the descriptive, the picturesque. One could readily suppose that Nicodé might have been more or less influenced by Rubinstein's "Ocean Symphony," but this is not at all the case. Nicodé's primary aim was the acquisi-tion of superb and startling effects by means of tone-color pure and simple. His technique is enormous. One of his strongest points is the ability to procure scin-tillating tints by means of multiple division of strings alone. By piling up a large number of independent and seemingly irreconcilable melodic themes one on top of the other, a marvellous effervescent polyphony is procured. The best example of pure tone effect is revealed in the movement entitled "Phosphorescent Lights." The modern symphonic orchestra is, of course, employed, being further augmented by an additional harp, and two tenor-tubas with the usual bass-tuba. The battery assumes gigantic proportions in that demand is made for two pair of kettle-drums, one pair of cymbals, a bass-drum, a triangle, a gong, and a set of bells. Even these additions do not satisfy the composer, for behind the stage is concealed a brass band of three trumpets, seven trombones and a bass-tuba.

IX.

(*) RICHARD STRAUSS (1864). It is universally conceded that the greatest master of orchestration after Richard Wagner is Richard Strauss. The latter's career thus far bears some affinity to that of Mendelssohn as regards early artistic surroundings, scholarly training in branches other than music, and exemption from monetary anxiety. But whereas Mendelssohn's affluent circumstances and prosperous career were undoubtedly detrimental to the development of profound pathos and tragic intensity, Strauss has made the demonstration that worldly cares and petty professional obstacles are not the essential stimuli for herculean artistic growth embodying the portrayal of experiences not personally experienced.

(**Biography.**) Strauss was reared in a schooling so orthodox that not even his severest critics can venture to deny his mastery of traditional usages, — indeed, in his earlier works Strauss has given tangible proof of his ability to compose in conservative forms. He is the son of a French-horn player of rare genius, whose memorable performance of his son's horn concerto first taught the present writer the latent possibilities of that instrument. Strauss is said to have produced a polka at the age of six, whereas already during his boyhood days he devoted his spare moments to writing orchestral overtures, choruses, sonatas, and the like. Although enrolled as a student at the Gymnasium and for one year at the University of Munich, he was simultaneously given opportunity to develop his musical talents along the prescribed lines of practical training. His public career as a composer may be said to have begun when two of his choruses were given at a school concert. In 1880 he succeeded in having three of his songs sung at a public concert. He was then only sixteen years old. These minor achievements, however, fall into insignificance in comparison with the recognition awarded him in the following year, when Benno Walther, concertmeister of the Munich Opera, produced the string quartet, op. 2, in the course of the annual series of chamber concerts. Walther's quartet was at that time highly authoritative in musical circles. In the same year Hermann Levi performed the symphony in D minor. Strauss next drew attention to himself with a serenade, op. 7, for thirteen instruments, and thereby interested no less a person than Hans von Bülow. This was destined to influence Strauss' entire career, for in 1885 he was engaged as musical director at Meiningen in a subordinate though honorable position to von Bülow himself. It was von Bülow, therefore, that gave Strauss his initial training as an orchestral conductor, a branch of art in which he has now attained proficiency only secondary to his powers as a composer. At Meiningen he was enabled to assimilate not only von Bülow's magnetic technique and

(*) See Appendix of Musical Illustrations, Examples 97 to 103.

authoritative interpretation, but was also led to grasp Wagner's ideals of conducting. In addition he also appeared occasionally as a concert pianist, and meanwhile completed his more or less conservative symphonic phantasy "Aus Italien." Here, too, he came in contact with the Wagnerian enthusiast, Alexander Ritter, an intimacy that had much to do with the subsequent moulding of his first distinctively original works, "Macbeth" and "Don Juan." Toward the close of 1885 he succeeded von Bülow as conductor of the Meiningen Orchestra, retained the post for one season, and then accepted a subordinate position in his native city under Levi and Fischer at the Munich Royal Opera. Like most prophets in their own country, he had to overcome the prejudice of some of the older gentlemen of the orchestra who had been colleagues of his father and had seen the son grow up. For three years he was now occupied with the rather thankless task of conducting lesser operatic performances, but devoted himself none the less with untiring effort to the development of his creative talents, which bore fruit in "Macbeth," "Don Juan" and "Tod und Verklärung." In 1889 he was called to the Weimar Opera, first as subordinate to Lassen, eventually as full-empowered potentate. He there married one of the operatic singers, Pauline de Ahne, daughter of a Bavarian general. While at Weimar he wrote his first opera, "Guntram." In 1894 Strauss returned to the Munich Opera in a capacity more responsible than formerly. His services as a conductor of unusual ability were by this time much in demand for special concert performances in European musical centres. The atmosphere of his native city must have been particularly inspiring to his creative Muse, for from 1894 to 1899 no less than four mighty orchestral works emanated from his pen — "Till Eulenspiegel," "Also sprach Zarathustra," "Don Quixote," "Ein Heldenleben." In 1899 he was called to the Berlin Opera as an associate with Muck. It is here that he at present wields the baton with unflagging zeal, in spite of his restless activity as a composer. Thus far his most important contributions to the twentieth century have been the opera "Feuersnoth" and the "Symphonia Domestica." [7]

Such are the biographical outlines of an epoch-making composer, an eminent conductor, and a well-trained pianist who has but entered upon the fifth decade of his lifetime. Before proceeding to an examination of the aims and ideals that are at the root of Strauss' huge orchestral conceptions, some comparisons between him and his predecessors as suggested by Richard Aldrich will bear citation: —

"At forty Strauss is the most commanding figure in the musical world of to-day. It will be an interesting disclosure for future years to make as to how much of his lifework he has already accomplished, and whether the salient characteristics are already fixed and contained in what he has done, or whether this is but a preparation. We may be reminded that on their fortieth birthdays Mozart

[7] See footnote on page 118 in reference to "Salome."

and Schubert had put the final seal upon their work, Mozart five years before, Schubert nine. Beethoven had given to the world his first six symphonies, his 'Fidelio,' and the 'Leonore' overtures, the 'Coriolanus' overture, the 'Egmont' music, the five piano concertos and the violin concerto, nine string quartets, including those dedicated to Count Rasoumoffsky; the 'Kreutzer' and the earlier violin sonatas, the 'Waldstein' and the earlier piano sonatas. Wagner had written 'Rienzi,' 'The Flying Dutchman,' 'Tannhäuser,' 'Lohengrin,' 'Eine Faust Ouvertüre,' and had conceived and partly executed 'The Ring of the Nibelung.' And yet these two had not given the finest fruitage of their genius. What Strauss has done in his younger manhood will not, perhaps, be counted of greater worth. Whether, like these two at his age, he will go on to further development may also be curiously questioned, and whether he will turn aside from the path in which he has already started. On that path he seems already to have reached the furthest confines of the territory he has traversed."

X.

(**Classification of Compositions.**) Similar to the works of most composers who have a genuinely original message to give to the world, those of Strauss may be divided into distinct groups of differentiated creative periods. He has progressed step by step through various stages of development. Conforming at first to the conservative romanticism founded upon traditional forms of Mendelssohn and Schumann, he soon came to admire and emulate the doctrines of Brahms — an influence that has never been effaced from his subsequent writings even though his associations with von Bülow and Ritter caused him to lean more and more upon Wagner and Liszt for the dominating thought of his conceptions. With one stroke, however, "Macbeth" and "Don Juan" went far beyond the tenets of the Weimar coterie, though the succeeding productions "Tod und Verklärung" and "Guntram" suggest what has been called a *reaction* toward Liszt and Wagner. But with "Till Eulenspiegel" and "Also sprach Zarathustra" Strauss inaugurated a permanent and ever advancing method of procedure distinctively individualistic and unprecedented, that has so far culminated in the vast realistic tableaux of "Don Quixote" and "Ein Heldenleben."

(*1st Period.*) Reference has already been made to his youthful efforts. After the small choruses, the songs, the string quartet, op. 2, and the symphony in D minor, there appeared some interesting experiments in various fields of composition. The list includes a pianoforte sonata, op. 5; a sonata for violoncello and pianoforte, op. 6; the serenade, op. 7, for wind-instruments, patronized by von Bülow; a violin concerto, op. 8; "Stimmungsbilder" for pianoforte, op. 9; the French-horn concerto, op. 11, already referred to; a symphony in F minor, op.

12; a pianoforte quartet, op. 13; and "Wanderers Sturmlied," for six-part mixed chorus and orchestra, op. 14. This choral work has been called "a broadly flowing stream of polyphonic vocal harmony against an elaborate and independent orchestral accompaniment that was something quite unprecedented." The above compositions comprise what might be termed the first of Strauss' creative periods, having all been written before he was twenty. They present a conventional though rapid development of and graduation from the dominating influences of Mendelssohn, Schumann, Brahms, as suggested above, and gradually point more and more toward Berlioz, Liszt, and Wagner.

(*2d Period.*) The symphony in F minor, written in 1883, may be looked upon not only as the culmination of these earliest attempts, but also as the first of Strauss' really significant orchestral compositions. Its maiden performance took place not in Germany but in this country, when, in 1884, Theodore Thomas produced it in New York with the Philharmonic Society.

Several years now elapsed before Strauss was ready to offer to the world the first of his great symphonic tone-poems: "Aus Italien" — sinfonische Phantasie, G-dur (op. 16, 1886). This was a marked advance upon the previous symphony, but though it reveals the subsequent path Strauss was to pursue, and embodies complex polyphony and increased command over the technics of orchestration, it is still dominated by Mendelssohn's and Schumann's subjective idea of program-music.

(*3d Period.*) Not until von Bülow and Ritter had fathomed the true depth of their young associate's latent powers did he proceed to evolve his conceptions in a language that has startled the entire musical world.

"Macbeth" — Tondichtung nach Shakespeare's Drama (op. 23, 1887), is the first of these vast color-pictures. Although "Don Juan" is to be recorded as opus 20, Friedrich Rösch, the authoritative reviewer of "Ein Heldenleben," places it after "Macbeth," although classifying it also as opus 20. He gives the date of its completion as 1888. Dr. Riemann's Dictionary of Music, which is the most accurate book of its kind in existence, seems for once to be at fault in stating the various dates at which Strauss penned his creations. "Macbeth," like its successors, at once displays a wealth of melodic utterance in all the principal orchestral voices, a prolific number of themes and sub-themes, and the most intimate acquaintance with the specific characteristics of the various instruments as well as with orchestral combinations and the resultant mixture of tonal tints thereby to be obtained. Like Berlioz, Strauss secures dramatic effects by means of vivid orchestration. The themes are arrayed in a kaleidoscopic sequence of instrumental color rather than being subjected to elaborate thematic treatment, and climaxes are reached by means of dynamic effects instead of by melodic evolution. An elaborately conceived program justifies the requisition for vast orchestral resources.   There is further evidence of genuine inspiration, of a true gift for thematic development forming a marvellous filigree of contrapuntally interwoven leading motives, of intellectual power, philosophical reflection, poetic revery, and naïve humor.   The following themes from "Macbeth" demonstrate the wide range of thematic conception Strauss possesses:

No. 1.

No. 2.

No. 3.

(*) Most of these examples have been selected from the transcriptions in skeleton form of Friedrich Rösch. Nos. 16 and 19 were suggested by Richard Aldrich. Nos. 34, 35, 36, 37 were prepared by Strauss himself.

The first consists of a flowing cantilena evolved on broad and dignified lines.   The second is a striking example of freely used chromatic intervals.   The third follows Wagner's precedent in deploying instruments of brass in forceful and incisive utterance.

"Don Juan" — Tondichtung nach Lenau (op. 20, 1888), belongs to the same creative period as "Macbeth" and follows the same general outlines of philosophical, structural, and orchestral procedure.   The following four representative themes are suggestive not only of "local" coloring but reveal the highest attribute of a genuine composer in that their very nature suggests the general type of instrument to be employed.   Proof is thus to be had that Strauss simultaneously conceives his subject-matter and the orchestral garment in which it is to be attired.

No. 4.

No. 5.

No. 6.

No. 7.

(*4th Period.*)   "Tod und Verklärung" — Tondichtung (op. 24, 1889), is classified with the opera "Guntram" for embodying a certain reactionary trend on the part of the author.   There is no lack of intricate polyphony, daring harmonic combinations, complex rhythm, startling contrasts, monumental climaxes, and clever orchestral devices; but in these works Strauss has exercised more restraint than in the preceding "Macbeth" and "Don Juan," whereas the acme of his extreme realism was not reached until after he began his following and mightiest series of symphonic poems beginning with "Till Eulenspiegel." To quote the refined language of Herman Klein: "In 'Tod und Verklärung' is depicted the death struggle of a man before whose mental vision there passes the panorama of a wasted life followed by the man's transfiguration, as his redeemed soul passes out of earthly existence into a higher state." Of the three themes from "Tod und Verklärung" appended below, it is interesting to note that the first of these (No. 8) was subsequently interwoven into the introductory theme of "Ein Heldenleben," and appears as the third phrase of the *Motiv* representing "Der Held." (See page 113, example 22, bars 6 and 7.)

Strauss has not been so conspicuously successful with his operas as with his orchestral works, [8] but the following themes from "Guntram" disclose the general nature of his operatic conceptions.

(*5th Period.*) The most radical exposition of modern orchestration is discovered in the fifth period of symphonic creations beginning with "Till Eulenspiegel's lustige Streiche" — nach alter Schelmenweise in Rondo-Form (op. 28,

[8] See footnote on page 118 in reference to Strauss' latest dramatic production.

1895) [a] and culminating thus far in "Ein Heldenleben." Of the following two themes from "Till Eulenspiegel," No. 16, representing the titular character, is a brilliant specimen of horn-writing, as embodied in the Rondo.

No. 15.

No. 16.

Flowing cantilena, perverted rhythmic effects and still another illustration of virile horn-writing are presented in the following examples from the musical exposition of Zarathustra's philosophy under the title of "Also sprach Zarathustra" — Tondichtung frei nach Nietzsche (op. 30, 1896). [b]

No. 17.

No. 18.

No. 19.

Among the most characteristic of Richard Strauss' pictorial themes are the following two from his portrayal of Cervantes' rueful hero: "Don Quixote" — phantastische Variationen über ein Thema ritterlichen Characters (op. 35, 1897):

No. 20.

No. 21.

(a) Appendix, Ex. 102, 103.
(b) Appendix, Ex. 97 to 101.

XI.

(**Æsthetics.**) Similar to the orchestral works of Wagner, those of Strauss are worthy of exhaustive critical analysis. To carefully examine them all, however, would require an entire volume by itself. It is therefore proposed to select as typical only a few of the most characteristic points from one of the most characteristic of Strauss' orchestral works: "Ein Heldenleben" — Tondichtung (op. 40, 1898).

In order to appreciate the magnitude of his undertakings, let us first see how he maps out and elaborates upon the programmatic theme chosen for musical setting. The nuclear thought of "Ein Heldenleben" is the simultaneous portrayal of a combined mortal and mental hero belonging to both a worldly and a spiritual realm, or as Friedrich Rösch expresses it: "Eine harmonisch gesteigerte Zusammenfassung eines Volks-und Kriegshelden und eines von künstlerischer Schaffensfreude beseelten Übermenschen aus dem Reiche der Phantasie."

The "program" of "Ein Heldenleben" contains six general divisions:

I. DER HELD.
II. DES HELDEN WIDERSACHER.
III. DES HELDEN GEFÄHRTIN.
IV. DES HELDEN WALSTATT.
V. DES HELDEN FRIEDENSWERKE.
VI. DES HELDEN WELTFLUCHT UND VOLLENDUNG.

No. I is comprised of two general groups of thematic material. The first group is in reality one single and broadly constructed main theme, — the synthesis of five distinctive motives. The second group is made up of four contrapuntally interwoven and super-imposed secondary themes. After these nine themes have been duly presented, they are subjected to recapitulation and development. A tenth figure, based upon previous material, is also introduced.

The first group of themes, given out by low stringed-instruments, horns, etc., begins as follows:

The first theme of the second group is assigned to divided first violins, beneath which wind-instruments intone the second theme.

No. 23.

No. II contains five sharply contrasted and interwoven themes. (No. 24.) The piercing accents of the wood-wind in their shrillest and most blatant range are here drawn into requisition, and are legitimately suggestive of Wagner's "Beckmesser" orchestration. The section subsequently embodies five modified expositions from the first leading theme of No. I.

No. 24.

No. III is ushered in by a tender theme for solo violin:

No. 25.

This is followed by an exposition of five themes of intentional similarity, which depict the varying moods of the hero's courtship. These themes are further enhanced by characteristic and contrasted orchestral tone-color.

No. 26.

The section further embodies some six motives that are either reminiscences from former or anticipations of subsequent thematic material. Rösch calls attention to an interesting passage at the close of this section, a passage that cannot be justified by any rules of harmony. He suggests that in modern orchestration many seemingly irreconcilable harmonic combinations become perfectly logical if the auditor train himself to follow the harmonic corollary of complex counterpoint "horizontally" instead of "vertically." The passage in question consists of a protracted chord, G flat major, sustained by muted strings, while various instruments of wood super-impose a number of independent themes whose concentrated effect forms chords entirely foreign to the underlying key of G major. The present writer, however, is inclined to regard this hazy film of string-tone as nothing more than a tonic and dominant organ-point with the third of the triad unobtrusively added.

The "program" of No. IV is symbolic of martial strife, the depictment of which, sub-divided into three parts together with an introduction, extends almost to the end of the movement, when a coda in two short divisions portrays victory and embodies a hymn of praise. From a musical standpoint, No. IV may be looked upon as that section of the entire symphonic poem in which the leading themes are subjected to systematic and elaborate musical development. In addition, one finds some ten new themes, such as a striking fanfare for trumpets behind the scenes (No. 27) and other warlike strains, of which Nos. 28 and 29 represent the missiles of the enemy.

This fanfare (No. 27) exhibits one of the most remarkable mixtures of three simultaneously combined keys that has ever emanated from the mind of man:

No. 27.

By examining the first trumpet part by itself:

one discovers a perfectly harmless figure in the key of B flat major.   The second trumpet, however, holds tenaciously to the key of G flat major:

The third trumpet is unquestionably in the key of B flat minor, or, at a pinch, in its relative major — D flat:

The resultant cross-relation caused by such an amalgamation of otherwise unoriginal figures excites a most remarkable impression.

The next two examples embody characteristic employment of wood-wind instruments:

No. V is primarily noteworthy for the poetic fancy that impelled Strauss to embody no less than twenty-four motives from his preceding symphonic poems, as well as from "Guntram" and from "Traum durch die Dämmerung."   These themes are, of course, not presented in a row, but are joined together or subtly interwoven or contrapuntally super-imposed one over the other, and one might again suggest that they must be listened to horizontally and not vertically.   Incidentally it might be added that this Division V of "Ein Heldenleben" draws into requisition every single example given above from No. 1 to No. 21 inclusive, with the exception Nos. 16 and 19.   Wagner pointed the way for such a procedure by introducing the opening bars from "Tristan und Isolde" into the "Meistersinger." Strauss, however, went much further, and in the course of *Des Helden Friedenswerke* he has drawn freely upon "Macbeth," "Don Juan," "Tod und Verklärung," "Till Eulenspiegel," "Zarathustra," and "Don Quixote." He further elaborates upon two practically new themes (Nos. 30 and 31), although an anticipation of the second of these themes is already to be found in Division III.

No. VI brings this noble creation to a fitting end. With the exception of an episodic anti-climax, the movement is dominated by calm and majestic peace, as exemplified by themes No. 32 (evolved from No. 31) and No. 33.

Such are the vast dimensions of Richard Strauss' orchestral tableaux! His other works are evolved on similarly broad lines. "Ein Heldenleben," with its six well-defined divisions, includes no less than seventy themes. The score makes demand for one hundred and five instrumentalists: —

16 first violins; 16 seconds; 12 violas; 12 violoncellos; 8 double-basses.

2 harps.

1 piccolo flute; 3 flutes; 3 oboes; 1 English horn (also as 4th oboe); 1 E flat clarinet; 2 B flat clarinets; 1 bass-clarinet; 3 bassoons; 1 contra-bassoon.

8 horns; 5 trumpets; 3 trombones; 1 tenor-tuba; 1 bass-tuba.

Kettle-drums; bass-drum; side-drum; military drum; cymbals.

XII.

Since composing what might be called the Tetralogy of mighty productions that have been classified together as belonging to the *5th Period*, Strauss has written two further important works: the opera "Feuersnoth" and the "Symphonia Domestica." The latter is still in manuscript, [9] and but recently had a hearing in this country under the composer's personal direction. It is as yet too

[9] Since published.

early to suggest a sixth period in Strauss' style of writing.[10]   What is more, the two recent offerings have too little in common to justify classifying them together. "Feuersnoth" has shared the fate of its predecessor, "Guntram," in that it has been granted no more than a respectful hearing, and is not to be compared as a work of art with Strauss' symphonic undertakings.   As to the "Symphonia Domestica," the very topic chosen for exposition gives rise to some misgivings as to whether it justifies the expenditure of so much vital creative energy.   The subject and the elaborate means employed to depict it would appear somewhat incongruous.   The sub-title of this paradoxical essay reads: "Ein Tag aus meinem Familienleben," and the orchestra is required to expound upon the charmingly naïve topics of Papa, Mama, and Bébé.   Incidentally, one passage introduces the worthy aunts as exclaiming in chorus, " Just like his father "; the uncles, " Just like his mother."   The "Symphonia Domestica " is further paradoxical in that the score includes no definite programmatic commentary, and Strauss himself has been quoted as saying emphatically, "This time I wish my music to be listened to purely as music."   The work is therefore intended to be accepted not as a symphonic poem but as a symphony " In einem Satz " like Mendelssohn's "Scotch " or Schumann's D minor symphony.   In the face of all this we find a program, and a positive one at that, at the root of the matter!   In reality, its only claim to the title of "symphony" rests upon the general outlines of its formal structure, which is comprised of three main divisions preceded by an elaborate introduction.   But it is assuredly not "absolute" music.   On the other hand, its thematic continuity is far more closely knit together than that of the above-mentioned symphonies of Mendelssohn and Schumann.

In the "Symphonia Domestica" we recognize the personal element that asserted itself, though in an unobtrusive manner, in "Ein Heldenleben." Humorous inclinations, characteristic of "Don Quixote," are also in evidence.

The Introduction is an exposition of the three principal themes.   The theme for the father is comprised of three contrasted sections (No. 34, a, b, c).   The mother is characterized by a lively and perhaps slightly undignified theme (No. 35).   For the child's theme (No. 36) Strauss makes use of an oboe d'amore.   The tone of this practically obsolete member of the wood-wind is veiled and tender, and the instrument found favor with Bach who assigned to it an important rôle

[10] Since the above lines were written, a sixth period was assuredly entered upon with the opera "Salome," first performed at Dresden in the fall of 1905 under the magnetic baton of Schuch, director of the Royal Opera.   The work, which has since been given throughout Europe and in New York, has universally created a sensation to which nothing in the annals of the musical stage furnishes a parallel unless it be the initial performances of "Tristan und Isolde" in Munich in 1865.   "Salome," by reason of its overwhelming dramatic force, the sureness of Strauss' marvellous use of representative themes, together with an orchestral color-scheme beyond anything he has used before, not only marks an epoch in the career of this still young composer and an epoch also in his orchestration, but becomes a landmark in the form of opera as evolved from and built upon the Tetralogy of Wagner.

in his mass in B minor, — in fact two oboi d'amore are employed for accompanying the bass solo "Et in Spiritum Sanctum."

The following sportive Scherzo or first main division proper presents a sprightly development of the three primary themes and especially of the child's theme. The movement is finally brought to a restful ending.

The succeeding Adagio enlarges upon the father's theme and pictures him alone as if in a revery. The music is reflective and dreamy, at times restless and impassioned as well.

The Finale embodies a lively double-fugue (No. 37, a and b), of which the principal theme consists of a diminution of the child's theme (No. 36). The close of the work is calm and peaceful.

By thus analyzing the programmatic foundation of two of Strauss' latest orchestral conceptions one can obtain at least a superficial idea of the somewhat eccentric though intensely original range of his imagination. The philosophical aspect of the "Symphonia Domestica" is, of course, far simpler than that of "Ein Heldenleben" and its companions, nor would it seem to possess the same scope or exert the same fascination that his nobler and more serious works do. The orchestration, however, leaves nothing to be desired. There is no retrogression in the deployment of the instruments whether as solo or in combination. Strauss is in command of an orchestral technique so deep-rooted that it can never fail him. One would have supposed that his works prior to the "Symphonia Domestica" had made requisition for practically every legitimately available instrument in existence, but the addition of an oboe d'amore together with four saxophones proves that Strauss has an insatiable craving for ever novel tonal tints, and whereas "Ein Heldenleben" requires 105 instrumentalists, the symphony demands 108.

Before proceeding to sum up the cardinal features of Strauss' orchestration, it is desired to call attention to his highly commendable foresight in evolving his songs with pianoforte accompaniment on comparatively simple lines, thereby greatly enhancing their effectiveness for vocal utterance as well as their adaptability for extensive rendition. It is a rare attribute of genius to possess the faculty of colossal orchestral language and at the same time of simple and pathetic song-speech.

XIII.

(**Instrumentation.**) The marvellous subtleties of Strauss' instrumentation and the irresistible sweep and large contour of his orchestration have already been so thoroughly aired by prominent critics the world over, that there is little further to say beyond epitomizing in a few brief sentences the general concensus of opinion. Founding his art of scoring upon that of Berlioz and Wagner, Strauss evidently has also made a careful study of the means and methods of his eminent contemporary, Saint-Saëns, for the performances of "Samson et Dalila" at the Berlin Royal Opera, when controlled by Strauss' magnetic force, are a source of artistic delectation. The fundamental reason that makes his scoring so effective is his intimate acquaintance with the characteristics of each individual instrument even to the minutest detail of mechanical limitation or latent potentiality. Therefore his instrumentation pure and simple as distinct from orchestration *en masse* is unhesitating and authoritative. In thus appreciating the imperative necessity for an exhaustive study of the instruments themselves, Strauss has done no more than to follow the precepts of his illustrious model, Wagner. Strauss would be entitled to but little credit had he not advanced beyond his master, for proportionately, Wagner established a far greater number of unalterable precedents than Strauss has since been able to add to. The criticism has been advanced that Strauss' demands upon the technique of the performers are excessive, and that he is given to force the instruments, and especially those of brass, into unnatural registers. Such points, however, would appear to be for the gentlemen of the orchestra to decide, and the enthusiasm and grim determination with which they overcome seemingly insurmountable difficulties at rehearsal, and the suavity and verve with which the performances of his works by first-class orchestras are carried through, may be looked upon as tangible proof that Strauss knows what he is about. The performers may complain of the demands made upon them, but they realize that the page before them bears the impress of a master of instrumentation whose music is written with special regard for the very instrument they are playing, — can and must therefore be played. And they accordingly respect the author of their arduous though fascinating task. Finally, if the now childlike simplicity of Schubert's orchestration proved a stumbling block to the Viennese orchestra only fifty odd years ago (as stated on page 75), and furthermore Wagner's "Tristan und Isolde" shared the same fate at a still more recent date, it will not be difficult to realize that Strauss fifteen years ago taxed the virtuosity of the performers with passages that are already no longer dreaded. As to the details of instrumentation, he has strengthened and elaborated upon the methods of his predecessors, assimilated the procedures of his contemporaries, besides resuscitating various obsolete instruments and initiating numerous novelties of his own.

The flexibility of execution that formerly was expected only of a first violinist is now imposed upon all five sections of the string band, and each member finds before him the pages of what looks like a concerto.[c] To the wood-wind are assigned passages that Wagner would have hesitated to write.[d] What Strauss demands from them, Beethoven might have demanded from the strings. Most prominent of all is the attention bestowed upon the deployment of the brass as initiated by Wagner.[e] The trumpets are treated with unprecedented freedom, and are expected to perform passages either of flowing melody or of rhythmic intricacy in the fastest of tempos. The horns are taught to display the agility of violoncellos. In four-part writing, the fourth horn is much used as a deep bass-instrument absolutely apart from the three upper horns. The trombones are employed as much for unallied melodic utterance as for combined harmonic effects, and the intricacy of their parts constantly necessitates the use of three staves in the partitur. Incidental mention might also be made of such devices for acquiring weird tonal tints as obtained from muted trombones. Similar to Wagner's procedure in the "Meistersinger" Vorspiel, the tubas — and particularly the tenor tuba — are constantly detached from their conventional association with the trombones, for the purpose of giving expression to flowing cantilena. Novelty in the use of instruments of percussion is restricted to rhythmic peculiarities and original combinations with other instruments of more variable pitch; for Wagner's general methods of handling the battery cannot be improved upon.

(c) Appendix, Ex. 100.   (d) Ap. Ex. 102.   (e) Ap. Ex. 103.

In a word, the three choirs of the orchestra have respectively advanced one step higher. The string band are graduated to the plane of so many virtuoso soloists. The wood-wind replace the strings and are themselves replaced by the brass. The battery acquire prominence such as the classicists formerly allowed to the trumpets and trombones.

(**Orchestration.**) The numerical distribution of Strauss' orchestra is, of course, consistent with the modern custom of employing quartets of uniform tone-color. But he advances yet further by making permanent Wagner's occasional incorporation into the orchestra of a second harp, an E flat clarinet, a double quartet of horns, five instead of four trumpets, and a tenor-tuba in addition to the bass-tuba. The occasional addition of unusual instruments such as an oboe d'amore and saxophones has already been referred to.

The sum total of Strauss' orchestration as a whole consists of what has been termed its "exposed" quality, resulting in a "vast piece of chamber music." [f] The extensive range of his imagination reveals itself in constantly novel combinations and kaleidoscopic variety of effects that are unprecedented. His command of dynamics is superb. His synthesis of thematic counterpoint in all the voices of the different choirs is at times so reckless that the euphony of its harmonic corollary is endangered and the resultant effect presents a chaos of cacophony unless the auditor accustom himself to follow the Melos not vertically but horizontally. The orchestration is the most vivid in existence. Realism is accentuated. The tonal tints are scintillating and glowing. Every single instrument in the orchestra has an indispensable rôle assigned to it. The scores abound in clever orchestral devices, in startling contrasts, powerful crescendos and exciting climaxes, and disclose the mind of a master possessed of poetic fancy, natural humor, artistic culture, strong individuality, philosophical insight and intellectual power.

The titanic achievements of Richard Strauss have caused him to appear as the most conspicuous living musician, and in the arrangement of a modern program, his works are at present the accepted companions to those of his models in rich and massive orchestration, Wagner and Liszt; to those of Brahms, conservator of classic models and loftiest ideals; to Saint-Saëns' scintillating and unrivalled tableaux; to Tschaikowsky's sombre tone-pictures, to Dvořák's brilliant and vivacious portrayals, to Grieg's poetic and popular conceptions.

[f] Appendix, Ex. 97.

XIV.

It is high time to bring this fascinating subject of modern German progressiveness to a close; otherwise there is no knowing whither this history might lead us. In these days even a secondary composer is supposed to be thoroughly conversant with every subtlety in the art of orchestration. Germany still leads the van; the number of her eminent masters of modern instrumentation is legion. The ambition of the ultra-modern school is to out-Wagner Wagner. It will suffice to make mention of Max Schillings' "Ingwelde" or of Cyrill Kistler's "Kunihild und der Brautritt auf Kynast" with its poem in alliterative verse in strictly Wagnerian lines by Graf Sporck. The same exaggerated sense of morbidness and pessimism has found its way as well into other fields of German composition as discovered in certain ones of Hugo Wolf's intensely modern and magnificent songs, or in Max Reger's organ works of questionable worth with their atrocious harmonic mixture, their intricacy of contrapuntal treatment, and their extreme difficulty of execution.[11] These restless signs of evolution are perfectly logical and eminently proper. In many instances the results have been highly successful, but again they have not. On the other hand, a number of living German composers could still be cited who are possessed of sufficient poise to accept the spirit of modern progression without allowing their convictions to carry them to extremes. One of the most successful of these is Humperdinck, whose "Hänsel und Gretel" acquires its effectiveness primarily by means of the orchestra. The exceedingly simple vocal parts are founded entirely on Volksmelodien; *Leit-motiven* add coherence to the opera as a whole, whereas the scoring is amazingly complicated and elaborate though ever lucid and euphonious.[12] Ludwig Thuille [13] has earned deserved success with his charming "Lobetanz," and Kienzl has captivated the masses with "Der Evangelimann," a work that is both dignified and uplifting in spite of its eclectic appropriations from Meyerbeer, Wagner, Gounod, and even Mascagni. Georg Schumann, also, is to be commended for the "healthy" tendencies of his orchestral works, of which both the symphonic chorale variations and the "Liebesfrühling" overture have been heard in America.[14]

[11] At the present moment Max Reger is exciting increased comment by reason of his continued revolutionary ideas expressed through the medium of the orchestra.

[12] Engelbert Humperdinck directed by invitation his opera "Hänsel und Gretel" at the Metropolitan Opera House, New York, during the season 1905–1906.

[13] Ludwig Thuille died since the above lines were written.

[14] Gustav Mahler, from 1897 to 1907 director of the Opera at Vienna, has of late invited comment throughout the musical world because of the colossal form and daring orchestration of his symphonies. His present activity in New York should give American critics an excellent opportunity to estimate the importance of his contributions to musical art. Leo Blech is commanding favorable criticism particu-

XV.

The reader will pardon the appendage of a few final remarks relating to the progress of lighter German music during the nineteenth century, for otherwise these records would not be complete.   By retracing a few of our steps we find that the more important successors of Kreutzer (who was mentioned on page 73 of Chapter IX, and lived from 1780 until 1849) were Lortzing, Nicolai, Flotow, Suppé, and Johann Strauss junior.   For charming originality and for naturalness of expression Lortzing (1801) stands head and shoulders above the remaining composers of this list.   His works show the unmistakable influence of Weber, and just this romantic tendency accounts for the universal popularity of his "Czar und Zimmermann," this tendency being, moreover, still more marked in his best work: "Die beiden Schützen."   Nicolai (1810) wrote in the conventional Italian style.   "The Merry Wives of Windsor" is still one of the popular comic operas of the day.   Flotow (1812) earned notoriety through "Stradella" and "Martha." His aims are not high, neither is his music on a par with that of Lortzing; he displays, none the less, a happy faculty for instilling warmth of sentiment into his works.   Suppé (1820) has acquired the nomenclature of "The German Offenbach" by reason of his pleasing operettas and vaudeville.   Johann Strauss junior (1825) owes a world reputation to his sprightly "Fledermaus."   These are the men who have been instrumental in transplanting the daintiness and refinement of modern light French opera into indigenous German productions.   The results have been directly beneficial.   Not only has this transplantation of exotic principles tempered the general taste of the German public for an all too heavy and sedate form of melodic and structural treatment, but quite especially has German orchestration reacquired thereby much of that lightness of touch it apparently had lost after the culmination of Mozart's career.   French instrumentation, in spite of certain of its superficial tendencies, is assuredly a very important factor in the evolution of orchestral music, and its continued development during the second half of the nineteenth century affords a fruitful topic for discussion as outlined in the next few pages.

larly by his opera "Das war ich," while d'Albert's highly effective operas "Die Abreise" and "Flauto solo" are being performed on nearly every operatic stage in Germany.   "Flauto solo" is winning popularity only secondary, perhaps, to that of Lehár's internationally favored operetta "Die lustige Witwe," which is at present going the rounds of the United States under its Anglicized title of "The Merry Widow."

(Summary on page 176.)

CHAPTER XII.

FRANCE AND ITALY.

I.

France. It will be recalled that Chapter VIII treats of the flourishing conditions of musical art in France at the time when it was undergoing a series of metamorphoses that embodied nascent modern tendencies. The standard of sacred music was being elevated by Cherubini; French opera in serious vein as well as French instrumentation had acquired distinctly indigenous characteristics through the efforts of two native composers, Méhul and Lesueur; the development of the lighter lyric style as bequeathed by Grétry lay in the hands of the Frenchmen Boieldieu, Auber, Hérold, Halévy; finally, a renewed interest for grand opera was awakened by the so-called historic school of Spontini, which was followed by the enthusiastic reception of Rossini's melodious and emotional productions, and of Meyerbeer's sensational and spectacular presentations. Of momentous purport was the influence that these three foreigners, Spontini, Rossini, and Meyerbeer exerted upon French orchestration. Meanwhile an absolutely novel aspect of musical activity was being developed by Berlioz, who, as one of the founders of the "New Movement," has already been treated in Chapter XI in connection with Liszt and Wagner. In resuming and concluding the topic now under discussion, it would be well to keep the above brief review clearly in mind, in order that the simultaneous evolution of musical art in France and Germany may the better be compared.

With the exception of Berlioz, Félicien David and Gounod, few French writers have, until recently, applied themselves to independent orchestral music as one of the primary objects of their ambition. In France, the operatic stage ever has been and still is the centre of attraction. Even the most recent of her composers can with difficulty be separated into distinct groups that shall represent exclusive devotion to dramatic writing only or to sacred music or to concert works. Nevertheless, the present writer, having attempted to bring order out of the rather heterogeneous array of nineteenth century French composers, has classified them according to that particular branch in which they have been conspicuously successful.

II.

Prominent contributors to instrumental and orchestral music are Onslow, Reber, David, Franck, Lalo, Reyer, Godard, d'Indy.

Onslow (1784) enjoyed an honorable reputation during his lifetime as an exponent of classic models. He was a prolific writer of chamber music, but his style, though correct, was cold, and his three comic operas are of small importance. Reber (1807) may be regarded as the successor of Onslow in that he also restricted himself to traditional forms. He was an excellent contrapuntist as well as one of the most cultured musicians France has produced; as a result, his compositions reflect the refinement of his character. Moreover, his conservative and careful style was modelled after that of the German classicists, and the constitution of his orchestra is like Mozart's. Practically all modern instruments, all instruments of percussion excepting kettle-drums, and even trombones are excluded from most of his orchestral works. He wrote four symphonies, one overture and one suite, besides chamber and salon music in various forms.

Although Félicien David (1810) is best known to the general public on account of his opera "Lalla Rookh," he was at his best as an exponent of graceful and buoyant instrumentation. Not that his orchestration can be regarded as epoch-making when compared with that of his contemporary, Berlioz, for of the two, David was the more faithful to French traditions, and his scoring is more like that of Haydn than any other French composer. On the other hand, David, like Berlioz, introduced certain scenic qualities into his orchestration, which is ever poetic, supple, and varied. Berlioz's aim was to re-echo the thoughts of the grand romantic poets, whereas David was *par excellence* a dreamer in the realm of picturesque imagination, of tender love, of ardent passion. In consequence of his extensive journey through the East as an apostle and missionary of Saint-Simonism, David acquired an insight and knowledge of Oriental melodies that caused him to be the first to introduce genuinely Eastern characteristics into Western music, as strikingly displayed in "Lalla Rookh." The effectiveness of this opera is largely due to its fine orchestration, for though the musical contents are clear and simple, the ideas themselves occasionally lack force, whereas the harmonies are somewhat meagre. However, David possessed, in addition to the characteristic feature of *clearness*, a highly developed talent for artistic disposition of his plans, for poetic picture-painting, and for rich and descriptive orchestral color. Of especial significance is his aptitude for accompanying a solo voice with daintily embroidered counterpoint. David contributed substantially to the development in France of independent orchestral music, and displayed, among other things, a commendable appreciation for well-marked rhythmic effects. His list of instrumental works includes a symphony in F, twenty-four string quintets, and two nonets for wind instruments.

César Franck (1822) might be compared in two respects with Cherubini. Both of them, though foreigners, are rated as French composers, and the dignity and solidity of their respective styles isolate them both from the more usual methods of their respective eras. Franck differs from his French contemporaries by reason of what might be termed the masculine severity of his inspiration, together with monumental mastery of polyphonic design and exhaustless command of orchestral resources. These attributes have earned him the title of "The French Bach." The opera "Hulda" is a forceful exposition of the gloomy Viking subject, but Franck rose to the height of his creative power in his chamber music, and in the symphonic poem with chorus: "Les béatitudes." That he was influenced by Liszt and Wagner is undeniable. Not only do his productions give evidence of a reserved use of guiding themes, but also his orchestration has affinity to that of "Tristan" so far as intricacy is concerned.

This mention of Wagnerian influence suggests an interesting comparison between the styles of César Franck and of Lalo (1823). The latter was a professed admirer of Wagner, and applied such of his theories as are restricted to "Tannhäuser" and "Lohengrin." This is particularly noticeable in the opera: "Le Roi d'Ys." In antithesis to Franck's severe and somewhat solemn style of writing, that of Lalo betrays a fund of spontaneous invention, curious rhythmic effects, charming and sprightly instrumentation, and great aptitude for imbuing his works with the necessary local coloring. Both the violin concerto styled "Symphonie éspagnole" and the "Rhapsodie norvégienne" for orchestra are distinctively characteristic. His chamber music is likewise written with sentient regard for euphonious effects and artistic requirements, but it is conspicuously in the art of orchestration that Lalo displays his individuality to the best advantage.

Reyer (1823) belongs more properly under the heading of operatic composers, since he devoted himself primarily to that branch of musical art. He is nevertheless mentioned at this point in consequence of the interest attached to his odesymphony "Le Selam," which, though not an imitation of David's "Le Désert," is intended as a sequel to it. He is ranked as a conspicuous representative of the young French romantic school. Reyer's reputation is generally confined to France, whereas Reber's eminent pupil, Godard (1849), has become widely known as a prolific writer possessing marked individuality. This foreign recognition is due to his works in smaller form, being a *genre* of composition in which he excels. In France, however, Godard has occupied a conspicuous position on the programs of orchestral concert music. His activity in this direction has been indeed prodigious, and the results should command a more extensive acquaintance by virtue of their charming musical ideas and graceful instrumentation. These orchestral works bring to light the varied range of his imagination, and for this very reason some of the most characteristic titles will bear citation.   In addition to a pianoforte concerto and a "Concerto romantique" for violin, Godard has written an orchestral suite: "Scènes poétiques," a "Symphonie-ballet," an "Ouverture dramatique," a "Symphonie gothique," a "Symphonie orientale," a "Symphonie légendaire," the lyric scena: "Diane et Actéon," and the dramatic poem for soli, chorus and orchestra: "Le Tasse."   The last named is considered to be his best work.   His chamber music also merits just commendation.   It is evident, therefore, that Godard's already extensive foreign reputation is overshadowed only by the broader recognition awarded him in France.

An examination of the works of Vincent d'Indy (1852) reintroduces the subject of contemporary musical art in one of its extreme phases.   In earnest endeavor and in faithful adherence to high ideals d'Indy has proved himself a worthy successor to his teacher, César Franck, whom he copies in exceedingly complicated development of subject-matter.   Not content with incorporating in his works the most advanced tenets of Wagner, he further has explored the pathway opened up by Brahms.   Wagnerian tendencies have crept into all modern French music, whereas Brahms has as yet found few imitators among the composers of the Romance nations.   Like each and every French writer, d'Indy has tried his hand in operatic lines; his chamber music, too, is surprisingly clever and effective.   Nevertheless, he is essentially a symphonist; "Wallenstein" is evolved on broad and dignified lines, and displays a masterful deployment of orchestral resources.   "Le Chant de la Cloche," dramatic legend adapted from Schiller, is perhaps the most remarkable of d'Indy's works; it shows marked resemblance to Wagner's later style by reason of its elaboration of detail and intricacy of orchestration.

Before turning from this series of composers, it is again desired to emphasize the peculiar fact that all French writers both past and present have been consistent in first experimenting in the dramatic field before settling down to the exacting requirements of equally arduous and perhaps intellectually higher orchestral and chamber music.   That the authorship of a more or less important opera has been conceded to every one of the above-mentioned composers need therefore excite no further comment.

III.

A little coterie of Frenchmen have distinguished themselves by almost exclusive devotion to the lightest of operatic forms.   Just as Lortzing and his contemporaries rendered incalculable service to German musical art by clothing their vivacious productions in dainty orchestral raiment, so has France been the gainer through the efforts of Adam, Maillart and Delibes.

Adolphe Adam (1803) was a most productive writer. The distinctive features of his talent are opulence of melody and rhythmic grace. The best known of his works is, of course, the "Postillon de Longjumeau." Maillart (1817), pupil of Halévy, winner of the Prix de Rome, and author of six operas, was, strange to say, most successful in composing a work that appeals especially to the German mind. "Das Glöckchen des Eremiten" still retains its place in the standard repertories of Germany. Delibes (1836), composer of the sprightly comic operas: "Le Roi l'a dit" and "Lakmé," and of the charming ballets: "Sylvia" and "Coppélia," enriched the world with a far higher type of composition than either Adam or Maillart. His music, by virtue of its grace and refinement, is of such intrinsic value as to entitle Delibes to be ranked among the foremost composers of the nineteenth century. Application to lighter forms only by no means excludes sterling musicianship. Delibes' music is typically French, and by its very naïveté, descriptive powers and clever instrumentation overcomes the impediment of a frequently faulty libretto.

IV.

It is proposed to classify under one distinctive and decidedly exclusive heading the names of six truly eminent composers, who, as worthy contemporaries and successors of Berlioz, may, with him, be regarded as the foremost French representatives of the nineteenth century. These are Thomas, Gounod, Saint-Saëns, Bizet, Chabrier, and Massenet. All these men have become famous as dramatic writers, but the scope of their genius is such as to entitle them to almost equally high rank as composers of orchestral and chamber music. It is further proposed to single out Saint-Saëns as being undoubtedly the greatest French orchestrator since Berlioz, although the present writer is inclined to believe that Chabrier would have equalled him, had not his career been abruptly ended.[15] At all events, Saint-Saëns and Richard Strauss are at present the undisputed living masters of orchestration.[16]

In order to discover to what extent Saint-Saëns has been aided by his immediate compatriots, one must turn to the sound methods and sterling achievements of AMBROSE THOMAS (1811–1896). A worthy exponent of lyric opera, Thomas possessed like Gounod a high degree of musical intelligence. His music contains the essence of polish and refinement, but its very elegance is at times detrimental

[15] Another interesting and rather bold point of view in reference to the significance of Chabrier's undertakings is to the effect that "Chabrier was an inspired experimenter, but would never have become a master; nevertheless, his experiments are more valuable to art than the mastery of Saint-Saëns."

[16] See footnotes on pages 137 and 161 in reference to the masterly orchestration of Debussy and of Elgar.

to emphatic utterance, to dramatic strength, to intensity of passion. Certain Italian formulae are in evidence. German influence is also apparent. Neither of these characteristics, however, predominates over Thomas' personal individuality and French methods of artistic development. "Mignon" is veiled in a filmy haze of poesy, owing to the delicacy of its orchestration. "Hamlet," which is in reality a grand lyric tragedy, represents an extreme phase of French grand opera. Wagnerian principles are here frankly espoused, whereas the solidity and vigor of the orchestration display an advance upon the scoring of "Mignon" and "Françoise de Rimini." Thomas never overloaded his scores. The orchestration is clear in *ensemble*, ingenious in detail, always interesting, appropriate, varied. Characteristic tone-color and poetically conceived combinations reveal the skilful hand of a competent master.

GOUNOD (1818–1893) stands as the most illustrious recent representative of lyric opera. Like Thomas, he was strongly influenced by contemporaneous German progression, but in some ways Gounod exhibits greater conservatism and again greater license than Thomas. This composite style of writing is undoubtedly due to the fact that Gounod diligently studied the works of two composers of differentiated views — Berlioz and Schumann, allowed himself further to be influenced by Weber and Wagner, and yet accepted in a measure the prevailing Gallic conventionalities of his day as well as the traditions inherited from Meyerbeer. Compared with Meyerbeer, however, Gounod possessed a far keener insight into those essentials that lead to the construction of a genuine music drama. Not that Gounod's operas embody such essentials to a degree sufficient to dignify them with the title of music dramas, for they lack structural continuity, contain an overabundance of set arias, are frequently guilty of harboring superficially composed accompaniments, and betray carelessly developed inner details. On the other hand, Gounod displays a rare gift for melody and euphony, his feeling for genuine expression and characterization is sincere, the tone-colors are admirably adapted to the requirements of the situation, and his thematic development toward some ultimate climax is often superb. In a word, Gounod stands midway between the classical and the popular. His music is not quite pure, being tainted by a suggestion of the sentimental and of the *chanson* style. In the art of orchestration, however, Gounod exhibits the unusual attribute of attaining excellent results without apparent effort. His scoring may not disclose material increase of orchestral resources, since it follows the general path indicated by Auber and Meyerbeer; but it further shows that he possessed a considerable knowledge of the German science of instrumentation which he used to good advantage. The lyric operas "Faust," "La Reine de Saba," "Roméo et Juliette," as well as the oratorios "Mors et Vita" and "The Redemption" abound in interesting instrumental details and clever orchestral devices. Not only are the vocal parts admirably supported and characterized, but the orchestra also frequently reveals hidden emotions and passions of the stage characters by means of subtle thematic reminiscences from earlier scenes. This suggestive trait is pointedly illustrated in "Faust" when the muted violins break in upon Marguerite's vain attempt to pray, with the dainty waltz theme of her former joyous days. Another striking feature of Gounod's orchestration is its refinement, and as already intimated, few have excelled him in ability to procure rich effects with comparatively simple means. Thus the "Redemption" is scored for but eight instruments of wood, four horns, two trumpets, three trombones, kettle-drums, bass-drum, cymbals, together with strings and organ. Even when the organ is silent, the results are remarkably full and sonorous in spite of the absence of triplets of wood instruments, of English horn, of bass-clarinet, of bass-tuba, and of the harp. In all of Gounod's works it will be found that particularly the brasses are made to yield soft harmonies of limpid purity, whereas the instruments of percussion are reserved to reproduce novel and picturesque effects. Incidental mention must further be made of his free use of the harp, as illustrated, for example, by the slow scale for that instrument in the middle of the introduction to "Faust."

(*) SAINT-SAËNS (1835), greatest of living French composers and mightiest of her orchestral exponents after Berlioz, is assuredly a modern composer in the full sense of that expression. Yet the background of his principles differs but slightly from those of Thomas and Gounod. Plainly in evidence are the outlines of Meyerbeer's operatic forms, in spite of Saint-Saëns' obvious desire to break away from recognized models. On the other hand, the suppression of detached numbers and the adherence to representative and guiding themes disclose his involuntary leanings toward the doctrines of the Bayreuth master, notwithstanding his openly avowed avoidance of such intentions beyond the willingness to accept the advanced spirit of the age. But as to this, it has even been claimed that Saint-Saëns was the first French master to apply Wagnerian principles, even though doing so with discretion. Finally, this peerless contemporary seems to have appropriated to himself all the virtues of eclectic orchestration without one mitigating vice, and crowns this achievement with the indelible impress of his own intensely original individuality to an extent that is verily epoch-making in the history of orchestral evolution. The dual aspect of his symphonic works presents a unique contrast, displaying, as it does, their author's versatility. Saint-Saëns has expressed himself both in symphonies and in symphonic poems. There are four of each on record. Of the former, that in C minor may be looked upon as the most interesting. It contains no programmatic idea, and at first sight would appear to embody a departure from classic form in that it is laid out in two grand divisions. Closer scrutiny, however, reveals a faithful adherence to accepted usage, for the first division con-

(*) See Appendix of Musical Illustrations, Examples 76 to 82.

tains an introduction, an allegro, and an adagio, whereas the formal structure of the second division can be analyzed into what are in reality a scherzo and a finale. Reminiscent themes and episodes from the first division reoccur in the second, in order to give coherence and organic unity to the work as a whole. Another interesting feature of this symphony is the adaptation of Wagner's "Lohengrin" methods for the wood-wind. The score also includes parts for organ as well as for pianoforte. The four symphonic poems are none of them of the same magnitude and significance as those of Liszt; but just as Liszt's form is simpler and more readily to be grasped than that of Berlioz, so Saint-Saëns' formal structure may be regarded as advancing yet further, if clearness and compactness be the desired objective. "Phaëton" [a] and "Le rouet d'Omphale" [b] display marvellous skill in scoring; "La jeunesse d'Hercule" [c] is the most elaborate, whereas the "Danse Macabre" [d] is the most characteristic as well as the most popular. Saint-Saëns' chamber music affords an interesting study in diversity of style between it and that of his eminent contemporary, Brahms. Both styles display a master's touch, but Saint-Saëns' chamber music is conspicuous for its simplicity of treatment and admirable clearness. He has given still further proof of versatility in a series of memorable concertos. Had Saint-Saëns been content to write nothing beyond such sterling instrumental works as just referred to, his reputation would not have suffered. But the full strength of his greatness reveals itself in attainments of still wider significance. In addition to several oratorios, including the so-called Biblical opera "Le Déluge," no less than nine operas must be accredited to his pen, and of these, "Samson et Dalila" looms up as the ideal embodiment of Saint-Saëns' highest creative genius. Lofty imagination, naturalness of expression and dramatic intensity join in making this opera his greatest masterpiece. Unique is the opening chorus for the captive Hebrews in oratorio style, whereas the ballet in the last act presents an effective adaptation of the peculiar Eastern scale. The orchestration is elaborate, rich and varied, — intricate without being obtuse. Saint-Saëns wields his large orchestral forces with unerring judgment; the score abounds in effects now scintillating or impassioned, now melancholy or heroic. The addition to the usual couplets of wood-wind of a third flute, an English horn, a bass-clarinet and a contra-bassoon again demonstrates the indispensability of triplets of related instruments. Opportunity for obtaining pure tone-color in independent harmony from each family of the brass is effected by employing four horns, by the union of two trumpets and two cornets, by adding to the three trombones a bass-tuba, and by making further requisition for two opheicleides, which together with the bass-tuba are capable of independent deployment. The strings are reënforced by two harps. The array of instruments of percussion would appear rather formidable; nevertheless, they are never used aggressively. This

(a) Ex. 79.   (b) Ex. 76, 77, 78.   (c) Ex. 82.   (d) Ex. 80, 81.

group includes three kettle-drums, a bass-drum, cymbals, tam-tam, a triangle, a Glockenspiel, a tambour de basque, and *crotales* or castagnettes made of wood and iron. May Saint-Saëns live to enthrall the world a second time with a work that shall rival if not surpass in beauty the rare seductive charm of "Samson et Dalila"!

No opera has won greater universal popularity than that which has immortalized the name of its author, BIZET (1838–1875). What is more, this unreserved approval is merited and will endure. An elaborate discussion of his style would be futile; every professional, every amateur is thoroughly familiar with it. The prevalent custom of French composers to build upon French traditions, but to allow German truthfulness of expression and interpretation to dominate their works was consistently followed by Bizet. The complaint has been made that the traditional disconnected forms of "Carmen" hamper the dramatic action of an otherwise perfect creation. Continuity of music might, perhaps, enhance its already unexcelled effectiveness, but such questionable criticisms are indeed paltry in the face of such melodic and harmonic originality, such dramatic intensity, such orchestral color! Bizet's skill in discovering novel traits of instrumentation was little short of marvellous. The orchestra prepares, accompanies, and moralizes upon the action. There is a wealth of rhythm and color; absolutely truthful characterization and the finest of feeling for artistic details are revealed on every page. It is to be regretted that "L'Arlésienne" has not been considered worthy of more frequent performance. Though its libretto cannot be compared with that of "Carmen," Bizet's setting of "L'Arlésienne" is in some respects more artistic than that of his masterpiece. Its orchestration is practically inseparable from the drama itself, whereas a considerable portion of "Carmen" can be given on the concert stage with good effect. Parenthetically it might be added that the former work contains in its prelude a highly ingenious solo for the rarely heard saxophone.

In the repertoire of a few progressive European stages is to be found a work of exceptional genius entitled "Gwendoline" by EMMANUEL CHABRIER (1841–1894). So highly imaginative and poetical are its attributes as to warrant the assertion that "Gwendoline" is the best recent French opera, if not the most advanced exposition of existing Franco-German music dramas. No less an authority than Reyer, was, in spite of his usually conservative views, moved to criticise this masterpiece in the following favorable terms: "Je me trouve en présence d'une oeuvre extrêmement intérressante, renfermant des pages superbes et qui dans ses parties les moins saillantes, porte quand même la griffe puissante d'un compositeur admirablement doné." Chabrier did not devote himself seriously to music until he was nearly forty years of age. Shortly before deciding to become a professional, he had been quite successful with an opéra-bouffe called "L'Étoile." "Gwendoline," however, developed at one stroke his dormant creative powers in a manner truly remarkable. (Charming though inconsistent is the adaptation of an Irish melody in one of the most picturesque scenes.) An enthusiast for Wagner, Chabrier nevertheless branched out into a style that is distinctly his own. The libretto of "Gwendoline" may, perhaps, bear some resemblance to "Der Fliegende Holländer" and to "Lohengrin." Gwendoline's recital of her dream in the first act is suggestive of Senta's, whereas in the second act, the love scene after the pagan marriage ceremony recalls the similar episode between Elsa and Lohengrin. Not so with the music. Striking originality, daring harmonic innovations, and above all marvellous skill in orchestral treatment constitute the distinctive features of Chabrier's individuality. The present writer has had opportunity for studying the manuscript score of "Gwendoline" after its revision by the eminent Bayreuth and Munich director, Hermann Levi. Judging from previously heard performances, there had been pictured a monumental accumulation of black notes and an intricate web of interwoven polyphony. These expectations were not justified. Needless to say that the instrumentation is not that of a Mozart, nor are the usual complicated and massive resources of modern orchestration lacking at the necessary moment. On the other hand, the reticence displayed during most of the accompanying polyphony to the vocal parts rivals that of Wagner's highest attainment as embodied in the first act of "Die Walküre." Effects that suggest to the listener the union of peculiar composites of tone-color, resolve themselves on paper to perhaps a few simple chords for flutes in their low range, extending across the entire page; or again to the gentle undulations of muted strings deployed in keys of many signatures, whereby subdued and grayish tints are procured. Chabrier's orchestration suggests a progressive yet peculiar phase of Wagnerism enveloped by a tinge of melancholy and softened by the delicate touch characteristic of the French. Masculine scoring as embraced in the rather brutal overture is the exception rather than the rule. The first act of a second unfinished music drama entitled "Briséis" was edited a few years ago by Levi, but in spite of its undeniable originality, it proved a disappointment to the present writer. Chabrier further wrote a comic opera: "Le Roi malgré Lui," which, though daintily scored, is also inferior to his masterpiece. The orchestral rhapsody "España" with its wonderful exhibition of skilful instrumentation constitutes his only really popular work, but it is to be hoped that the time may not be far distant when the musical world shall awake to the significance of "Gwendoline."

In marked contrast to the limited appreciation shown for Chabrier's eminent accomplishments is the universal fame enjoyed by MASSENET (1842) during his lifetime. Essentially a dramatic writer, the latter has tried his hand at both comic and grand opera. Of the former, "Manon" is a general favorite; of the latter, wide-spread interest has been excited by "Hérodiade," "Le Cid," and

"Werther." The music to De Lisle's "Les Erinnyes" deserves notice if for no other reason than the peculiar antique coloring that permeates the orchestration. Massenet possesses above all a highly developed feeling for sensuous charm. His style is distinctly poetic and presents no exception to the prevailing custom of embodying both the guiding theme idea as well as the more general philosophical and orchestral principles of Wagner. Unreserved acceptance of such theorems in their extreme phase reveals itself in the recently presented "Werther." Much of Massenet's harmonic treatment displays undeniable traits of originality, and his scoring is rich and variated. His activity also as a composer for the concert stage has been untiring, but he is at his best as an operatic writer, nor do his orchestral works approach those of Saint-Saëns. As to this, however, neither has any other modern French composer as yet equalled Saint-Saëns, even though several younger writers, and notably Debussy, are successfully demonstrating possibilities quite beyond the scope of Saint-Saëns' achievements. Of Massenet's orchestral works, the most important to be recorded are the two suites, the "Hungarian" and the "Scènes pittoresques," besides the overture to Racine's "Phèdre." This last is undeniably Massenet's representative concert piece, embodying as it does virile force, impassioned sentiment and exceptional orchestration.

V.

As in Germany so in France has the array of sterling composers belonging to the nineteenth century assumed such extensive proportions that the historian's well-meant intentions to be concise are in danger of being frustrated. Only with regret can the temptation to search for further indications of orchestral innovations be set aside. On the other hand, one is obliged to concede that the recent progress of French instrumentation is entirely due to the series of eminent composers with which we have just been occupied, nor has the art of orchestration advanced as yet beyond that of Saint-Saëns and of Chabrier, unless we accept the efforts of Debussy as rich in promise as well as in interest. Omitting, therefore, the names of a host of other worthy aspirants, there remains only the seemingly indispensable mention of two secondary composers of recognized merit: Dubois and Paladhile; — of the eminent expounders on orchestration: Gevaërt and Lavoix; — of the literary writers and champions of the new school of thought: Vidal, Benoit and Joncières; — of the organist-composers: Guilmant and Widor; — of the representatives of the fair sex: Augusta Holmès and Cécile Chaminade, together with one of the most recent comets on the dramatic horizon: Gustave Charpentier.

The works of Dubois (1837) bear the stamp of exceptional ability and versatility. In addition to a successful grand opera entitled "Aben Hamet," the list includes an oratorio "Paradise Lost," a ballet "La Farandole," a concert overture "Frithjof," a pianoforte concerto, and several orchestral suites. Paladhile (1844), a pupil of Halévy, has made himself popular with "Mandolinata," besides winning the respect of the professional world in the cosmopolitan field of grand and comic opera, symphonies, masses, and minor works.

By a strange coincidence the three standard expositions of practical instrumentation and æsthetic orchestration are conceived in the French language, — the authors of these works being, of course, Berlioz, Gevaërt and Lavoix. Gevaërt (1828) merits the reputation not only of a musical savant but of a prolific composer as well. His "Nouveau Traité de L'Instrumentation" is not only a worthy sequel to Berlioz's, but has to a great extent actually displaced it. Of an entirely different stamp but equally indispensable to the student of orchestral evolution is the comprehensive "Histoire de L'Instrumentation" by Lavoix (1846). Further eulogistic comments upon these world-renowned treatises would seem superfluous.

The literary writer, Vidal (1820), must also be mentioned as an authority in one branch of instrumentation by virtue of his voluminous work entitled "Les Instruments à archet." It contains an admirable account of stringed instruments as well as of their makers, their performers, their composers. Benoit (1834) is identified with the advancement of musical art in Flanders, and the nature of his teachings emphasizes his strong Germanic convictions. He set to music several Flemish melodramas, but is especially to be commended for an essay on "L'École de Musique Flamande et son Avenir." The unflinching attitude of Joncières (1839) in favor of the Bayreuth master contributed materially in overcoming both dogmatic and racial prejudice. His literary writings reveal the mind of a keen musical critic, but his compositions lack significance in spite of being extremely modern.

The ascendency of modern French organ playing has been brought about by Guilmant, Widor, and their associates. But this is not their only claim to recognition, for their creative efforts bear directly upon the art of orchestration. Guilmant (1837) has displaced the classical organ concerto with string accompaniment by creating a more pliable form under the heading of "symphony for organ and orchestra." Widor (1845) has likewise shown a progressive spirit in his various organ, chamber, and orchestral works, which are notable for their artistic skill and for their display of poetic imagination.

To be looked upon as the first of the gentler sex to hold a conspicuous position among modern French composers is no small honor. This privilege has been granted to both Augusta Holmès and Cécile Chaminade. What is more, their achievements entitle them to a footing equal in rank to many of their most eminent masculine rivals. Not content to restrict themselves only to smaller forms of composition, both of these women have aspired to higher flights in the realm even of symphony and opera. Nor have their efforts been futile, for they both have written masterpieces of enduring worth. Augusta Holmès, also known under the nom de plume of Hermann Zenta, was a pupil of César Franck. In consequence, her style and orchestration have acquired a certain solidity and dignity that act as an admirable counterpoise to the lightness of touch and dainty scoring that are to be expected from a woman. The opera "Héro et Léandre" and the symphonic poems "Irlande" and "Pologne" may be looked upon in the light of her most representative works. Better known in America is her sister-composer, Chaminade, whose charming songs and pianoforte pieces appeal to both professional and amateur. The fact of her being Moszkowski's sister-in-law has its significance in the plausible assumption that his example and guidance may have aided the full development of her creative powers. The most characteristic phase of her individuality finds expression in a pianoforte concerto and in the symphonie-ballet "Callirhoé." Both these works present much that is interesting, and are, moreover, effectively orchestrated.

It is yet too early to judge whether the fame of Gustave Charpentier (1860) is destined to be effervescent or enduring. At the present moment both the opera "Louise" and his orchestral efforts have most assuredly excited more than passing comment. Other contemporary Frenchmen, however, such as Fauré, Chausson, Bruneau, Debussy, have in turn also attracted attention, but with the exception of Claude Debussy (1862), none of them prove worthy of retaining more than the respectful esteem of the public.[17] Charpentier's "Louise" is conspicuous for its incidental episodes that are full of action, and the work in its entirety presents an attractive series of contrasted tableaux. The opera embodies an interesting experiment in that the lines of the libretto are of a decidedly colloquial *genre*. The music is modern in the extreme and suggests Wagnerian influence as pronounced as that of any other French composer with the possible exception of Chabrier. The latter, however, appropriated to himself little more than Wagner's fundamental distribution of orchestral forces, whereas Charpentier has unquestionably permitted the distinctive atmosphere of "Die Meistersinger" to permeate portions of his opera. The vocal parts are designedly declamatory rather than melodic, unvocal, and exces-

---

[17] During the past two years particularly, Debussy's orchestral compositions have awakened much interest in France and in the United States, while his opera "Pelléas et Mélisande" to-day shares critical favor in Paris with Charpentier's "Louise." Both these operas are being performed in New York during the present season of 1907–1908.

The orchestration of "Pelléas et Mélisande" strengthens the previously formed conviction that Debussy is proving a worthy elaborator upon Saint-Saëns' lucid and refined methods. The key-note is transparency combined with an all-sufficient sonority. In a word, the cardinal feature of Debussy's scoring is the indispensability of each note, each phrase, each melody, even when assigned to the so-called secondary instruments of the orchestra — and this is by no means invariably the case in the scores of even such masters as Wagner, Elgar, Richard Strauss!

sively difficult.   The regisseur of the Munich Opera, Anton Fuchs,[18] declares that in all his experience at Bayreuth he never found a more knotty problem to solve than in teaching the singers the correct intonation of some of Charpentier's vocal cues. "Louise" is scored with the same due regard for proper effect that in these days is required of all meritorious composers.   Although the orchestration may at times be somewhat noisy and overburdened, it reveals numerous insignia of characteristic individuality.   Charpentier's orchestral music which M. Colonne has recently been presenting to the American public is on the whole analogous to that of "Louise," and the instrumentation is imbued with delicacy and refinement.

VI.

The attitude of the French public toward orchestral concert music has undergone a radical change during the last fifty years.   Habeneck's efforts during the first half of the nineteenth century were indeed praiseworthy and productive, but to the modern conductors, Pasdeloup, Lamoureux, and Colonne belongs the honor of having placed concert music in France on a par with that of the drama.   The story of their unprecedented activity has been frequently recorded but will bear repetition in consequence of its wide significance.   The peculiar fact that until recent times practically all French composers won distinction in operatic lines before attempting orchestral works has already been sufficiently emphasized. It will be remembered, however, that even in the eighteenth century determined efforts had been made to establish orchestral concerts on a permanent footing, though they could not then hope to rival the allectations afforded by the dramatic stage.   Retrospection shows us that in 1725 a brother of the composer, François Philidor, founded the "Concerts spirituels," which were subsequently fostered by Mouret and other worthy conductors.   In 1770 the "Concerts des Amateurs" as established by Gossec proved such a success that he followed up the enterprise by reorganizing the venerable "Concerts spirituels."   With the advent of Cherubini, French concert music received a still more powerful impetus, and through his resistless energy "La Société des Concerts du Conservatoire" sprang into existence.

This is the organization that gave Habeneck (1781–1849) an opportunity to distinguish himself.   He repaid the debt with interest, for these concerts owe their subsequent world-wide fame primarily to him.   Dating approximately from the year of Beethoven's death, new life was infused into this reorganized institution by reason of Habeneck's contagious enthusiasm, and it was he who initiated the French people into the inner mysteries of Beethoven's immortal creations.

[18] It is but justice to accord Anton Fuchs a large measure of credit for the recent successful series of performances of Wagner's "Parsifal" in New York at the Metropolitan Opera House.

In 1851, two years after the death of Habeneck, there was founded a second concert organization that was destined to bring both inspiration and recognition to many a young composer of the modern French School. It was founded by Pasdeloup (1819–1887) and went under the name of "Société des jeunes artistes du Conservatoire." It is not to be confounded with the "Concerts du Conservatoire" which continued to exist in connection with the conservatory proper. Out of this "Société des jeunes artistes" emanated in 1861 the "Concerts populaires de musique classique," which, as the name implies, was a further progressive step in affording the general public opportunity for hearing good music at popular prices. Pasdeloup's undertakings had for their original object the rendition of the best classical works. But the productions of contemporaneous composers both native and foreign were by no means excluded, and so such men as Lalo, Bizet, Saint-Saëns and Massenet were not slow to be the gainers thereby. That Pasdeloup was eventually forced into the background by Lamoureux and Colonne is but another proof of the fickleness and gross ingratitude of the general public. In vain did Pasdeloup in 1886 duplicate Godard's previous attempt to revive the "Concerts populaires," and this signal defeat undoubtedly hastened his end which took place one year later.

The career of the violinist and conductor, Lamoureux (1834), has been triumphant from the time when in association with Colonne he established a society for the performance of chamber music up to the time of his retirement in 1897. In 1873 he established an oratorio society which went under the name of the "Société de Musique sacrée." Subsequently he became conductor at the Grand Opéra as well as of the Conservatoire concerts. His crowning achievement was the founding in 1881 of the "Nouveaux Concerts," better known as the "Concerts Lamoureux."

Colonne (1838), greatest of all exponents of Berlioz and a zealous interpreter of Wagner, instituted in 1874 a series of performances under the name of the "Concerts du Chatêlet" that have since made his name famous. At the present day he still ranks as the most eminent contemporary French conductor. His activity shows no signs of abatement, for season after season finds him and his orchestra furthering the cause of French music in the musical centres of Europe as well as in America.

Neither the orchestras of Lamoureux nor of Colonne can be excelled in smooth and velvet-toned string playing, or in the purity, the sympathy, and at times the pathos that distinguish the quality of the wood-wind instruments. In French orchestras, however, the brass does not always possess that solidity and richness found in representative German orchestras. This defect may be due to the retention of at least one alto trombone, whereas the Germans now use either three tenor trombones, or two tenor and one bass. The bass-tubas also are frequently too light and small.   Particularly in some renditions of Wagnerian works is the undue prominence of inadequately balanced brass occasionally noticeable.   Finally, the metallic quality of the kettle-drums, which effects the coloring of the entire orchestra, sounds foreign to ears accustomed to instruments of less pronounced incisiveness.   These criticisms are equally pertinent to Italian orchestras, but do not appear to be objectionable to the composers of either France or Italy.   In a word, therefore, the performance of French orchestras displays a marvel of refinement and finish even to the minutest of details, but lacks ideal balance and fulness in loud *ensemble* passages.

Such is the story of French musical progression during the nineteenth century! Though she inaugurated no such reforms as those that signalize the "Sturm und Drang" period in Germany, France has a record to show that is indeed an enviable one.   Formerly surpassed by the parent of Romance nations — Italy, France has in recent years left that country far behind in matters both artistic and musical.   For half a century Italy has now been represented by but one luminary of the first magnitude.   Conspicuous in his solitary grandeur, this versatile hero has captivated in turn the hearts of all peoples, whether Latin, Germanic, or Anglo-Saxon.   In every clime is the name chosen for our following discourse a familiar household word,—the name of that wonderful melodist, Verdi.

ITALY.

VII.

The last extended reference to Italian music is to be found in Chapter VIII, which treats of the contemporaries of Beethoven.   Those pages call attention to Spontini's historic grand opera, to Rossini's seductive charm, and to the "mellifluous fabrications of Donizetti and Bellini with which undramatic productions must be classed also the earlier works of Verdi in consequence of their voluptuous melodic exuberance."

VERDI (1813–1901) exhibits in the development of his creative power a series of progressive stages that are in some respects analogous to Wagner's evolutionary periods.   Just as Wagner's operas and music dramas can be separated into three general groups, so may Verdi's productions be subjected to similar analytical treatment.   It will be remembered, however, that the orchestration of Wagner necessitated a second independent classification which partially ignores the æsthetic and philosophical aspect of subject-matter.   With Verdi, on the other hand, dramatic style, musical treatment and orchestration matured simultaneously and gradually.

There is no call to refer to works anteceding "Nabucco," which launched

Verdi on his unprecedented career. The first group may therefore include such operas as "Nabucco," "I Lombardi," and "Ernani." The sole claim to merit that these works can offer is in their wealth of melody, further enhanced by considerable rhythmic variety. Displaying closer resemblance to Meyerbeer's style than to *il bel canto* of Rossini, they further embody reminiscences of Bellini, and their favorable reception may have been aided by these very reminiscences. From an artistic standpoint they contain little worthy of commendation. They lack depth of feeling, whereas both form and instrumentation are conventional and commonplace. Orchestral color depends largely upon violent and frequently illogical dynamic contrasts.

Typical of the second group are "Rigoletto," "La Traviata," and "Il Trovatore." A further division might have been made in consequence of the superiority of "Il Trovatore" over "Rigoletto." Such exact distinctions, however, do not seem necessary in this discussion. These works show more earnest search for truthful and impressive expression, greater harmonic variety, and freer treatment of the inner and lower parts. The dramatic effects are of an intensity rarely surpassed. The music is, however, not only passionate but violent, and the tonal effects often suggest unnecessary noise rather than satisfying sonority. As Ferris expresses it: "Verdi storms the ear and captivates the senses, but does not subdue the soul." "Rigoletto" shows increased regard for judicious orchestration and that particularly in the deployment of the wood-wind. The scoring of "La Traviata" is picturesque and consistent. "Il Trovatore" presents passionate outbursts of feeling, a certain striving after effects, whereas the instrumentation reflects in its not infrequent coarseness the brutal tendencies of the subject-matter itself. As a whole, however, the orchestration possesses more independence and richer tonal variety than that of Verdi's preceding works.

The third and last group is comprised of the "Manzoni Requiem," the operas "Aïda," "Othello," and the lyric drama "Falstaff." The last named might almost be classified by itself, representing as it does the extreme phase of Verdi's involuntary adaptation of Teutonic dogmas both ancient and modern. In spite of his obvious intention to make this his masterpiece, it presents a line of departure not suited to his most felicitous style of writing. However, this *dramma lirico* has borne fruit in so far as to be a source of inspiration to Puccini, Mascagni and Leoncavallo, although *their* effusions take the form of "tragic operettas." In spite of the display of virile power in "Falstaff," Verdi reached his highest development in the orchestration of the Requiem, in the musical contents of "Aïda," and in the dramatic continuity of "Othello." In all these later works one finds unquestionable evidence of Wagnerian influence, at the least in respect to externals. Notwithstanding Verdi's repudiation of any such intentions, no composer surrounded by the spirit of the times could do other than progress. The most noticeable improvements in the third group consist of freer use of the dissonant element, better declamation, higher regard for faithful interpretation, painstaking finish of minor details, and above all an extreme advance in the art of instrumentation. The functions of the orchestra become more and more important, and the tonal colors acquire a richer and warmer hue. The scoring of the Requiem is dignified, religious, yet emotional. That of "Aïda" breathes the very atmosphere of its Egyptian setting. In "Othello," the orchestration is essentially dramatic and impassioned. "Falstaff" accepts the fundamental principles of Gluck, and the orchestra is raised to prominence equal to that of the voices. As a result of this concession, Verdi found Wagner's orchestral resources indispensable to his needs, and the resultant modern effects are a pleasant surprise. The vocal parts and the orchestra are here logically balanced, though Verdi's marvellous gift as a writer of pure and limpid melody continues in evidence.

With the evolution of this third period was instituted one of the mightiest transformations in the history of Italian opera. That country has as yet been unable to replace him. The efforts of Ponchielli, Gomez, Boïto, Sgambati, Buonamici, Puccini, are certainly praiseworthy, but sink into insignificance when compared with the splendid attainments of their venerable and venerated model. As to the rocket-like ascent and descent of Mascagni together with the present notoriety of Leoncavallo, time alone will decide whether the path they have chosen be meritorious or meretricious.

VIII.

It will take but a few words to conclude the record of musical activity displayed by the recent representatives of the Latin races. They have done practically nothing for the cause of orchestration other than to branch off into infrequented by-ways that have necessitated corresponding orchestral treatment. These final remarks must therefore deal not with the subject of instrumentation proper, but rather with the æsthetic and philosophical aspect of modern Italian music, the influence it has exerted, and the direction it is taking.

Ponchielli (1834) owes a foreign reputation to his opera "Gioconda," but endeared himself to his countrymen not alone as a dramatic writer but also as the author of the "Garibaldi Hymn," written in 1882, four years before his death. He enjoyed the reputation of being the greatest modern composer of Italian opera after Verdi. Since the Brazilian, Gomez (1839), practically adopted Italy as his home, he is mentioned in this connection. He was a painstaking composer, but his music frequently reminds one of Verdi's, whose ardent admirer he was. Boïto (1842) possesses not only the talents of an excellent composer, but of a highly gifted poet as well. He was the first prominent Italian to accept without reserve the fundamental principles governing the Germanic music drama, and thus became the head of the Wagnerian party in his own country. His "Mefistofele" did not succeed without a struggle, but it is now accepted as a standard opera of universal fame. The orchestral efforts of Sgambati (1843) are analogous to Boïto's adaptation of exotic principles bearing on operatic forms. To Sgambati belongs the honor of being the first Italian composer of the nineteenth century devoted to purely instrumental music and large orchestral forms. Already in his youth he attracted attention in consequence of an interesting pianoforte quartet. His structural form, moulded on classic lines, is logical and well proportioned, nor is it devoid of distinctive characteristics. His music embodies clear melodic delineation and free harmonization. The orchestration is, however, its best feature. It displays sound judgment, sentient appreciation for variety, contrast, and tone-color; these results are, moreover, attained by means of a comparatively small orchestra. Concert overtures, chamber music and the like are comprised in the works of Buonamici (1846) who was a pupil of both von Bülow and Rheinberger. His chief claim to recognition, however, like that of Puccini, depends upon his dramatic effects, which have attracted considerable attention. At the present moment Puccini is generally regarded by his countrymen as the foremost living Italian composer. His orchestration is rich and full, but his music, in spite of its pleasing melody and impassioned utterance, betrays the influence of Ponchielli who in turn drew inspiration from Verdi.

What shall be said about Mascagni and Leoncavallo? What have they done even indirectly for the cause of orchestration? Chronologically, Leoncavallo (1858) precedes Mascagni (1863), but without "Cavalleria rusticana" to establish a precedent, "I Pagliacci" might never have created the furor that it has. A discussion as to the relative merits and defects of their notorious productions would be here out of place. As to their relative orchestration, that of Mascagni shows, on the whole, a lack of genuine musicianly training. Although it must be conceded that he elicits highly dramatic and intensely passionate accents from the orchestra, the substance of his orchestration has, on the whole, a false ring to it and is of a hoarse quality of tone. It lacks balance, lacks taste, lacks judgment, and is at times coarse even to brutality. That of Leoncavallo is decidedly more refined and original. Here again the key-note is a striving after unnatural effects; but the orchestra is at least full of life, impassioned, descriptive.

The earlier achievements of Ponchielli, Boïto and Sgambati are assuredly of more enduring worth. These three representative men may be regarded as the only noteworthy Italian composers born after Verdi and before 1850.[19] Such is

(19) Although Giacomo Puccini (1858) has long since been held by his countrymen at his true valuation, it is only during the past few years that the world at large has come to realize that his productions are more significant than those of Mascagni and Leoncavallo who, until 1896, had won an international

the present meagre record of a country that can boast of an illustrious throng of preceding prodigies! [20]

reputation that temporarily overshadowed that of Puccini.   Even though Puccini lays himself open to criticism as to the æsthetic value of his choice of librettos in which ultra-sensationalism frequently plays so conspicuous a rôle, there is no longer any doubt that his operas "La Bohème" and "Tosca" have now been permanently admitted to the standard repertoires of the dramatic stage, and, together with his recent success, " Madam Butterfly," have caused the entire musical world to put their stamp of approval upon the earlier verdict of Puccini's countrymen in regarding him as a worthy successor to Verdi and as the most gifted living representative of Italian operatic art.

[20] Wolf-Ferrari (1876) is probably the youngest living composer to whom already more than fleeting recognition has been accorded.   It is not an easy matter to decide under what classification he should be placed.   With a German father, his mother an Italian, and married to an American, his instincts are Italian, though he owes the stability of his musical training to Rheinberger at Munich.   His melodic form is conspicuously Italian, while his harmonic substructure is more or less Teutonic.   His orchestration is eclectic; on the other hand, its cardinal characteristic consists of a happy appropriation of Mozart's naïve touch.   In a word, one might go yet farther and say that it is precisely this naïveté, not alone in orchestration but in musical substance as well, that makes Wolf-Ferrari's music so refreshing. He owes the opening up of his career to the opera "Die neugierigen Frauen," which has enjoyed a notable and wide-spread popularity in Germany, whereas he has already demonstrated his ability to handle large vocal and orchestral forces for concert performance by his setting of Dante's "La vita nuova," which has also excited favorable comment in Germany and has just been performed in New York with success.

(Summary on page 178.)

CHAPTER XIII.

HUNGARY AND BOHEMIA; SCANDINAVIA AND RUSSIA;
ENGLAND AND AMERICA.

I.

Hungary. The music of Hungary with specific relation to orchestration calls for but brief comment beyond what has already been said in connection with Liszt on page 92 and with Goldmark on page 85. It will be remembered, however, that Liszt's Hungarian origin revealed itself not so much in an indigenous style of composition as in the propagation of those musical characteristics peculiar to his race. This adaptation and development of native dance tunes received plastic form in his "Hungarian Rhapsodies." Goldmark, on the other hand, cannot properly be regarded as an Hungarian composer at all. His music is German rather than Magyar, eclectic rather than local. He revels in the insidious atmosphere of the Far East. These two men are, however, the only composers of unusual eminence Hungary has produced. A small group of men may have remained more faithful to Magyar traditions than Liszt and Goldmark, but the results of their efforts are not significant. What these secondary composers did accomplish can be embraced in a few words. Before doing so, however, it might be well to settle upon the exact definition of "Hungarian" music. A quotation from Parry's "Art of Music" would appear to answer this question to the best advantage: "The original Hungarian music is extraordinarily characteristic in rhythm and vigorous in melody, but devoid of ornament. The recognized musicians of Hungary are gypsies, who are of Oriental descent, and are well known for their taste for finery and ornamentation all the world over; and in their hands Hungarian music has become the most ornamental thing of its kind that Europeans are acquainted with. The ornaments are perfectly meaningless, except as implying singular dexterity of manipulation and an extraordinary aptitude for purely superficial invention in the decorative direction. Hungarian music belongs to the illustration of making a special rise to the highest point in the middle or early in the latter part of a tune. With the Hungarians both the dance tunes and local tunes are so full of energetic intervals and rhythms that even when there are no crises the impression produced is often emotional."

Representative adherents to Magyar characteristics are Franz Erkel (1810), Mosonyi (1814), Albert Doppler (1821), his brother, Karl Doppler (1826), and Czibulka (1842). By admitting the cosmopolitans, Liszt (1811) and Goldmark (1830), this list of Hungarian composers is sufficiently complete for all present purposes. Erkel and the elder Doppler are looked upon as the leading national opera composers. Of the two, Erkel displayed the greater originality. Author of no less than nine operas, he reached his highest attainments in "Bank Bán" and "Hunyadi Laszlo." The latter combines native traits with German and Italian operatic and orchestral traditions. Albert Doppler's foreign reputation is primarily due to his extensive concert tours as a flute virtuoso. His additional activity as a composer, however, gave him high standing in his own country. The present writer recalls an interesting conversation with his brother, Karl Doppler — late Kapellmeister at Stuttgart — in reference to the opera "Erzébeth" written jointly by Erkel and the two Dopplers. He described the work as "Gelegenheitsmusik"; such was the haste demanded by the attending circumstances, that the first act was put into rehearsal before the last act was completed, whereas Karl Doppler himself was still busy scoring (in Italian style) on the very day appointed for performance. Erkel's contemporary, Mosonyi or Michael Brandt, displayed considerable versatility in forms both small and large, whereas Czibulka represents a later generation of Hungarian composers. His position as bandmaster at Vienna gave him opportunity to cultivate his native attributes in the guise of dance music, in addition to which he wrote an operetta entitled "Pfingsten in Florenz."

It cannot be said that the collective efforts of these composers have developed a national style of orchestration. There is plenty of color and variety in their scoring, but the latent charm of their works is the result of melodic and rhythmic novelty, and not of instrumentation.

II.

Bohemia. In marked contrast to the above-mentioned limitation is the evolution of Bohemian orchestration, especially when one considers the fact that the pioneer, Smetana, was content to build upon Mozart's system of scoring, whereas already in the next generation his illustrious pupil, Dvořák, developed that art to a point excelled by none. To mention these two men is synonymous for both the birth and the maturity of a native Bohemian school of composition. They both relied upon the Folk-song as a basis for operation, but Dvořák advanced far beyond his master. A worthy successor to these two men has not yet appeared upon the horizon, even though Dvořák's pupil, Joseph Suk, reveals latent possibilities for future prominence.[21]

SMETANA (1824–1884) is a typical Czechish composer. Though he studied for a short time under Liszt and showed himself an enthusiastic follower of the "New Movement," his melody and rhythm are thoroughly Bohemian; moreover, his music, like his orchestration, occasionally reveals a certain naïve touch of Mozart. Smetana wrote as many as eight operas, but the very first of these, "Die verkaufte Braut," not only gave him his foreign reputation, but has proved the best and most enduring of them all. The overture of this work, with its magnificent fughetta, forms an admirable concert number by itself. It might be incidentally added that this overture contains horn attacks of such difficulty as to have proved a stumbling block at public performance to no less an orchestra than the Royal band in Munich under Levi's magnetic baton some fifteen years ago. Smetana's affiliations with Liszt bore fruit in a worthy series of symphonic poems, whereas his native inheritance is emphasized in his national dances for pianoforte.

III.

(*) DVOŘÁK (1841–1904) shares with Saint-Saëns, Tschaikowsky and Richard Strauss the distinction of having done more for the advancement of modern orchestration than any other composer since Wagner. For his conservation of classic symphonic forms he might be ranked as an extreme classical-romanticist, but he has gone far beyond Brahms or Rheinberger in that his harmonic progressions are novel and daring, his orchestration varied and rich. Moreover, his music is conspicuously national in character and embodies the very essence of Bohemian melody and rhythm. But though Dvořák's form may be orthodox, it is nevertheless subjected to differentiated transformations according to the particular branch of composition that is being treated. In this he resembles Saint-Saëns, and some interesting comparisons might be made between the latter's symphony in C minor and Dvořák's "From the New World." It will be recalled that this successful experiment of Saint-Saëns allows of but two grand structural divisions, which, however, reveal the outlines of the traditional four movements. Organic unity is obtained by reintroducing important subject-matter from the first part of the work into the second. Neither Saint-Saëns nor Dvořák make use of a dramatic scheme like Berlioz's "Symphonie fantastique" with its *l'idée fixe*, but as

[21] Joseph Suk (1874) continues to command critical favor, as evidenced, for example, by his successful appearance on the concert stage of Berlin in the fall of 1906. Particularly his "Scherzo fantastique" is widely known and well received.

(*) See Appendix of Musical Illustrations, Examples 90 to 96.

Krehbiel, the eminent New York critic, states it: "Dvořák in his symphony entitled "From the New World," in which he has striven to give expression to the American spirit, quotes the first period of his principal subject in all subsequent movements, and then sententiously recapitulates the principal themes of the first, second and third movements in the finale; and this without a sign of the dramatic purpose confessed by Berlioz."

Dvořák's chamber music presents still another phase of the subtle manner in which he retains and yet remodels the outlines of classic form. In regard to musical contents, the essence of national melody and rhythm is ever in evidence, but whereas in their original shape these folk-tunes are frequently commonplace and even vulgar, Dvořák's brilliant imagination transforms them into worthy conceptions that are both dignified and noble. These he adorns with vivacious yet refined orchestration.

Yet another illustration of Dvořák's versatility is displayed in the "Spectre's Bride," which embraces in a felicitous manner the supernatural element peculiar to the works of Spohr and Weber.

As has been already intimated, the paramount accomplishment of this modern luminary was his colossal development of orchestral resources. One can point to his symphonies as models for brilliant scoring. The "Spectre's Bride," the Stabat Mater, the Requiem abound in beautiful combinations. The orchestration is warm and rich [a] without being overburdened, interesting and varied, yet appropriate and consistent. Minor details receive careful attention. The string writing is clear and bright,[b] whereas in the handling of the wood-wind instruments Dvořák shares with Brahms the tendency to fall back upon Schubert's methods.[c]

One by one our great contemporary masters are passing away. Be it hoped that at a not far distant day Bohemia may again send forth a missionary to our climes worthy of rank with Dvořák!

SCANDINAVIA AND RUSSIA.

IV.

Scandinavia. Analogous to the development during the nineteenth century of Hungarian and Bohemian folk-tunes is that of the Scandinavian countries. Just as Germany can point to her *Lied* and France to her *chanson* as the basis for scientific secular music on the Continent, so is the recognition of the younger musical countries dependent upon the distinctive features of their native

(a) Ex. 93, 96.   (b) Ex. 91.   (c) Ex. 90.

melodies. America presents a unique exception to this rule. For variety and expression, Norwegian and Swedish folk-tunes compare favorably with those of Russia. A conspicuous characteristic of early Scandinavian folk-tunes is the progression to the minor seventh of the scale through its fifth. Again, many peculiarities popularly regarded as Grieg's exclusive property constitute in reality the fundamental characteristics of the original source from which he has drawn his inspiration. The national music of all three countries, Denmark, Norway, Sweden, embodies shortness of theme, reiteration of the same interval, shifting tonality, alliance of binary and ternary rhythm, and the plaintive fall of the leading tone to the dominant. To Denmark belongs the honor of having produced the pioneer exponent of native melodies and native characteristics — Gade. His achievements have since been eclipsed by Norway's sturdy representative — Grieg. In the earlier part of the century several Swedish composers made a creditable showing, but in recent years Norway seems to have established her ascendency. After Gade, the only Danish composer who has attracted especial attention beyond the boundaries of his own lands is Enna. Few modern Swedish composers have risen conspicuously above their predecessors, Lindblad, Hallström and Södermann. Norway, on the other hand, possesses not only Grieg, but Svendsen and Sinding as well. The racial affinity disclosed by the music of all these composers makes possible a collective review of their achievements in chronological order.

V.

Already in the initial Swedish productions are national tendencies to be found. Subject-matter, coloring, harmonic and rhythmic structure all reveal the same general source. Lindblad (1801) became known as the teacher of Jenny Lind and also as a composer of songs. His melody and harmony are original and characteristic. His more ambitious works include a violin sonata and a symphony; the latter was performed at a Gewandhaus concert. Hallström (1826), in addition to national songs, wrote seven operas as well as a memorable Idyl for soli, chorus and orchestra entitled "Die Blumen." Less widely known is the name of Södermann (1832); nevertheless his efforts are ambitious and comprise an operetta, a mass, an overture for orchestra, and incidental music to the "Jungfrau von Orleans." He owes his German reputation largely to a composition for four female voices, called "Bröllop," which went the rounds of that country and was popular in its day. At least passing reference is at this point due to Normann (1831) in consequence of the important services he rendered to his country as an orchestral conductor.

Though GADE (1817–1890) stands as the pioneer of Scandinavian composers and as chief representative of Denmark, his works do not present unadulterated indigenous characteristics. The influence of Mendelssohn as well as of Schumann is plainly in evidence; consequently he is classified on page 77 among the direct followers of romanticism. The substance of Gade's music suggests Northern coloring and surroundings, but the presence of native melody, harmony and rhythm is less conspicuous. He adhered to the symmetry of sonata form, though his thematic development is free and his musical treatment unfettered. Gade first became known through the overture "Nachklänge aus Ossian" and the first symphony in C minor. The "Crusaders" still belongs to the standard cantatas of the present day. He had early been a careful student of representative scores, and developed high efficiency in the art of orchestration. Appreciation of the possibilities as well as of the limitations of each instrument, successful application of "local coloring," and a ready pen stamp the pages of his numerous symphonies and orchestrally accompanied choral works.

Turning to the representatives of Norway belonging to a later generation than Gade's, one naturally recalls the name of Grieg. Nevertheless Svendsen (1840) was born three years before Grieg, and holds a position of eminence only secondary to that of his Danish predecessor or of his Norwegian contemporary. A violinist as well as a composer, he possesses a gift for spontaneous and flowing melody. His music rests on a sound harmonic basis, is cleverly developed and skilfully orchestrated. It reveals national coloring though not to excess, and reflects the mind of a cosmopolitan musician. Svendsen's sphere of creative activity embraces various orchestral works, besides chamber music and smaller pieces. Prominent among these are the four Norwegian rhapsodies, and he has been particularly happy in arranging many Norwegian, Swedish and Icelandic melodies for small orchestra.

GRIEG (1843) represents one of the few recent composers who have not been conspicuously influenced by ultra-modern tendencies beyond appreciation for the necessary alliance of poetry and music. The exact value of his attainments is not easy to define. D. G. Mason has been rather hard on him in his thoughtful essay entitled "From Grieg to Brahms," and in Germany there is also a disposition to regard much of his music as superficial. None the less, Grieg's style has a charm about it that is irresistible, and this charm goes far to silence the grumblings of critics more scientifically and profoundly trained than he. But it is precisely this naïve spontaneity, this guileless yet poetic touch, this flow of fancy emanating straight from the heart that endears his music to the more appreciative and emotional amateur. Though a pupil of the Leipzig Conservatory, Grieg early took a firm stand against the lukewarm Scandinavianism of Gade, and bestirred himself in a search for musical utterance that should present the indigenous characteristics of his own people in the most favorable light. His solution of this problem brought into existence a distinct Northern school of composition. As previously suggested, many peculiarities of his music are but the adaptation of time-honored Scandinavian characteristics. But though the strength of his works rests upon the development of Danish, Norwegian and Swedish Volkslieder, he has imbued these with an element of poetic coloring, of tender melancholy, of mystery, of quaint humor, of grotesqueness even to eccentricity that are all his own. Grieg's style is frequently lacking in breadth, nor does he possess the powers of a great orchestral composer. Nevertheless, his writing for strings alone is of surpassing beauty, with its multiple division of parts, its polyphonic voice-leading, and its impassioned deployment of violas and violoncellos. When at his best, Grieg handles his larger orchestral forces with similar rare skill. The orchestration of Björnsen's unfinished drama "Olaf Trygvason" and that of the music to Ibsen's "Peer Gynt," conceived as a melodramatic scene-painting, is tender, fervent, weird, brilliant, stormy, popular, effective. Notwithstanding all that has been said, Grieg stands as one of the most original and healthy composers of the nineteenth century.[22]

Of the younger Norwegian composers, Sinding (1856) has given evidence of a fertile imagination that finds expression in some pleasing chamber music and other works in small form. To judge from his popular "Frühlingsrauschen," he must be counted among the admirers of Wagner. His Danish contemporary, August Enna (1860), has devoted himself to a more ambitious form of composition. His opera "Heksen" was brought out at Copenhagen in 1892, and at Berlin in the ensuing year. Two further operas of recognized merit have emanated from his pen — "Cleopatra" and "Aucassin og Nicolette." [23] The Scandinavians are not conspicuously dramatic, but Enna's grandfather was an Italian, which may account for the grandson's histrionic talent. There are other names worthy of mention, [24] such as Tor Aulin and Wilhelm Stennhammer [25] of Sweden; up to

[22] Edvard Hagerup Grieg died in Bergen, Norway, on September 4, 1907.

[23] Enna's recently composed opera "Aglaia" has yet to await the favorable verdict of the general public. Taking into consideration the kindly and patriotic disposition of his own countrymen toward all serious artistic efforts on the part of their native composers, it is reasonable to predict that "Aglaia" will eventually receive the same cordial reception as its predecessors, at least in so far as the Danish audience is concerned. (During the past year the present writer has had repeated opportunity to note the attentive attitude of the public in the Danish capital toward aspiring home talent, — a national trait of such exceptional virtue that it cannot be sufficiently commented upon.)

[24] This would appear to be a fitting place for mention of the Finnish composer, Sibelius (1865), who has, during the immediate past few years, added a new name to the list of modern Northern writers for the orchestra, besides being distinctly the first composer of Finland to acquire international reputation.

[25] In the fall of 1905, Stennhammer's opera "Das Fest auf Solhaug" was heard for the first time at the Royal Opera House in Berlin. A condensed version of Ibsen's drama constitutes the libretto. From the very beginning of the introduction to the final note of the last act the listener is primarily

the present moment, however, none have proved worthy to be ranked with the greatest of Scandinavian composers — Grieg.

VI.

Russia. Among the phenomena of the nineteenth century must be reckoned the wonderful artistic evolutions in Russia and in America. Of the two countries, Russia has thus far forged ahead by reason of her indigenous melodic wealth, whereas America has no similar source to draw from. Again, the melancholy and semi-barbaric coloring of Russian folk-tunes appeals more readily to the world at large than do the assuredly more healthy though somewhat eclectic offerings of the young American school. None the less, the artistic future of the latter country is to be regarded in the most optimistic light, and this certainly will be subsequently enlarged upon under its proper heading.

Russian folk-songs embody certain characteristics that are likewise at the root of Scandinavian folk-songs. In their natural and unadorned state they suggest the rhythmic freedom of Scandinavia, and their dance forms are similarly wild and irresistible. Further characteristics that are more distinctly Russian consist of odd modulations, of plaintive minor cadences, of harmonies resolving abruptly into the unison, and of the frequent recurrence of a principal theme alternating with various reiterated phrases. A possible reminiscence of the Lydian and Dorian modes of ancient Greece might also be suggested. This is the basis upon which an epoch-making school of highly-seasoned dramatic and orchestral music has been reared.

Cultivated Russian music may be properly divided into three distinctive groups. First came the old lyric-school of Glinka, Dargomizski and Seroff, followed by the neo-Russian school which includes Dargomizski in his maturity, together with Borodin, Cesar Cui, Balakireff, Mussorgski, Rimski-Korsakoff, and their associates. A third classification is required for Rubinstein and Tschaikowsky in consequence of their less national than cosmopolitan attributes. It is by no means intended to convey the idea that Tschaikowsky was not intensely Russian, but his broad education and his intellectual classicism distinguish him from his compatriots. Rubinstein, on the other hand, was more a Teutonic classical-romanticist than a Slavonic composer. This exposition will therefore first treat of the typically native composers, leaving Rubinstein and the unrivalled Tschaikowsky for the end.

impressed by and almost solely interested in the limpid pureness and delicacy, the masterly finish of detail both inner and outer, and the sensitive appreciation for the suppression of dynamic excess as revealed in its *orchestration*. But the immaturity in the literary form and style of this earlier conception of Ibsen precludes the possibility of more than momentary interest for Stennhammer's opera, unless, perhaps, within the confines of Scandinavian shores.

VII.

GLINKA (1803–1857) accomplished for his country what Smetana and Gade did for theirs. A further unique comparison can be made in that the labors of these three men in each case paved the way for subsequent herculean development in the hands of one conspicuous successor of even greater talent — respectively Dvořák, Grieg, Tschaikowsky. Although Glinka, like Gade, devoted himself to the propagation of national melodies, it is the local coloring rather than subject-matter that gives his music a character of its own. In this he again resembles Gade. His very first opera "Life for the Czar" proved a triumphant success, and, together with its successor "Ruslan and Ludmilla," gave Glinka the right to be called the first great opera composer of Russia. His music may not be especially dramatic, but is significant for having elevated and perpetuated popular airs, which are clothed in rich harmonies and surrounded by a distinctly Russian atmosphere. The orchestration calls for but little comment excepting that it is clever and at times even brilliant. Glinka's position in musical history has been accurately described by Riemann when he says: "Glinka is the Berlioz of the Russians, the man who attempted something new with definite meaning; but to his countrymen he is still more, namely, the creator of a national musical tendency striving toward independence."

Dargomizski (1813), second representative of the old lyric-school and eventually a convert to the new Russian movement, stands as a noteworthy example for gradual artistic expansion. Clinging at first to the forms prevalent in France and in Italy, he gradually came to attach greater importance to *recitative*, and finally went even too far. This extreme as to absence of melody as well as of structural form reached its culmination in his posthumous opera "The Marble Guest," which has since been most effectively orchestrated by Rimski-Korsakoff. The work is advanced both in thought and treatment, and may be regarded as the initiatory modern Russian opera. Two of Dargomizski's minor orchestral compositions, the "Finnish Fantasia" and the "Cossack Dance," acquired considerable popularity. Dargomizski is particularly to be commended for his attitude as a patron of the young Russian enthusiasts whose tendencies were inclined toward Berlioz, Schumann, Liszt and Wagner.

Serow (1820) — usually spelt Seroff in the English language — belongs properly to the earlier school, although he was a zealous disciple of Wagner, and, like him, prepared his own librettos. The style of his music is such as to carry us almost imperceptibly across the short bridge joining the first and second groups of Russian composers.

VIII.

As just stated, the second group of young composers found a champion in their senior, Dargomizski. The tenets of the "New Russian Movement" are closely allied to those of the "New German Movement." The programmatic and philosophical theories of Berlioz and Liszt applied to the dramatic orchestra, and the unreserved adaptation of Wagner's speech-singing and instrumentation form the basis for their creed. On the other hand, they demand that all "program-music" shall be of such intrinsic merit as to withstand the test of being deprived of its program. Prominent among these innovators was Borodin (1834). His originality displayed itself conspicuously in independent orchestral music as exemplified by his two symphonies. The style is attractive and polished, whereas a wealth of orchestral effects and instrumental tone-color is at his command. Further proof of his fertility is revealed in the opera "Fürst Igor," in the symphonic poem "Mittelasien," and in his chamber music. Cesar Cui (1835) holds a position of prominence only secondary to that of Rubinstein and Tschaikowsky. He was an ardent literary advocate for Berlioz, Schumann and Liszt, whereas his vocal writing is in reality the exposition of a style akin to the requirements of French prosody. Balakireff (1836) and Mussorgski (1839) also belong to this second group of Russian composers. The former has been called the direct successor of Glinka. The compositions of the latter display daring originality and a gift for charming melody, although the harmonization is not always skilful. Nevertheless, both these men are outranked by Rimski-Korsakoff (1844), whose eminence is fully equal to that of Borodin and Cesar Cui. His works include several remarkable symphonies, three operas, chamber music and salon pieces. Special attention should be called to the program-symphony "Antar" and to a legend for orchestra, "Sadko." One of the youngest exponents of combined melodic and declamatory styles is Arensky (1862), and the interest recently excited by the third symphony in C minor of Glazounoff (1865) entitles him also to recognition under this heading.

This discussion may evoke the criticism that thus far too little has been said about orchestration proper and nothing whatever about the details of instrumentation. As to this, however, it must be remembered that modern Russian orchestration owes its fundamental characteristics to only one man — Tschaikowsky; consequently, the examination of these characteristics has been reserved for discussion in connection with *his* titanic achievements. All contemporary and sequent orchestral treatment in the hands of his countrymen is but the reflection of Tschaikowsky's style combined with the further progressive methods of German and French orchestration. It is the indirect influence these other composers have exercised upon the art of orchestration rather than their actual instrumentation that has needed elucidation.

IX.

For convenience, Rubinstein and Tschaikowsky have been classed together as representing a third group of Russian composers. Theoretically they possess nothing in common other than their cosmopolitan proclivities.

RUBINSTEIN (1830–1894), regarded in the light of a Russian composer, cannot be compared with Glinka as an operatic writer or with Tschaikowsky as an orchestrator. Regarded as a classical-romanticist, he must be included in the list of composers following traditional forms. What is more, he was an extremist in his antagonism to the innovations of the New German Movement. This hostility exerted a baneful influence upon his instrumentation. His intentions were high, but the results of uneven value. His music reveals a search after fulness of contents, passionate strength, and a certain predilection for the peculiar. Euphony and rounded form are less pronounced, though occasional evidence of delicacy and even of tenderness is not lacking. Rubinstein cannot be eulogized as a dramatic writer, although "Feramors" is a pleasing lyric opera, and the Biblical stage-play "Sulamith" presents a poetic idyl imbued with Eastern color. Interesting is the embodiment of seven movements in the "Ocean Symphony," a work that holds high rank in musical literature. In string writing, Rubinstein revealed fine appreciation of tone-color. The instruments are handled with rare skill and that quite especially in his chamber music. But in spite of a not infrequent display of superb power, his orchestration, on the whole, was hampered by the narrow prejudice which limited his horizon.

The history of Slavonic music up to the present day will be concluded with the following brief remarks concerning (*) TSCHAIKOWSKY (1840–1893). Though he is mentioned last, one must not forget that his activity covers the same period as that of the originators of the neo-Russian school.

The composite of his high-strung and intensely æsthetic nature may be summed up by saying that at heart he was in sympathy with Liszt; his structural form rests upon the intellectuality of classicism; his conceptions emanated from Muscovite melodies but are stamped with the insignia of genius all his own; his style is essentially lyrical, and betrays the delicacy and refinement of a cultured Russian. What is more, there are momentary suggestions even of coyness that are again strikingly contrasted by a certain barbaric element worthy of a barely-civilized Cossack.

The peculiar fascination exerted by his music may be traced first and foremost to its dominating melancholy character, although this plaintive strain is again set off by a certain vigor, which Henderson calls "the outcome of a certain grim

(*) See Appendix of Musical Illustrations, Examples 83 to 89.

determination always present in the Russian heart." It has also been described by Dannreuther as "fiery exultation on a basis of languid melancholy." The means which Tschaikowsky found to express himself in a language of profound pathos embodied the free use of sombre chromatic harmony, of minor modes, and above all of weird and gloomy orchestration.[a] The general outlines of Tschaikowsky's music embrace melodic subtleties, bold modulations, florid figuration, strongly marked rhythm and cadences peculiar to his own land, huge dimensions, fantastic portrayal, broad dignity of utterance, and magnificent orchestral effects. The embodiment of native folk-music in no way interferes with his own intense originality and genuine spontaneity.

One of the most astounding features in Tschaikowsky's scoring is the extreme modern effect secured from virtually the same orchestra of moderate size that Beethoven employed. To the uninitiated auditor, the wealth and variety of tone-color produced would appear to require a mighty aggregation of instruments; but the "Symphonie pathétique," for example, makes requisition for no more instruments than those used in Beethoven's grandest symphonies, excepting the addition of a bass-tuba.[b] As for an increased number of strings, the increase remains in force for modern performances of the classics as well. In regard to obtaining what has been called "a gloomy eloquence of instrumentation," this is effected by drawing upon the deeper accents of the orchestra.[c] Tschaikowsky employed such combinations as horns and bassoons alone; English horn, bassoons and violas; the lower tones of flutes and clarinets also accompanied by violas; the unison of English horn with low strings as in the *cantabile* of the overture-fantasy, "Hamlet," — a combination to which Henderson calls attention in his admirable little book on the orchestra. (This work, by the way, is skilfully written for the delectation of cultivated amateurs.) Other important contributors to Tschaikowsky's subdued coloring are the clarinets in their lower range and the bassoons in their upper range.[d] The best exemplification of orchestration essentially mournful in character is discovered in his last great work — the "Symphonie pathétique" already referred to. On the other hand, a magnificent specimen of forceful writing is presented in the final movement of particularly the C major symphony.

Recent development in Russia of orchestral resources is bearing delectable fruit; but without Tschaikowsky to point the way, this would not have been possible. He still reigns supreme as the greatest interpreter of Slavonic ideals. Tschaikowsky in Greater Russia, Grieg in Scandinavia, Dvořák in Bohemia, Saint-Saëns in France, Wagner and Richard Strauss in Germany, — these are the men of the nineteenth century who have caused the art of orchestration to

[a] Ex. 83, 86, 89.

[b] Ex. 85.   [c] Ex. 84, 88.   [d] Ex. 87.

acquire distinctively national characteristics suited to the needs of differentiated national music. In return, composers of all countries are seizing upon every possible device introduced by these innovators, and the twentieth century gives promise of results cosmopolitan in nature and superb beyond description.

ENGLAND AND AMERICA.

X.

England. Although the recent growth of Russian music is of vast significance, neither have the Anglo-Saxons been idle. England can also point to a long series of sterling composers belonging to the nineteenth century. Among the representative musicians who have helped to develop a native style of composition and orchestration should be mentioned Balfe, Macfarren, Bennett, Barnby, Sullivan, Bridge, Mackenzie, Parry, Cowen, Stanford.

At the head of this sturdy list stands Balfe (1808), whose continuous application to operatic forms presents an exception to the more varied labors of most English composers. Neither the substance-matter nor the instrumentation of his works merits the distinction of having furthered the cause of indigenous English music. The style is essentially Italian. Balfe possessed fluency of expression and displayed aptitude for pleasing melody. Depth and power were not among his attributes.

An entirely different atmosphere pervades the numerous productions of Sir George Macfarren (1813). This eminent pioneer of nineteenth century English music had the honor of being born in the same year with Wagner. The cosmopolitan range of his compositions is noteworthy, and his tireless activity in the face of an affliction that eventually ended in entire blindness entitles him to unstinted praise. His works are among the most important contributions to the literature of English music, covering as they do every branch of music from opera, oratorio and cantata to symphony, chamber music and sacred pieces.

The reader will remember that on page 77 of Chapter IX, particular mention was made of Sterndale Bennett (1816), in view of his association with Mendelssohn and Schumann. The pith of the remarks embodied in that paragraph will, however, bear repetition, owing to the significance attached to Bennett's influence upon modern English music. The acknowledged heir of Purcell, he clothed his individuality in the language promulgated by the early Romanticists; but though his works bear the undeniable impress of Mendelssohnian characteristics, they are none the less original and of enduring worth. His field of activity as a composer was extensive. Outside of England, his oratorio "The Woman of Samaria " is, perhaps, the best known of his various choral works, symphonies and concertos. The high regard in which he is held by his countrymen reveals itself in his title of "Founder of a New English School."

To mention Barnby (1838) in these pages may appear somewhat out of place. Sacred music is the line in which he particularly distinguished himself. In addition to writing magnificent hymns and anthems, he developed his best gifts in such works as his psalm "The Lord is King." Nevertheless, it will be noticed that from a chronological standpoint Barnby heads the list of the more recent English exponents of progressive ideas, and his advanced convictions entitle him to recognition in this discussion if for no other reason than for his zeal and perseverance in having given in London two concert performances of "Parsifal" as early as in 1884. The date of this achievement is significant when one considers that the initial dramatic performance of "Parsifal" at Bayreuth had taken place but two years before.

The most widely known English composer of the nineteenth century is, of course, Sullivan (1842). This renown has been won by virtue of a unique talent for writing comic operas that are gems of the first water. On the other hand, Sullivan has again and again revealed his latent powers for composition in serious vein. Had he elected to consecrate himself to the nobler form of art, he might have become the greatest of all English composers. As it is, he has done much for the cause of Anglicized music and especially of Anglicized orchestration. The author of no less than fifteen operettas that are famed in England, America, and to a lesser degree in Continental Europe, he has clothed these works in charming orchestral garment. The instrumental combinations at his command were small, but he was never at loss how to use them to best advantage. It was his peculiar custom to postpone the orchestral scoring until all modifications as suggested by preliminary rehearsals had been decided upon. Taking the "Mikado" as a favorable example, it is seen that the local coloring demanded by the setting depends chiefly upon the orchestra. The quaint opening chorus for men at the very beginning of the operetta proves the truth of this statement. Sullivan based his methods of instrumentation upon those of Mozart, but occasionally copied Gounod and even Berlioz. When, however, Sullivan employs larger orchestral forces, his musicianship, dramatic power and command of resource seem to expand in proportion. Notable illustrations of original and effective scoring are to be found in his representative oratorios and above all in his grand opera "Ivanhoe."

John Bridge (1844) displays sound scholarship in a respectable list of sacred music, cantatas and orchestral works, but his attainments cannot be compared with those of Mackenzie (1847). The latter is first and foremost an orchestral writer, in fact one might say that his conceptions are wholly orchestral. His is the realm of realism rather than of idealism. His style reveals no great depth or pathos. There is a mixture of Mendelssohnian and Wagnerian externals. His melody has been styled angular; his harmonic structure is inefficient, and his rhythm monotonous. Mackenzie's orchestration, however, is unusual. Its many excellences afford a striking contrast to the mediocrity of subject-matter. It is powerful and effective, allowing also commendable freedom to the wood-wind. Some interesting passages for flute and oboe in combination with low clarinet arpeggio effects are contained in the cantata "The Story of Sayid." Among Mackenzie's most notable achievements should be mentioned two operas, two Scotch rhapsodies, and his magnum opus, a dramatic oratorio entitled "The Rose of Sharon."

There is a double interest in examining the musical compositions of Charles Hubert Parry (1848) in consequence of his having enriched the world with a scholarly and broad-minded work entitled "The Evolution of the Art of Music." This standard book has been quoted from more than once in the course of these pages. Parry has tried his hand at all forms of composition, including chamber music, symphonies and oratorios. There is a natural hesitation to pass individual judgment on these works, so the criticism of two contemporary Englishmen will be referred to instead. These two are Willeby and Stanford. In general terms, Willeby speaks of Parry as a man of wide experience and absolute sincerity, and as one "devoted to liberation." He then goes on to say that Parry's works show traces of Beethoven, especially of Brahms, somewhat of Händel and Mendelssohn, whereas his earlier "Prometheus Unbound" is conceived in the "Tristan" style; but the "human" element is lacking. The most complex methods are employed to attain the desired results. The obvious avoidance of natural cadences is carried to an extreme. The melodies are stately and self-possessed but become monotonous. So much for Parry's style. As to his orchestration, the opinion of Dr. Stanford is presumably authoritative and is appended *verbatim:* "His orchestral sense is by no means his most highly developed sense, for while there is no lack of sonority in his scoring, there is not infrequently all too little of 'fancy.' What leanings he has in this art are certainly more toward Wagner than Berlioz, and sometimes the incongruity of Wagner in the orchestra and Brahms in the music is by no means compensated for by what there is of Parry in both." [26]

Cowen (1852) stands as one of the representative English exponents of both absolute and programmatic symphonic writing. Of his five characteristic sym-

[26] A. Goring Thomas (1851) should, chronologically, be referred to at this point in view of the present continued popularity and frequent performance in the United States of his cantata "The Swan and the Skylark," even though the work is said to have been orchestrated by Stanford. On the other hand, more pronounced independence is evidenced in such of Thomas' representative works as the opera "Esmeralda" and the choral ode "The Sun Worshippers." The general substance of his compositions displays delicacy and refinement in orchestration and the possession of a real melodic gift.

phonies, special reference is due to the "Scandinavian," No. 3, the "Welsh," No. 4, and the one in F, No. 5. The fact that this later symphony, No. 5, contains no programmatic idea, leads to some conjecture as to what Cowen's motive was in returning to the conservatism of pure and abstract music. This work embodies considerable depth of sentiment, sombre orchestral coloring, and a possible touch of Chopin. Cowen has written several operas, but special significance is attached to his choral work "The Sleeping Beauty," in that it incorporates Wagner's principle of representative themes together with their skilful thematic development. The orchestra plays an exceedingly important rôle, even to the occasional detriment of the vocal parts.

Having listened to what Stanford had to say about Parry, let us see what Stanford's music has to say for its author. Here again one discovers the accomplished scholar rather than the artistic dreamer. Stanford (1852) has proved himself an eminent conductor and professor, but as composer, his emotional capacity is evidently limited, and his music lacks the very essentials of ideal love and impassioned sentiment so conspicuous, for example, in Félicien David's ardent conceptions. Compare the glowing colors in David's "Lalla Rookh" with those in Stanford's opera "The Veiled Prophet of Khorassan." The latter does, indeed, suggest "local" color, but there is no evidence of sensuous Eastern charm. Stanford's right to share with Cowen the rank of representative English symphonist is undisputed. His fertile pen has produced an honorable series of orchestral works that include a festival overture and four symphonies. Prominent among these is the "Irish Symphony," which again reveals a striving after characteristic portrayal. Willeby also makes reference to this in the following terms: "Here, for the obtainment of local color, he has called to his aid all kinds of melodies and 'modes.' The 'Aeolian' mode transposed, which consists of the scale having its semitonic intervals between the second and third, and fifth and sixth degrees, and the 'Mixolydian,' with its semitones between the third and fourth, and sixth and seventh degrees, are both extensively used." [27]

During the last few years a new star has risen on the British horizon, one that promises to become a permanency, — Edward Elgar (1857). His talent is conspicuous, and he is fast winning his way through sheer merit. Henderson goes so far as to write of him as "the most promising of modern composers," though this is a matter of opinion. At all events, Elgar stands out in marked contrast to his more self-restrained countrymen in that he dares to break through the barriers of

[27] The favorable comment excited a few years ago by the cantata "Hiawatha" by H. Coleridge-Taylor (1875) has proved to be of more than passing endurance. Mention of his activity, which includes also such works as an operetta, "Dream Lovers," is therefore in place. Coleridge-Taylor is the first composer of African descent to command serious recognition.

British good form by employing a language of emotional eloquence and dramatic intensity. His handling of vocal forces does not by any means discard the time-honored doctrines of Bach and Händel so tenaciously adhered to in England, but he combines classic polyphony with modern expedients of unfettered chromatic harmony and throbbing orchestration. His "Dream of Gerontius" and his "The Apostles" should convince his compatriots that heretofore they have been content to compose in a manner all too sedate and unemotional. Bennett founded a "new school" of English music in the early part of the nineteenth century. It may be that the time has now come for a second "new school" which shall meet the requirements of the twentieth century.[28]

AMERICA.

XI.

In undertaking to set forth the present conditions of American musical art it is realized that little can be said beyond that with which professional American musicians are already perfectly familiar. But the future of indigenous American music gives promise of a significance so wide that the reader will concede the indispensability of embodying in this book at least a bird's-eye view of an evolution that is destined to lead to glorious results. Moreover, to refrain from repeating well-known facts for fear of presenting trite material would indeed appear as an inexcusable and glaring omission should these pages ever come into the hands of a foreigner.

In order to cover the entire ground, it would be necessary to touch upon the rather doubtful experiments of our forefathers during the seventeenth and eighteenth centuries:— to examine into the tardy emancipation of religious music from the dogmatic fetters of Puritanism, to follow the gradual development of American hymn-tunes, and to ferret out the initial encroachments of beneficent

[28] Elgar's "The Apostles" is the general title of a cycle of four works for voices and orchestra, of which Part II, named "The Kingdom," was completed and performed since the above was written. "The Kingdom" further discloses the remarkable individuality of Elgar's style, which in turn bespeaks the exalted spiritual nature of the man.

Each successive work that emanates from Elgar's pen emphasizes his monumental command of polyphonic structure in its largest dimensions, clothed meanwhile in the most realistic of orchestral garments. It would be going too far to aver that Elgar approaches Richard Strauss as an orchestrator; on the other hand, it will hardly be questioned that there are three prominently conspicuous composers of the present day who, having put themselves in close touch with the ideals of Richard Wagner and agreeing to a more or less degree with the tenets of Richard Strauss, stand forth as the recognized vancouriers in their respective countries for the most advanced phase of orchestral art:— Elgar, Debussy, MacDowell.

Teutonic influence. Such preliminaries may here be dispensed with. America has no native folk-tunes. The experiments of our illustrious guest, Dvořák, to adapt so-called negro melodies as the basis for future operation are certainly masterly, — nevertheless illogical. MacDowell's poetic "Indian Suite" draws upon still another source for the same purpose. Racial characteristics and local coloring are indeed suggested, — but the desired objective is not attained. Of similar purport are the exhaustive researches of Farwell. His deductions are intensely interesting, frequently picturesque, — but again prove that the primitive tunes of the American Indian do not meet the requirements for a national form of melody. It is evident, therefore, that American composers are obliged to rely upon their own individual efforts. What is more, no marked individuality displayed itself before the nineteenth century. Anyone desiring detailed information pertaining to the infancy of American music may be referred to Ritter's book on that subject as well as to Louis C. Elson's "History of American Music." Furthermore, since the main theme of this discussion is orchestration, it will not be possible to more than touch upon the sterling achievements of the already large list of nineteenth and twentieth century composers who are so worthily furthering the artistic cause of their country. Detailed biographies of these men are also to be found in Elson's work as well as in Rupert Hughes' "Contemporary American Composers."

During the nineteenth century America produced no less than some hundred native born composers, conductors, performers and pedagogues who are worthy of unstinted praise and enduring recognition. It is, however, an extremely difficult matter to single out those who may be looked upon as America's representative writers for the orchestra. At the present moment one might suggest the names of six men who have been exceptionally fortunate in being granted the opportunity of showing the world what they can do. These fortunate ones are Paine, Buck, Foote, Chadwick, MacDowell, Parker, of whom no less than four are claimed by New England. The word "fortunate" is used advisedly, for without detracting in the least from the hard-earned and well-merited laurels of these conspicuously successful composers, many another American could be pointed to who even now is worthy of being classed in the first rank and who would undoubtedly rise to epoch-making greatness were the *opportunity* but granted him. Selecting a few names merely at random, the present writer has had occasion to peruse the orchestral pages of such men as Father Bonvin (a Jesuit priest of Canesius College, Buffalo, N. Y.) and Professor Leo R. Lewis of Tufts College, — the breadth and power of whose scoring would command widespread admiration were the authors natives and residents of Continental Europe. Further proof of native independence and strength is revealed in the deplorably rare opportunities of listening to the orchestral works of our younger aspirants such as F. Converse, H. H. Huss, H. K. Hadley, Rubin Goldmark, not to mention the scholarly productions of the older and reputed leaders of the country such as Gilchrist, F. G. Gleason, Foerster, Beck, E. S. Kelley, Schoenefeld, Zeck.

No country in the world makes such unreasonable demands upon the range of professional capacity as does America when begrudgingly bestowing her patronage upon her musicians. To be an "all-round" musician one is supposed to be a proficient organ and pianoforte player, a vocal teacher, a trainer of boy choirs, of solo quartets, of denominational church choir singing, and a choral as well as an orchestral conductor; one is supposed to be familiar with all matters pertaining to church services, to have some knowledge of orchestral stringed instruments, to be versed in subtleties theoretical and pedagogical, to have business executive ability, and to be — incidentally — a composer! It is therefore not easy to classify our contemporary musicians into distinctive branches of activity. John Knowles Paine, for example, is first and foremost the pioneer of America's great composers. On the other hand, were he to be deprived of this tribute, there would still remain divers possible classifications under the headings of organist, of pioneer educator, of theorist, lecturer, and teacher. Consequently, the following group must, like that of the French composers in Chapter XII, be accepted with considerable reserve; for, as in that chapter, the different composers are but arbitrarily classified under the particular branch in which they would appear to have excelled. It is also to be understood that where no statement to the contrary is made, the composer under discussion is a native born American.

XII.

(1) **Pioneers and Promoters.** Prominent among our indefatigable workers of the nineteenth century born prior to 1850 are: Lowell Mason, Bristow, Dr. William Mason, Gottschalk, C. C. Converse, Dr. L. Damrosch, Paine, B. J. Lang, Emery.

Lowell Mason (1792–1872) was for many years the president of the Händel and Haydn Society of Boston, where he founded an academy of music, and displayed untiring activity in initiating conferences of music teachers and in the cause of American musical art in general. Bristow (1825) deserves mention not only for his activity as a pianist, teacher, and conductor, but also for his ambitions as a composer in large forms. These works include two symphonies, two oratorios "Daniel" and "St. John," and an opera "Rip van Winkle." Dr. William Mason (1829) proved himself worthy of the heritage entrusted to him by his father, Lowell Mason, and is looked upon as one of the chief factors in the evolution of American music. His compositions, though clever, are conservative and somewhat pedantic, but his influence as an educator cannot be overestimated. Gottschalk (1829) devoted his exceptional talents as a concert pianist largely to the dissemination of his own salon music, which is brilliant though sentimental, being, moreover, unquestionably dominated by Spanish characteristics. Converse (1832) is recognized as a typical American and has won esteem as the author of a large number of hymn-tunes. Dr. Leopold Damrosch (1832) was among the earlier Germans who adopted the United States as their home. He left his indelible impress upon the artistic life of New York City and bequeathed the fruits of his labors to his sons, Walter and Frank, who have piously preserved and extended them. Paine and B. J. Lang are mentioned in this connection by virtue of their indomitable perseverance in behalf of improved musical conditions in the earlier period of their respective careers when the general attitude of the American public toward true musical art was even worse than it is at present. Emery (1841) owed his reputation originally to his talents as a pianist, but his primer of harmony has since made his name a familiar one in almost every household.

This list may rightfully include the name of a more recent benefactor of native composition — the pianist, Sherwood (1854), who was one of the first to insist that the American public should become acquainted with the slighted creative talents of her artistic sons. He put this noble resolve to practical test by devoting large portions of his programs to the compositions of his compatriots, and was able to command the attention and respect of his audiences not alone by his sterling technique and refined interpretation but by his charming personality as well.

Many other names such as Carl Zerrahn and Theodore Thomas could be added here. They have, however, been classified under their more pronounced specialities.

(2) **Master of Orchestration.**

PAINE (1839). As Hughes fitly expresses it, Paine is the venerable dean of America's truly great composers. Dr. Riemann also is not far wrong when he declares that Paine's earlier works breathe a classical, the latter ones a romantic spirit. This unwearying composer is at his best in large forms — indeed, his supreme devotion to large undertakings has left him little time for smaller works. His artistic career displays a steady growth not unlike that of Wagner or Verdi. Grounded in the conservative principles of sound Germanic classicism, as revealed in his powerful and dramatic oratorio "St. Peter," he has pressed onward through various stages of legitimate program music, represented by such works as the "Spring Symphony," the symphonic poem "The Tempest," the overture to "As You Like It," the setting of Keat's "Realm of Fancy," Milton's "Nativity," and, most important of all, the "Oedipus Tyrannos of Sophokles." Having reached the height of his power in these lines, Paine advanced yet further and concentrated his energies upon not only the music but the libretto as well of a dramatic conception that should head the list of a genuine American school of opera. The recent completion of "Azara," with its dramatic continuity, irresistible climaxes, dignity and beauty of musical contents, consistent and effective orchestration, is of epoch-making significance. The exasperating obstacles placed in the way of its performance both here and abroad are, alas, too well known to require additional comment. Until a production of this work shall have been an accomplished fact, our country justly merits the existing condemnation of foreign musicians who declare that America has not the slightest conception of her duties either to her artistic development or to her native composers who have sacrificed the best years of their lives in the hope of stimulating that development. Not without justice do the Germans declare that the American public at large possess no artistic instincts whatever, since they force their native composers to turn to foreign lands for encouragement.[29]

BUCK (1839) is conspicuously identified with the evolution of American church music. As a composer he is at his best in religious composition in smaller forms. On the other hand, his important contributions to the branch of larger choral works with orchestral accompaniment must not be overlooked. His scenes from Longfellow's "Golden Legend" were deemed worthy of winning one of the coveted prizes at Cincinnati. The cantata for male chorus "Columbus" displays masterly command in the deployment of men's voices, whereas the "Light of Asia" is one of the standard works of America. Buck has rather neglected the field of purely orchestral music, but the scoring of his choral compositions reveals the firm hand of a master.

FOOTE (1853). Turning to a younger generation who have sturdily maintained the high standard set before them, one naturally recalls the name of one who may perhaps be regarded as the most satisfactory exponent of the efficiency of two American teachers, Paine and Lang, the most significant representative of an exceptional class of musician — the native trained composer, Arthur Foote. It is generally conceded that Foote is possessed of unusual powers in writing for men's voices. Widely known is his "Skeleton in Armor" with its forceful utterance, as well as his poetic setting of "The Farewell of Hiawatha." Again, in the field of song lyrics he has endeared himself to the worthy army of singers by virtue of a notable series of exceptional and widely contrasted productions. His true strength would, however, appear to reveal itself in the noblest vehicles of musical thought — the quartet and the orchestra. Foote does not aim to produce sensational effects, in fact his orchestral canvass has, on the whole, a grayish hue. The seriousness of his purpose, the serenity of his ideals, and the unmistakable impress of a cultured University training are faithfully reproduced in the nobility, the

[29] John Knowles Paine died in Cambridge, Massachusetts, on April 25, 1906. He did not live to hear a complete performance of his opera, although after his death a concert rendition of most of the music was given as a memorial in Boston under the direction of B. J. Lang.

breadth, and the sober though appropriate coloring of his artistic conceptions. The present writer is inclined to regard him as the Brahms of this country.

CHADWICK (1854). In contrast to Foote's domestic education, **Chadwick** stands among the first of that memorable list of students who served a rigorous apprenticeship under Rheinberger in Munich, and thereby helped to perpetuate his name in America. A mighty throng followed in Chadwick's footsteps, among whom were the composers Parker, Huss, Bullard, Atherton; the educators Lewis and Spalding; the organists and teachers John White, Howland, and Bertram Henry. Not only did Chadwick with one stroke make his individuality felt upon returning to his native land, — an individuality that has since been strengthened rather than lessened, — but his appointment to the directorship of the New England Conservatory of Music was a choice so opportune that that institution has since been raised to a standard of excellence it never before had enjoyed, and is becoming one of the recognized arbiters in the musical affairs of the country. Like Foote, Chadwick has tried his hand in divers fields of composition, being particularly successful in writing part-songs as well as songs with pianoforte accompaniment. Large choral works have, however, also claimed his attention, and are represented by his cantata "The Pilgrims," and again by "The Viking's Last Voyage" for barytone solo, male chorus and orchestra. It appears to be the fortune of American composers to become known primarily by their vocal compositions. This is also true of Chadwick. Nevertheless, he has given expression to his loftiest inspiration in a series of chamber and orchestral pieces that stamp him as a keen judge of those essentials required for large instrumental works. His form, though conservative, is well rounded. His orchestration is chaste and refined rather than sensational and glowing. His music is above all manly and energetic. Personally, Chadwick may not regard his operetta "Tabasco" with all too favorable eyes; yet the step taken was assuredly in the right direction. It is to be regretted that our contemporary American composers seem unable to take a firm stand in imperceptibly educating the public with a light yet artistic *genre* of music such as characterizes Chadwick's "Tabasco" or the earlier operettas of Victor Herbert and de Koven.

MACDOWELL (1861). In venturing the assertion that MacDowell stands apart on his exalted pinnacle of fame, there is not the slightest danger of incurring disparaging comparisons between him and his eminent contemporaries who have been classified under this heading. Paine's monumental achievements are unassailable. Buck occupies an honorable position as one of the foremost of our writers of church music. Foote and Chadwick have each of them established their respective individuality as composers of exceptional ability. Parker holds undisputed sway in his particular domain. What separates MacDowell from his colleagues is the difference between his perspective and theirs. His conceptions betray certain tendencies that are foreign to their Anglo-Saxon ruggedness with its Teutonic substructure. MacDowell's Scotch ancestry, his intimacy with Raff, his contact with the artistic life of Paris, — all these circumstances helped to mould his exceptional genius into a form distinctly original and unique. It is natural that the influence of his teacher, Raff, should predominate. But whereas Raff's programmatic expositions deal in the romance of enchantment, of the supernatural, of the fantastic, MacDowell pins his faith to the romance of poetic imagination symbolic of emotional realities. Lawrence Gilman, in a persuasive essay on MacDowell, eulogizes, together with other works, his symphonic poems "Hamlet and Ophelia," "Lancelot and Elaine," "The Saracens" and "Lovely Alda" as "the works of a master of imaginative expression, a penetrative psychologist, above all, an exquisite poet." The same writer further remarks that "MacDowell has chosen occasionally to employ, in the realization of his purposes, what seems at first to be precisely the magical apparatus so necessary to the older romanticism. Dryads and elves inhabit his world, and he dwells at times under faery boughs and in enchanted woods; but for him, as for the poets of the Celtic tradition, these things are but the manifest images of an interior passion and delight. Seen in the transfiguring mirror of his music, the moods and events of the natural world and of the incessant drama of psychic life are vivified into shapes and designs of irresistible beauty and appeal. Both in theory and in practice, MacDowell stands uncompromisingly for music that is, of intention, persistently pictorial and impressionistic. . . . It is as much in his choice of subjects as in the peculiar vividness and felicity of his expression, that he is unique among tone-poets of the external world." The above citations present a faithful picture of MacDowell's philosophical reasonings. His chord formation, harmonic progressions, thematic treatment and structural form are all in accord with the psychological subtleties to be expressed.

It is particularly in orchestration that MacDowell discloses certain French characteristics. Many of his pages might have been written by Saint-Saëns himself, but the "solid" foundation inoculated by the exacting requirements of his German training is never entirely absent. As a result, MacDowell's scoring frequently surpasses even that of his illustrious French contemporary. MacDowell proves no exception to the rule in that his popularity is due not so much to his more significant orchestral works as to his smaller offerings such as his attractive and highly ingenious pieces for the pianoforte. He has still many years before him, and gives promise of ever increasing power and versatility. America may well be proud of him! [30]

PARKER (1863). In several respects Parker's orchestral and choral style

---

[30] The entire country mourns the premature death of Edward Alexander MacDowell, which occurred in New York on January 23, 1908.

bears some affinity to that of both Foote and Chadwick. His subject-matter, like theirs, is serious — at times even severe; his formal structures are conservative; his command of vocal forces is supreme. Again, his orchestral colors, like theirs, are accused of being cold and gray, — devoid of scintillating tints and glowing hues. This may be true to a certain extent. But when one considers the *genre* of choral composition to which these three composers are addicted, it will be readily seen that a radical readjustment of their orchestral pages in favor of warmer coloring would be inconsistent with the nature of their oratorical settings. Among the most conspicuous of Parker's productions are the overtures "Regulus" and "Count Robert of Paris," the ballad for chorus and orchestra "King Trojan," and, of course, his masterpiece "Hora Novissima." Parker shares with Mac-Dowell the good fortune of having already won enduring recognition in foreign lands, — Parker in England, MacDowell in France, Germany and Russia. Yale University was one of the first institutions of this country to follow Harvard's lead in establishing a chair of music, and showed sound judgment in selecting so eminent a composer as Parker to occupy that chair.

As already intimated, the country is further represented by a dignified array of American born composers for the orchestra, who are working against fearful odds in behalf of improved conditions for native art. Gilchrist (1846) was, like Arthur Foote, trained in this country, and is identified with the city of Philadelphia. His forte is choral and religious music, being, moreover, a remarkably successful prize winner. His symphonic attempts show sound scholarship, but are conservative and non-programmatic. The name of F. G. Gleason (1848) is highly respected in Chicago. His works display harmonic rather than melodic strength, and were frequently performed by Theodore Thomas. In Pittsburgh, Adolph Foerster (1854) has done fine work in both large and small forms. Of unusual interest are the scores of J. H. Beck (1856) in consequence of their novel effects and warm coloring. His early success in Germany justified the hope that he would become widely known, but he seems to have so far intentionally avoided the publishers. Arthur Bird (1856) cannot be blamed for preferring to live in the midst of the generous artistic encouragement of a European city. Of especial merit are his symphony in A and the ballet "Rübezahl." The representative composer of San Francisco is Edgar S. Kelley (1857). He was a pupil of Clarence Eddy, but studied also in Stuttgart. He is essentially a programmatic writer, possesses considerable originality and humor, orchestrates with skill and daring, and has been especially successful with his melodramatic music to "Macbeth." Henry Schoenefeld (1857) was a pupil of both Reinecke and Lassen, and was identified with Chicago. His undertakings are worthy of consideration in consequence of his adaptation and idealization of negro melodies in his Suite for string-orchestra, op. 15, before Dvořák's experiments of similar nature. Schoenefeld has since written an overture entitled "In the Sunny South." San Francisco can boast of yet another orchestral composer of repute — Frederick Zeck jr., who has written, among other things, several symphonies, a symphonic poem, and even a romantic opera.

Frank van der Stucken (1858) cuts a large figure in the evolution of American music. He is frequently though erroneously regarded as a German, but he was born in Texas, and studied not only in Leipzig but under Benoit in Antwerp as well. He first rose to prominence as director of the Arion Male Chorus Society of New York. In 1885 he instituted a series of "Novelty Concerts" that opened up new possibilities to America's neglected composers. Since undertaking the directorship of the Cincinnati Symphony Orchestra in 1895, van der Stucken has made himself a national benefactor by encouraging and repeatedly performing American productions. He is himself a composer of no mean ability, possesses decidedly modern tendencies, and orchestrates with unerring certainty. His compositions cover a wide field and include an opera " Vlasda," a symphonic prologue " William Ratcliff," and a Suite on Shakespeare's " Tempest."

Walter Damrosch (1862) has acquired the right to be ranked with America's orchestral composers on account of his grand opera "The Scarlet Letter," and Reginald de Koven (1859) knows how to enhance the scores of his comic operas with a lightness of touch and some clever devices. "Robin Hood" and "The Fencingmaster" are sprightly and refined even though guilty of occasional plagiarism.

Mrs. Beach is rightfully looked upon as an eminent leader among the women composers of America and is fully entitled to equal rank with her fair contemporaries in France, Cécile Chaminade and Augusta Holmès. Her "Gaelic Symphony" has been performed not only by the Boston Symphony Orchestra and by Theodore Thomas, but has been granted numerous performances by other representative organizations as well. Mrs. Beach's scores are exceedingly elaborate — possibly too much so. Nevertheless, her command of orchestral resources is remarkable, and in her Mass in E flat, op. 5, she has obtained impressive effects, rich colors and dramatic climaxes.

The scores of Bonvin and Lewis have already been referred to. The former evolves his conceptions by means of the most intricate polyphony and with an opulence of orchestral effects. Lewis has branched out into lines distinctly his own. A Brahms background of grayish orchestration is in evidence, but his rhythm is absolutely unfettered, his harmonies are bold, and his mastery of thematic treatment is unusual.

Of the younger composers born after 1860, much may be expected from F. S.

Converse of Harvard,[31] who is in close touch with the ultra-modern school of composition with all its attending freedom of form and emancipation from stereotyped pattern, for he has already excited attention both in this country and in England.[32]   A promising pupil of Rheinberger is Henry Holden Huss, who is essentially a dramatic and lyric composer.   The healthy and above all optimistic tendencies of Henry K. Hadley's compositions, as exemplified by his symphony "Youth and Life," stand out in sharp contrast against the morbidness and pessimism that have apparently won the upper hand in musical art during the last fifteen years.   Rubin Goldmark was born in New York and is living at present in that city.   He is possessed of a thoroughly artistic nature and has inherited much of his eminent uncle's originality and ability to impart luscious tone-colors to his orchestral tableaux.

Before concluding this classification of orchestral composers it is desired to remind the reader of the vast significance attached to the labors of Dvořák and X. Scharwenka during their sojourn in the United States.   Again, other foreigners who have cast in their lot with us, such as Loeffler [33] and Victor Herbert, are now practically regarded as loyal American composers.   Both these men are possessed of sovereign command of orchestration.   The one uses his art for portraying vivid realism, the other for the purpose of clothing his pleasing conceptions as evolved in daintier vein.

There are undoubtedly a number of important American composers whose names have been omitted from these pages.   The present writer desires to apologize for any such unintentional omission under the plea that it has not been his good fortune to have his attention called either directly or indirectly to their compositions in larger forms.

XIII.

(3) **Orchestral and Choral Conductors.**   The progress of a country's musical art rests largely in the hands of its orchestral and choral conductors.   America has been exceptionally fortunate in this respect, for her history presents an army of luminaries who are unexcelled the world over.   The concert and operatic stage of New York owes its very existence to such indefatigable workers as Carl Bergmann (1821), Dr. Leopold Damrosch (1832), Theodore Thomas

[31] See footnote, page 173.

[32] "The Pipe of Desire," a romantic grand opera in one act by F. S. Converse, was twice performed in Boston early in 1906, and reveals significant command of the modern technics of orchestration.

[33] The recently performed "Pagan Poem" (op. 14) of Charles Martin Loeffler (1861) would indicate that a list of the world's representative masters of modern orchestration made up five years from now would include his name.

(1835), Anton Seidl (1850), all four of whom were Germans. And at the present day, there are a number of eminent conductors in New York.

To Theodore Thomas more than to anyone else is due the present high standard of musical taste in America. At the head of an excellent virtuoso orchestra, he traversed the country in his earlier years, and revealed for the first time the value and meaning of the thoughts of the great masters, while toward Wagner, Tschaikowsky, Dvořák, etc., he performed the same mission. These were the days when the New York Philharmonic Society and the Harvard Musical Association in Boston were the only permanent institutions devoted to orchestral music. Theodore Thomas not only established a new standard of interpretation in this country, but so catholic was his taste and so far reaching his purpose that the debt to him can never be paid. During his entire career, his attitude toward the American composer was that of a helpful ally and friend. It was as conductor of the Philharmonic Society of New York for a term of years and particularly as conductor of the Cincinnati May Music Festivals and of the Chicago Orchestra that Thomas' maturer and later years were passed; and it is especially in these cities that his memory and influence will remain ineradicable.

In Boston prior to the establishment of a permanent symphony orchestra in 1881, Lowell Mason's initiative was zealously fostered by the two foreigners, Carl Zerrahn (1826), Bernhard Listemann (1839), and by B. J. Lang (1839), together with other tireless enthusiasts. The Boston Symphony Orchestra has since attracted the best the world can afford — Henschel, Gericke, Nikisch, Paur.[34] Inland, public-spirited citizens have made it possible to establish local symphony orchestras and have almost invariably been exceedingly fortunate in their choice of conductors. Theodore Thomas migrated to Chicago. Franz van der Stucken was called to Cincinnati, Frederic Archer, Victor Herbert, Emil Paur to Pittsburgh, Fritz Scheel to Philadelphia. Perhaps one of the greatest services to the education of the country has been rendered by that vast brotherhood of German Singing Societies which flourish from shore to shore. The high standard of their performances has been constantly sustained by men of splendid attainments such as, for instance, van der Stucken while in New York, John Lund while in Buffalo, Franz Bellinger in Indianapolis. In recent years American Choral Societies have forged to the front. Chicago owes much to Tomlins. Frank Damrosch and his colleagues are doing good work in New York; Mollenhauer, J. Wallace Goodrich and others in Boston. Similar conditions prevail in almost every large city in the Union. Neither may the beneficent influence of our military bandmasters upon the masses be overlooked. Considering the conditions that have existed in the past, no one can censure them for catering to the demands of the public. Never-

[34] Dr. Karl Muck was its conductor for the season of 1906–1907, and continues in the position for 1907–1908.

theless, they have little by little managed to interpolate numerous transcriptions from works of recognized merit. Such men as Gilmore, Sousa and Innes have done more for the cause of good music than is popularly supposed.

(4) **Songs and Smaller Forms.** One of the most favorable opportunities open to modern composers in their struggle for recognition is found in the field of songs and salon music. This is particularly the case in America. Consequently, all of our representatives produce such offerings, and that with success. A few composers, however, have made a special study of song writing and pianoforte pieces in lighter *genre*. Conspicuous among these are G. Templeton Strong, J. H. Rogers, Clayton Johns, Neidlinger, Ethelbert Nevin, Margaret Ruthven Lang, Fred Field Bullard, and Percy L. Atherton. Especial mention is due to Clayton Johns for the charming lyric quality of his songs; to Nevin for the fascination of his lighter pianoforte pieces, that nevertheless avoid triviality; to Miss Lang for the fairylike daintiness of many of her conceptions; to Bullard, whose promising career was prematurely cut off at the very moment when the rugged simplicity of his inspiring songs and choruses had won the hearts of his countrymen; to Atherton, who is, perhaps, the most talented of contemporary song writers in the realm of subtle psychological reasoning.

(5) **Organists and Church Composers.** It may be boldly asserted that America concedes the palm to none in the art of organ playing. Such is the skill in registration demanded in these days that that art is practically assuming the dignity of orchestration. This demand has been largely brought about by the need of finding an adequate substitute for concert orchestras. As a result, not only the large cities but almost every town in the Union possesses one or more modern organs presided over by executants of marked ability. In most cases these men devote themselves to church composition as well. Almost all the composers whose careers we have just been reviewing count church playing and church composition among their accomplishments. The only notable exception is MacDowell, who is, instead, a virtuoso pianoforte player. This is not the place to examine into the work of our many excellent church organists and composers. One is confronted by notable names wherever one turns. In Boston, Warren A. Locke has for many years held undisputed authority in matters pertaining to church services and boy choirs. Whitney and Whiting have done similar good work. Of the younger men, J. Wallace Goodrich displays an astounding technique, unexcelled either in this country or in France. The high standard of Episcopal church music in New York is due to such men as Samuel P. Warren, Richard H. Warren, Stubbs, Hall, etc. Among the prominent soloists are Eddy, Archer,* and Gerrit Smith. Shelley (1858) is widely known for his church compositions. He has also written large works such as the oratorio " The Inheritance Divine," but owes his popularity primarily to pleasing though rather conventional songs. Another

* Frederic Archer died since the above lines were written.

prominent church composer is Jules Jordan of Providence, whose interest is centered chiefly in oratorio. N. H. Allen, Marston, Hanscom and Coombs should also be mentioned under this heading.

(6) **Teachers and Theorists.** Teachers and theorists have found a fertile field in the United States, and in scientific educational matters the native American easily takes the lead. Already a dignified array of theoretical and pedagogical books have been added to the literature of music by such authors as A. J. Goodrich, A. R. Parsons, Goetschius, Wilson G. Smith, Matthews, Chadwick, Benjamin Cutter, Spalding, Norris. American teachers have won recognition in Europe as well. Goetschius found occupation in Stuttgart; Boise was for years an authority in Berlin.

(7) **School and College.** Of late, increased attention has been bestowed upon the study of music in the college curriculum. Harvard's lead is being followed, and chairs of music have been established on every hand. Harvard has been obliged to increase its staff of musical instructors, so that Paine is now assisted by Spalding and Converse.[35] Excellent work is being done by Parker at Yale, Lewis at Tufts, Gow at Vassar, Macdougall at Wellesley, Chadwick at the New England Conservatory, Pratt at the Hartford Theological Seminary. At Columbia, MacDowell has been succeeded by Rübner, who is ably seconded by McWhood. Smith College was one of the pioneers in musical affairs, being represented until recently by Blodgett, who was possessed of a peculiarly magnetic power. One of his prominent lieutenants, who is still in active service at Smith, is the pianoforte teacher and pedagogue, Edwin B. Story. He is one of the most fluent accompanists in the country. The enterprise of these college professors is making itself felt in the preparatory schools of the country, whereby the entire artistic morale of the public at large is being elevated. Credit is also due to the sound principles inoculated into the teaching of music in the public schools by such men as Frank Damrosch in New York or Tomlins in Chicago.

The writer has intentionally overstepped the bounds of orchestral composition for the purpose of emphasizing the prodigious activity displayed by our professional brethren on every hand. Throughout these pages there runs an undercurrent of discontent provoked by the listless attitude of the American public taken as a whole. The fickleness of their support seems to be at the root of our troubles. Everything conceivable is being done for this public. Music in the schools is encouraged. The colleges are alive to the needs of the hour. Many of our com-

[35] The retirement of Professor Paine not long before his death, and the recent resignation of Assistant Professor Converse for the purpose of devoting himself to composition, leaves the department of music at Harvard in charge of Assistant Professor Spalding.

posers are sacrificing their inner convictions on the altar of patriotism with the determination to write simply. Music lovers and philanthropists are enlisted in the cause. A high musical standard for religious worship is maintained. Orchestral performances can be listened to at moderate cost. Such renditions are as good as, frequently better than, those in Europe. How is it, then, that so many choral societies flourish for a few seasons, only to eventually die a lingering death? Buffalo's Symphony Orchestra is no more. Other cities have allowed similar mortifying conditions to come to pass.

On the other hand, the singer or the instrumental virtuoso reaps rewards that are out of all proportion to the tardy recognition and modest remuneration awarded to their colleagues — the composers, conductors, and organists — who are almost invariably possessed of an artistic education far superior to that of the soloist. A Rossinian era would appear to have reasserted itself! The larger number of these soloists are themselves rarely patriotic, for only with difficulty can they be persuaded to sing or perform even the finest of American productions. Orchestral conductors who come to our shores from abroad soon perceive that the public does not support home talent in a whole-hearted manner, and adjust their programs accordingly. With a few notable exceptions, they too are disloyal. Again, the worthy efforts of our comparatively few eminent newspaper critics in behalf of the American composer are constantly counteracted by the superficial and bombastic criticisms of their lesser brethren.

The American composer is to-day ready to enter the lists against the entire world. His own countrymen are impeding him. It is high time that the American public awake out of its lethargy!

(Summary on page 180.)

SUMMARY OF PART III.

CHAPTER IX. THE ROMANTIC SCHOOL.

The German composers of the nineteenth century are for convenience classified in three general groups: "The Romantic School," "The Classical Romanticists," "The New Movement." The so-called founders of the Romantic School, Spohr and Weber, were followed by such representative composers as Schubert, Mendelssohn and Schumann. The evolution of orchestration was conspicuously advanced by Weber. He stands at the head of modern instrumentation, for with him a new period began.

SPOHR was instrumental in awakening a keener interest for the supernatural, and he aimed to illustrate certain definite ideas by means of musical expression. He contributed to the evolution of orchestration proper but little that was actually new, but his development of violin technique stimulated at least a freer and more elaborate manner of employing the strings. The equilibrium of his orchestra is admirably preserved and the general color-scheme enriched by frequent use of soft harmonies for the brass.

WEBER'S true greatness lay in the power of orchestral portrayal and in rare appreciation of instrumental effects. Few composers contributed more than he to the independence of the wood-wind. He showed particular predilection for the clarinet as well as for horns, and was exceedingly modern in the use of small combinations. Weber's scoring is above all dramatic, and serves as a model for all later composers.

SCHUBERT displayed rare skill in the handling of orchestral instruments, whether in solo passages or in combination. His was the hand of a master who without hesitation knew what effects he desired and how to obtain them. Novel was his manner of writing for trombones, and the contrast of solo wood-instruments in dialogue.

MENDELSSOHN'S contributions to the details of instrumentation are both original and varied. The suavity of his melody, the purity of his form, and the delicacy of his scoring have been excelled by none. His orchestration is buoyant, transparent, and perfectly balanced.

SCHUMANN holds the unusual position of being one of the few great masters who did not excel in orchestration.

CHAPTER X. THE CLASSICAL ROMANTICISTS.

The representatives of classical romanticism are Raff, Rubinstein, Goldmark, Brahms, Bruch, Rheinberger. Although all of these men displayed rare skill in the application of orchestral resources, none of them can take rank with the more conspicuous exponents of instrumentation.

RAFF. Striking insignia of absolutely original scoring are not conspicuous in Raff's orchestration, but its entire character gives evidence of fertile imagination and sound judgment.

RUBINSTEIN. The instrumentation of the Russian, Rubinstein, is not of distinctive significance.

GOLDMARK, on the other hand, owes his reputation primarily to his gifts as an orchestrator. He atones for a certain lack of musical inspiration by mastery of material effects and power of vivid portrayal.

175

BRAHMS considered glowing orchestral color and sensational dramatic effect of secondary importance. In spite of his otherwise comprehensive and titanic achievements, one cannot point to him as a model for invariably felicitous instrumentation.

BRUCH possesses supreme command of modern orchestral resources, but is at his best in the art of accompaniment, which displays perfect taste, genuine expression and an abundance of energetic force.

RHEINBERGER'S orchestral works cannot be regarded in the light of important contributions to musical literature. The instrumentation is thoroughly refined, marvellously smooth, and perfectly rounded in every detail; but the essential elements of individuality and novelty do not enter into the orchestral scheme to any appreciable extent.

CHAPTER XI. THE NEW MOVEMENT.

The "New Movement" dates from the innovations simultaneously introduced by Berlioz in France and by Liszt and Wagner in Germany.

BERLIOZ was practically the first representative of the New Movement, but contrary to the natural course of evolution, he was not only its founder but at once its most radical exponent as well. The laying out of his musical scheme was inseparably connected with a *series* of events or ideas. As the chief French representative of romantic musical art, he combined dramatic and symphonic effects. His contributions to the development of "program" music and to modern science of orchestration loom up in gigantic proportions. One of the primary objects of his orchestral conceptions was to display tone-color in its own right, an object that was foreign to the more æsthetic ideals of the classicists. The distinctive features of his orchestration are power of musical description; new combinations, new effects, new treatment; insight into the characteristics of the instruments whereby their possibilities both individual and collective are demonstrated; excessive polyphony and complicated rhythm. Berlioz must be accredited with having anticipated many effects subsequently elaborated upon by Wagner, as discovered, for example, by his frequent use of homogeneous tone-color in independent three and four part harmony. Berlioz represents the ultra-realistic school of instrumental music and was the most daring orchestral writer that has ever lived.

LISZT. The importance attached to the rich and heavy orchestration of Liszt consists of the bearing it has upon the unfettered form, the freedom of tonality and the novelty of treatment that characterize the New German School. His scoring is masterful, highly colored and ingenious, but contains nothing conspicuously new. He was led to modify the cyclic form of the symphony which became transformed into the symphonic poem with its continuity of music, monothematic principle and absence of conventional formulas.

WAGNER. The highest ideals of German opera culminated in the music dramas of Wagner. He aimed to substitute a noble form of art in the place of mere pleasure-giving and sensational fabrications. Music, poetic ideas, action and stage setting were all to be worthy of the subject intended for presentation. By developing the so-called *Leit-motiv*, Wagner discovered a most potent factor for recalling past events, for emphasizing those present, and for anticipating those of the future. To-day Wagner stands forth as the accepted champion of dramatic reforms, as the most eminent composer of the nineteenth century, and as the greatest master of orchestration in the annals of the world. Although at first susceptible to tone-color as an end to itself, he learned to subordinate it to the demands of the musical and poetic ideas of the immediate dramatic situation. He emphasized solidity, made the orchestra firm and supple, increased its melodic as well as harmonic force, and used it for two definite purposes: to render emotion and to portray action and situations. His orchestration does not deviate from well-established and approved traditions, but the grouping and treatment of instruments are entirely new. Every phase of his inexhaustible variety in string writing is of surpassing beauty. The use of deep, sonorous basses never interferes with harmonic clearness or with the outline of melodic and rhythmic movement. The modern extreme development of unsupported wood-wind and their numerical distribution are entirely due to Wagner. The most radical changes are those affecting the brass. Of incalculable value was the permanent employment of valve-horns and valve-trumpets, the immense development in horn writing, the discarding of opheicleides, and the introduction of a complete group of tubas. Much of Wagner's warm and rich orchestration is due to a substratum of soft brass harmonies that are apparently not audible at all. No composer knew better than he how to obtain the best effects from instruments of percussion without overstepping the bounds of artistic refinement. Greatest of masters for the orchestra, Wagner brought that organization to its highest point of evolution.

Further prominent representatives of the "New Movement" are Cornelius, Bruckner, Lassen, Ritter, Draeseke, Weingartner, Nicodé, Richard Strauss. The masterful and ingenious instrumentation of Cornelius proves him a worthy follower of Wagner. Bruckner's orchestration, though clever, lacks buoyancy and warmth. That of Lassen, Ritter, Draeseke and Weingartner contains many sterling qualities, but has not advanced the evolution of orchestration to any perceptible degree. Nicodé's methods present some of the most interesting specimens of modern orchestration.

RICHARD STRAUSS. The greatest cosmopolitan master of orchestration after Wagner is Richard Strauss. He has progressed step by step through various stages of development. Conforming at first to the conservative romanticism of Mendelssohn and Schumann, he soon came to admire and emulate the doctrines of Brahms, but eventually leaned more and more upon Liszt and Wagner for the dominating thought of his conceptions. With "Till Eulenspiegel" and "Also sprach Zarathustra" Strauss inaugurated a permanent and ever advancing method of procedure distinctly individualistic and unprecedented that has so far culminated in the vast realistic conceptions of "Don Juan" and "Ein Heldenleben." His works embody flowing cantilena, intricate polyphony, freely used chromatic harmony, daring harmonic combinations, complex rhythm, startling contrasts, monumental climaxes, clever orchestral devices, and extreme realism. In order to grasp the true significance of the contrapuntally synthesized harmonic Melos it is of utmost importance to trace the complicated melodic delineations as independent factors flowing in a horizontal direction. His orchestral conceptions are vast color-pictures and display a wealth of melodic utterance in all the principal orchestral voices, a prolific number of themes and sub-themes, and the most intimate acquaintance with the specific characteristics of the various instruments as well as with orchestral combinations and the resultant mixture of tonal tints thereby to be obtained. Like Berlioz, Strauss secures dramatic effects by means of vivid orchestration, and displays an insatiable craving for the discovery of novel combinations. His themes are arrayed in a kaleidoscopic sequence of instrumental color rather than being subjected to elaborate thematic treatment, and climaxes are reached by means of dynamic effects instead of by melodic evolution. An elaborately conceived program justifies the requisition for vast orchestral resources. There is further evidence of genuine inspiration, of a true gift for thematic development forming a marvellous filigree of contrapuntally interwoven leading motives, of intellectual power, philosophical reflection, poetic revery, and naïve humor.

Germany still leads the van in the art of orchestration, of which she possesses many eminent exponents such as Max Shillings and Cyrill Kistler, — slavish imitators of extreme Wagnerism, and Humperdinck, Thuille, Kienzl, Georg Schumann, Mahler, — less extreme in their views but more successful in their results.

During the nineteenth century a small group of men were especially instrumental in transplanting the daintiness and refinement of modern French light opera into indigenous German productions. Conspicuous among these is Lortzing, supported by Nicolai, Flotow, Suppé and Johann Strauss junior.

CHAPTER XII.

(1) **France.** The French composers of the nineteenth century may for convenience be divided into several distinctive groups. After Berlioz, a number of representative writers devoted themselves with signal success to the development of orchestral concert music. Conspicuous among these are David, Franck, Lalo, Godard, d'Indy.

DAVID possessed, in addition to the characteristic feature of *clearness*, a highly developed talent for artistic disposition of his plans, for poetic picture-painting, and for rich and descriptive orchestral color, especially when portraying Oriental subjects. Like Berlioz, he introduced certain scenic qualities into his orchestration, which is ever buoyant, supple, and varied.

CÉSAR FRANCK differs from his French contemporaries by reason of what might be termed the masculine severity of his inspiration, together with monumental mastery of polyphonic design, exhaustless command of orchestral resources.

LALO. In antithesis to Franck's severe and somewhat solemn style of writing, that of Lalo betrays a fund of spontaneous invention, curious rhythmic effects, charming and sprightly instrumentation, and great aptitude for imbuing his works with the necessary local coloring.

GODARD. In France, Godard occupies a conspicuous position on the programs of orchestral concert music. His musical ideas and instrumentation are both graceful and charming.

D'INDY. In earnest endeavor and in faithful adherence to high ideals d'Indy has proved himself a worthy successor to his teacher, César Franck, whom he copies in exceedingly complicated development of subject-matter. Not content with incorporating in his works the most advanced tenets of Wagner, he further has explored the pathway opened up by Brahms. He is essentially a symphonist, evolves his conceptions on broad and dignified lines, and displays a masterful deployment of orchestral resources.

A little coterie of Frenchmen — Adam, Maillart and Delibes — have distinguished themselves by almost exclusive devotion to the lightest of operatic forms. Conspicuous among these is Delibes by reason of his naïve descriptive powers and clever instrumentation.

Thomas, Gounod, Saint-Saëns, Bizet, Chabrier, Massenet may be regarded as the foremost French composers of the nineteenth century and the greatest French orchestrator after Berlioz is Saint-Saëns.

THOMAS. The orchestration of Thomas is clear in *ensemble*, ingenious in detail, polished, refined and never overloaded. Characteristic tone-color and poetically conceived combinations reveal the skilful hand of a competent master.

GOUNOD stands as the most illustrious recent representative of lyric opera and exhibits the unusual attribute of attaining excellent results without apparent effort. His scoring follows the general path indicated by Auber and Meyerbeer, but it further shows that he possessed a considerable knowledge of the German science of instrumentation.

SAINT-SAËNS is the greatest living French composer and the mightiest of her orchestral exponents. The fundamentals of his artistic principles differ but slightly from those of Thomas and Gounod, and the outlines of Meyerbeer's operatic forms are also in evidence in his works. Nevertheless, Saint-Saëns discloses involuntary leanings toward Wagner. His symphonic poems, though not of the same magnitude and significance, are nevertheless clearer and more compact than those of either Berlioz or Liszt. Admirable clearness as well as simplicity of treatment characterizes his chamber music. His orchestration is elaborate, rich and varied, — intricate, at times, without being obtuse. It invariably reveals the soundest of judgment in the deployment of large or small orchestral forces. It is alternately scintillating, impassioned, melancholy, heroic. Among other details, his scoring frequently makes requisition for triplets of wood and brass instruments, and embodies the best traits of all contemporary orchestral writers both native and foreign.

BIZET followed the prevalent custom of building upon French traditions, enhanced by German truthfulness of expression and interpretation. He possessed a rare talent for discovering novel traits of instrumentation together with variety of rhythm and tone-color.

CHABRIER'S representative work " Gwendoline " may be rightfully looked upon as the most advanced exposition of existing Franco-German music dramas. Much of his orchestration suggests a progressive yet peculiar phase of Wagnerism enveloped by a tinge of melancholy and softened by the delicate touch peculiar to the French.

MASSENET appears at his best as a dramatic writer. His endowments embrace highly developed feeling for sensuous charm, a style distinctly poetic, and a manner of orchestration both rich and varied.

French art during this era has been further assisted by the sterling achievements of many secondary composers such as Dubois and Paladhile; by the orchestral expounders: Gevaërt, Lavoix; by the literary champions: Vidal, Benoit, Joncières; by the organist-composers: Guilmant, Widor; by the representatives of the fair sex: Augusta Holmès, Cécile Chaminade; and by the most recent aspirants to fame: Charpentier and Debussy.

The attitude of the French public toward orchestral concert music has undergone a radical change in the last fifty years. During the first half of the nineteenth century Habeneck reorganized and developed the "Concerts du Conservatoire." This was followed by the establishment of Pasdeloup's "Société des jeunes artistes" and its offspring, the "Concerts populaires." The persistent propagation of both indigenous and exotic works of art is largely due to Pasdeloup's initiative. In recent years, concert performances in France have been brought to a high state of proficiency through the untiring efforts of Lamoureux and Colonne.

(2) **Italy.** For half a century Italy has now been represented by but one luminary of the first magnitude — VERDI. His earlier scoring is conventional and commonplace. The orchestration depends largely upon violent and frequently illogical contrasts. Gradually, however, Verdi acquired increased regard for judicious and more independent instrumentation, and that more particularly in the deployment of the wood-wind. An extreme advance is discovered in his Requiem and later operas. Here the functions of the orchestra become more important, and the tonal colors acquire a richer and warmer hue.

Verdi's followers have done practically nothing for the cause of orchestration other than to branch off into infrequented by-ways that have necessitated corresponding orchestral treatment.

CHAPTER XIII.

The universal development of musical art during the nineteenth century is indeed unprecedented. Side by side with the rise and growth of the New Movement in Germany, side by side with the high development of French lyric opera enhanced by advanced Teutonic principles, side by side with the gradual unfolding of Verdi's melodious and impassioned conceptions stands the evolution of scientifically applied Folk-tunes belonging to the younger musical countries.

(1) **Hungary.** It cannot be said that Hungary possesses a national style of orchestration. Although Liszt and Goldmark were both Hungarians by birth, the former benefited his country not so much by developing an indigenous style of composition as by the propagation of those musical traits peculiar to his race. As to Goldmark's music, it is that of a German rather than of a Magyar. More faithful to native characteristics were the efforts of a small group of secondary composers. Their scores, like those of Liszt and Goldmark, contain plenty of variety and color, but owe their distinctive features to melodic and rhythmic novelty, — not to instrumentation. Hungary has, therefore, exerted no more than an indirect influence upon the art of orchestration.

(2) **Bohemia.** The development of orchestration in Bohemia affords a striking contrast to that in Hungary. SMETANA, the pioneer, was content to employ comparatively simple means, — indeed, his scores occasionally reveal a suggestion of Mozart's naïve touch. On the other hand, his eminent successor, DVOŘÁK, developed the art to a point excelled by none. The latter ranks among the four greatest orchestrators since Wagner. Like Smetana, Dvořák evolved his music from the native folk-song. He was, on the whole, an adherent to strict forms, but subjected these to the utmost freedom and originality of treatment. His greatest powers displayed themselves in the colossal development of orchestral resources. His orchestration is appropriate and consistent, varied, warm and brilliant. It abounds in beautiful combinations. It is rich but never over-burdened. Further distinctive features include clear and bright string writing, methods of employing the wood-wind similar to those of Schubert, and an occasional touch of the supernatural suggestive of Spohr and Weber. In a word, Dvořák was a master of vivacious and refined orchestration.

(3) **Scandinavia.** The music of Scandinavia is likewise evolved from native folk-melodies. The Northern composers are not particularly dramatic nor have they developed many novel traits of instrumentation. They resemble the Hungarians in having wielded but an indirect influence upon orchestration, this influence being restricted to the indigenous properties of their melody, rhythm and local coloring. Their chief representatives are GADE, the pioneer, and his illustrious successor — GRIEG. The former, under the beneficial influence of Mendelssohn, developed high efficiency in the art of orchestration. He appreciated both the possibilities and the limitations of each instrument, and revealed his nationality by the application of suggestive tone-color. Grieg's instrumentation is not conspicuously influenced by modern tendencies. Though he cannot be ranked as a great orchestrator, his writing for strings alone is of surpassing beauty, nor does his deployment of larger forces lack novelty and effectiveness.

(4) **Russia.** The gradual ascendency of Russian music is one of the phenomena of the nineteenth century. Here again the native folk-song forms the basis for scientific development. Russian composers may be divided into three classes: — the old lyric school, — the new Russian school, — Rubinstein and Tschaikowsky in a class by themselves.

GLINKA, pioneer of the old lyric school, accomplished for his country what Gade and Smetana did for theirs. His orchestration calls for but little comment excepting that it is clever and at times even brilliant.

The tenets of the "New Russian Movement" are closely allied to those of the "New German Movement." Chief representatives of this class are BORODIN, CESAR CUI, RIMSKI-KORSAKOFF. The orchestration of these men and their associates is, on the whole, but the reflection of Tschaikowsky's style combined with the further progressive methods of German and French orchestration.

RUBINSTEIN cannot be compared with Glinka as an operatic writer or with Tschaikowsky as an orchestrator. His instrumentation was hampered by his antagonism to the innovations of the New German Movement. In string writing, however, Rubinstein reveals fine appreciation of tone-color, and his full scoring at times displays superb power.

TSCHAIKOWSKY still reigns supreme as the greatest interpreter of Slavonic ideals. A remarkable feature of his scoring is the extreme modern effect secured with comparatively modest means. He expressed himself in a language of profound pathos which was in part due to the embodiment of weird and gloomy orchestration. He made prominent use of low wood-wind, which were constantly combined with the violas, and he evinced peculiar predilection for clarinets in their low range and bassoons in their upper range. On the other hand, many magnificent specimens of forceful writing are also in evidence in his scores.

(5) **England.** Of the ten men chosen as representative English composers of the nineteenth century, six are prominently identified with the evolution of English orchestration. The pioneer of these was Macfarren, whose cosmopolitan range of composition is particularly noteworthy. Bennett, a disciple of Mendelssohn, proved himself a worthy heir to Purcell, and is regarded as the founder of a new English School. Most widely known is Sullivan, who substantially aided the development of an Anglican style of orchestration. Sullivan based his methods of instrumentation upon those of Mozart, but occasionally copied Gounod and even Berlioz. He displayed sound musicianship, dramatic power, and a thorough command of orchestral resources. Mackenzie's conceptions are wholly orchestral. His scoring is powerful and effective, allowing also commendable freedom to the wood-wind, and suggests a mixture of Mendelssohnian and Wagnerian externals. Cowen is an exponent of both absolute and programmatic music. He shares with Stanford the rank of representative English symphonist.

The twentieth century gives promise of marked advance in English composition from an emotional and orchestral standpoint as discovered in the initial productions of Elgar.

(6) **America.** America and Russia are the two countries that have forged to the front in musical art during the past quarter century. Until the shackles of English conservatism and of Puritan dogmas were thrown off, little could be done in the way of preparing for a national school of composition. But with the ever increasing influx of German musicians, American composers were stimulated to extend their horizon, so that at the present day one can point to a host of cultured and highly educated musicians who are devoting themselves to the furtherance of national art. Many of them have displayed rare skill as orchestral writers, but comparatively few have as yet been sufficiently fortunate to acquire wide-spread recognition in this branch. The list of pioneer composers and promoters includes Lowell and William Mason, Bristow, Gottschalk, C. C. Converse, Paine, Lang, and Emery. A somewhat arbitrary selection of representative orchestrators includes Paine, Buck, Foote, Chadwick, MacDowell, Parker. The pioneer of America's great composers is Paine. His opera "Azara" may be regarded as his

representative work, and is conspicuous for its dramatic continuity, irresistible climaxes, dignity and breadth of musical contents, consistent and effective orchestration.   Buck is prominently identified with the evolution of American church music.   The orchestration of his choral compositions reveals the firm hand of a master.   Foote appears to best advantage when writing chamber and orchestral music.   He does not aim to produce sensational effects, yet clothes his artistic conceptions in appropriate orchestral garment.   Chadwick's music is above all manly and energetic.   His form, though conservative, is well rounded.   His orchestration is chaste and refined rather than sensational and glowing.   He has proved himself a keen judge of those essentials required for large instrumental works.   MacDowell's music possesses certain characteristics that distinguish it from that of any other American composer.   His education has been thoroughly cosmopolitan.   He aims to induce poetic imagination symbolic of emotional reality.   His chord formations, harmonic progressions, thematic treatment, and structural form are all in accord with the psychological subtleties to be expressed.   His orchestration is one of his strongest attributes; though founded upon that of Raff, it possesses also the charming touch of the modern French school.   Parker has risen to eminence through his choral writings, and is the best known American writer in England.   He wields his orchestral forces with no uncertain hand, but does not allow tone-color in its own right to predominate in his choral works.   Further prominent writers for the orchestra are Gilchrist, Gleason, Foerster, Beck, Bird, Kelley, Schoenefeld, Zeck, van der Stucken, Mrs. Beach, F. S. Converse, Huss, Hadley.   Until recently the larger number of orchestral conductors in the United States were foreigners, but the Americans are gradually taking the reins into their own hands.   The present display of musical activity in America is unprecedented.   The schools, the colleges, the churches, the concert hall, the dramatic stage are all preparing the way for the ascendency of the American composer.

CONCLUSION.

We have now traced the history of our modern art of orchestration through five great stages of evolution. (1) Under the head of "The Cradle of Instrumental Music," musical development among primitive men was attributed to two impelling forces: emotional expression and pagan religious rites. The nature of these early attempts at musical utterance can only be conjectured, but although we have no knowledge of its tonal aspect, extant relics and representations of primitive instruments among such races as the Egyptians, the Assyrians and the Jews correspond to the leading types of sound-producing apparatus belonging to civilized nations. Authentic history discloses the development of artistic music in India, in Greece and in early Rome. These efforts were essentially melodic. Rhythm was dependent upon poetic instinct, whereas the harmony of simultaneous sounds, though scientifically expounded, was put to but small practical use. Systems of harmony, notation and measure were eventually established, though circuitously devolved from the tedious experiments of the scholastic monks to the more tangible results of the troubadours and of the masters of the Netherland School. Lasso and Palestrina eventually pointed the way toward a settled tonality determined by harmonic considerations. (2) "The Dawn of Independent Instrumentation" treats of the further development of consistent tonality, of greater rhythmic freedom, of artistic structural form, and of the gradual ascendency of a secular style in connection with solo-singing and independent instrumental music. Independent instrumental music found its origin in the attempts at embellished organ accompaniment; solo singing devolved from the Miracle Plays, from the lyrics of the troubadours, and from the Florentine monody as developed by Peri and Cavalieri, whose theories contained the germ of opera and oratorio, for which instrumental accompaniment is a requisite. (3) The chapter entitled "Beginnings of Orchestration" marks the actual starting point for the nuclear thought of this book. Here the central figure is Monteverde, father of modern instrumentation. His methods were propagated by Carissimi in Italy, Schütz in Germany, Cavalli and Lulli in France. The greatest orchestral writer after Monteverde was Scarlatti. (4) The way was now prepared for the comprehensive "Classic Era," of which the central figures, as regards orchestral evolution, are Haydn, the father of modern orchestration, and Beethoven, — magnificently supported by Mozart, and to a lesser degree by Bach, Händel and Gluck. In the earlier part of this era, France owed the high standard of her indigenous music primarily to Rameau and Grétry.

The former stands as an exponent of serious opera, whereas the latter established *opéra comique* upon a permanent basis. Rameau found a worthy successor in the great orchestrator, Méhul. Grétry was succeeded by Boieldieu, Auber, Hérold, Halévy. Meanwhile the orchestration of Italy did not keep pace with that of Germany or France. The Italians were primarily engaged in composing church music and in writing operas that should satisfy the existing demands for vocal virtuosity. Pergolesi was a notable exception. Even though the art of instrumentation had originated in Italy, no important evolutionist of orchestration can be mentioned between Scarlatti (1659) and Cherubini (1760); the latter is moreover identified with France rather than with Italy. Spontini, Rossini, and the German, Meyerbeer, likewise won their laurels in Paris. Cherubini and Spontini stand as the chief Italian exponents of orchestration during the classic era, the one for the church, the other for the drama. (5) The classic era overlaps the rise and growth of the "Romantic Movement," for the highest attainments of Beethoven, Auber and Rossini were not reached until after Spohr and Weber had already entered the lists. These two early romanticists were shortly succeeded by Schubert, Mendelssohn, Schumann, by the classical-romanticists, headed by Raff and Brahms, and by the originators of the New Movement, Berlioz, Liszt, Wagner. Recent development of differentiated types of orchestration discloses the unique fact that almost every country of musical prominence is represented by a single orchestral writer of unusual ability whose success was dependent upon the initiatory work of one single predecessor. Italy is represented by Spontini and Verdi, France by Berlioz and Saint-Saëns, Bohemia by Smetana and Dvořák, Scandinavia by Gade and Grieg, Russia by Glinka and Tschaikowsky, Germany by Wagner and Richard Strauss.

The above epitome presents the historical aspect of orchestral development. Due credit has been given to those men who particularly helped to forge the connecting links in the evolutionary chain, irrespective of the intrinsic value of their own instrumentation. In antithesis to the above historical aspect, the following synopsis presents the purely practical aspect of orchestration proper as developed by thirteen men whose contributions thereto would appear to be of chief importance. They are named in chronological order without regard to evolutionary sequence or nationality. It is from their works that the specimens of orchestral scoring in the appendix to this book have been chosen. These thirteen representatives are: Monteverde, Scarlatti, Haydn, Mozart, Beethoven, Weber, Berlioz, Mendelssohn, Wagner, Saint-Saëns, Tschaikowsky, Dvořák, Richard Strauss. Monteverde aimed to obtain expressive and dramatic effects, established the orchestra on a permanent basis of stringed instruments played with a bow, and realized the necessity for an individualistic and differentiated style of writing for voices and instruments. Scarlatti divided his strings into four parts, properly dispersed and balanced, readjusted the relation of the wind instruments to the rest of the orchestra by employing them in pairs, strengthened and extended the structure of his opera-symphonies. Haydn established a perfectly balanced orchestra as a whole, realized the value of the wood-wind in their capacity of lending warmth and color to the orchestral canvass, employed them systematically in pairs, and regulated the proportion of the brass to the strings and wood. Mozart infused into the orchestra vitality and warmth, exploited the proper functions of the wood-wind with especial attention to those of the clarinet, and was the first to consistently mix the tonal colors of the orchestra. The evolution of the classic orchestra culminated in the symphonic writings of Beethoven. His scoring not only embodies the ideals of his predecessors, but treats each instrument also with characteristic individuality, subordinated, however, as a means for faithfully depicting the details of the composition proper. He pointed the way for the subsequent romanticists, and his descriptive music proves that even with comparatively simple means gorgeous tone-painting can be attained. Weber initiated a novel style of dramatic orchestration and contributed substantially to the independence of the wood-wind. Berlioz was the first of the great modern symphonists and represents the ultra-realistic school of orchestral program-music. He combined both dramatic and symphonic principles but also applied tone-color in its own right. His unique genius disclosed itself in the discovery of new combinations, new effects, new treatment, and in his power of musical description. The orchestration of Mendelssohn is invaluable for its finish of detail. It is buoyant, transparent, delicate, and perfectly balanced. Wagner brought the art of dramatic orchestration to its highest point of evolution. His orchestration does not deviate from well-established and approved principles, but the grouping and treatment of instruments are entirely new. He emphasized solidity, made the orchestra firm and supple, increased its melodic as well as harmonic force, and used it for two definite purposes: to render emotion and to portray action and situations. Saint-Saëns' methods emphasize the prevailing custom of his countrymen to combine French traditions and advanced German principles. Clear and compact form, comparative simplicity of thematic treatment, elaborate, rich, varied and above all scintillating orchestration constitute the cardinal features of his conspicuous attainments. The ideal representative of Greater Russia is Tschaikowsky. He secured a gloomy eloquence of instrumentation by drawing upon the lower accents of the orchestra, but was also a master of magnificent and stirring effects. Dvořák evolved his music from the Bohemian folk-song and was a master of vivacious and refined orchestration. His scoring is appropriate, consistent, varied, warm and brilliant. It abounds in beautiful combinations. It is rich but never overburdened. Richard Strauss is proving himself a worthy successor to Wagner as a result of his marvellous insight into the specific characteristics of each individual instrument and of his genius for combining them in a bewildering network of contrapuntally interwoven melodic themes. He possesses an hitherto unheard of orchestral technique, and taxes both the executive ability and the artistic attributes of the instrumentalists to the utmost. He makes use of elaborately conceived programs necessitating vast orchestral resources, is an extremist in the realm of realism, and secures powerful dramatic effects by means of vivid orchestration.

Orchestration in its present development would seem to have reached its highest possible attainment of effectiveness and virtuosity. The problem of the future, therefore, deals not so much with material increase of orchestral resource, as with what manner of thought and music the orchestra is destined to portray. What are to be the musical ethics of the twentieth century composers? The most subtle thinkers of the world have generally taken an idealistic view of the social mission of musical art. Eminent psychologists of Germany, France and England, who otherwise represent distinctive and frequently antagonistic schools of philosophy, all agree on this point, as illustrated by a few quotations selected from the writings of Hegel, Schopenhauer, Emile Montegut and Herbert Spencer. Music, according to Hegel, should "fill the heart and bring to consciousness everything developed and undeveloped which human feeling can carry, experience and bring forth, in its innermost and most secret parts; whatever the human heart in its manifold possibilities and moods desires to express or excite; and especially whatever the spirit has in its idea of the Most Essential and High; the glory of the Honored, the Eternal and the True." Schopenhauer declared that music "never expresses phenomena, but solely the inner being, the essence of phenomena, the will itself. It expresses, therefore, not this or that single and particular joy, this or that sorrow, or pain, or horror, or exultation, or hilarity, or repose of mind itself; but, as it were *in abstracto*, the essentials of these without their concomitants, therefore without their motives. Nevertheless, in such quintessence we understand it perfectly. Hence our fancy is so easily excited by it and tries to clothe this invisible spirit world, that speaks to us so immediately and eloquently, with flesh and blood, *i.e.* to embody it in an analogous example." Emile Montegut expresses himself to the effect that this magic sound of what is called music "pierces the material barriers which limit human words; it gives to hearts the means of communicating among themselves; it creates a language of which the most ignorant and the poorest perceive all the power and all the sweetness. Music speaks, and suddenly the hearts which were chilled with consciousness of their own isolation are thrilled with tenderness and radiant with happiness." Herbert Spencer believed that "music ought to take rank at the head of the fine arts because it is the one which adds most to human happiness. Not content with exciting powerfully our better instincts, it awakens sentiments lying dormant in us, of which we had not conceived the possibility, of which we do not understand the sense. This obscure presentment of an unknown happiness, which music awakens in us, this confused dream of an ideal and new life, all this is but a prophecy of something which music itself ought assuredly to accomplish." In contrast to the above enthusiastic utterances, how material and unsatisfying are the dreary speculations of such men as Leibnitz! The latter looked upon music as being but the "*exercitium arithmeticae occultum nescientis se numerare animi*"! The ideal mission of music, therefore, ever has been and surely should continue to be that of uplifting. It should present a moral synonymous for the æsthetic, the pure, the spiritual. It should reveal the highest ideals of the living soul. It should, according to Browning, express truth, not of the mind — knowledge, which is absolute, but of the soul — shifting. Music above all other arts interprets the innermost thoughts of the soul. It is being constantly re-created, whereas all other arts are but the images of what is already created. The imitative arts — sculpture and painting, can no longer be all-satisfying to the self-consciousness of an age influenced by the subjective thought of such men as Goethe and Schiller. Why, therefore, should modern music be reared solely upon a similar realistic basis of imitation instead of upon an idealistic one of representation? The fundamentals of music rest upon an acoustic element dependent upon absolute pitch. Since, however, an isolated tone cannot suggest a definite idea or image, it is necessary, in order that music should mean something, to connect a series of tones so as to produce melody, to combine several tones so as to form chords, and to group these chords so as to obtain contrasts of tonality and modes. This accomplished, there must be added rhythmic life, variety of tone-color, and dynamic contrast. Finally, the whole fabrication must be fitted into a framework of structural form based upon the science of logic. But all this is not enough. There exists an underlying psychological principle that cannot be disregarded. Appreciation for acoustic effects and the realizations of intellectual reflection are but the stepping stones to something higher. The first requirement of a composer is intuition or the spontaneous expression of musical instinct — an element more essential to musical creation than to any other branch of art. Further requisites are imagination, emotion, inspiration, and above all spirituality. There is a tendency among recent exponents of the most advanced school to declare that the possibilities of purely æsthetic music have been exhausted. Morbidness and pessimism dominate the creative conceptions of these recent experimentalists. They are leaning more and more toward the expression of concrete ideas concealing vague abstractions. The present writer is heartily in sympathy with the most catholic application of all legitimate resources so long as the primary object of musical utterance be not lost sight of. It goes without saying that descriptive, imitative, realistic and even morbid music has its proper place in the poetic conceptions of our contemporary tone-masters. Exception only is made to music that is primarily intellectual or pessimistic. On the other hand, it need not be primarily pleasure-giving. In a word, all such objectives should be made subjective to a purer motive. The portrayal of lesser sentiments and passions is legitimate only in so far as to form a background for the nobler, which are thereby thrown into relief. The ideal mission of music is to reflect the loftiest sentiments of the composer's soul, and to awaken similar experiences in the mind of the auditor so as to inspire and uplift him. Such were the ideals of Beethoven. May his example continue to be emulated!

APPENDIX

OF

MUSICAL ILLUSTRATIONS

MONTEVERDE.
(Page 16)

No. 1. L'Orfeo: Atto I—Toccata, (*che si suona avanti il levar de la tela tre volte con tutti li stromenti.*)

No. 2. L'Orfeo: Atto II—Ritornello. (*Questo Ritornello fù sonato di dentra da un Clavicembano, duoi Chitaroni, e 2 Violini piccioli alla Francese.*)

No. 3. L'Orfeo: Atto III. (*Orfeo canta al suono del Organo di legno solamente.*)

Ei dor - me, e la mia ce - tra, se pie - tà non im - pe - tra nel in - du - ra - to co - re,

No. 4.   L'Orfeo: Atto IV—Sinfonia,
(No instruments indicated.)

No. 5.   L'Orfeo: Atto V.   *(Apollo ed Orfeo ascende al cielo cantando.)*

Sa - liam, ...   Sa - liam . . . .

Sa - liam . . . .

(Pianoforte Arrangement.   No instruments indicated.)

SCARLATTI.

(Page 22)

No. 6. La Rosaura: Prologo-Sinfonia.

Allegro.

(*No instruments indicated.*)

(Mss. = b c♯)

No. 7. La Rosaura: Atto I — Scena II.

No. 8. La Rosaura: Atto II — Scena II.

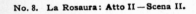

No. 9. La Rosaura: Atto II. — Scena IV.

Aria, a tempo.

(Climene sola.)

(Pfte Arr. Skeleton Score.)

ma non sia, chi di mia fe - de il can - dor . . . . ten - - - ti, ten - ti of - fus - car il can - dor . . . . ten - - ti, ten - ti of - fus - car.

HAYDN.
(Page 47)

No. 10. Symphony in D, No. 2 : 1st Movement.

No. 11. Symphony in D : 2d Movement.

No. 12. Symphony in D: 2d Movement.

No. 13. **Symphony in D: 2d Movement.**

No. 14. **Symphony No. 3: 1st Movement.**

No. 15. **Symphony No. 4: 1st Movement.**

No. 16.   Symphony No. 5 : 2d Movement.

No. 17. Symphony No. 6 : Adagio.

[*] N.B.

MOZART.

(Page 50)

No. 18. Jupiter Symphony: Menuetto.

No. 19. Jupiter Symphony: Finale.

No. 10. Jupiter Symphony: Finale.

No. 21. Symphony in G minor: 2d Movement.

MOZART.

No. 22. Symphony in E flat: 2d Movement.

No. 23. Symphony in E flat : Menuetto.

BEETHOVEN.

(Page 53)

No. 24. Fifth Symphony : 2d Movement.

No. 25. Fifth Symphony : 2d Movement.

No. 26. Fifth Symphony : 2d Movement.

No. 30.   Fifth Symphony : Finale.

No. 31. **Pastoral Symphony : 2d Movement.**

No. 32. **Pastoral Symphony : Shepherd's Song.**

No. 33. **Seventh Symphony : Allegretto.**

No. 34. Seventh Symphony: 3d Movement.

No. 35.   Seventh Symphony : 3d Movement.

WEBER.

(Page 71)

No. 36. Der Freischütz: Overture.

No. 37. Der Freischütz: Overture.

Molto vivace.

No. 38.   Der Freischütz : Overture.

No. 39. Der Freischütz: Overture.

Molto vivace.

No. 40. Der Freischütz: Overture.

Molto vivace.

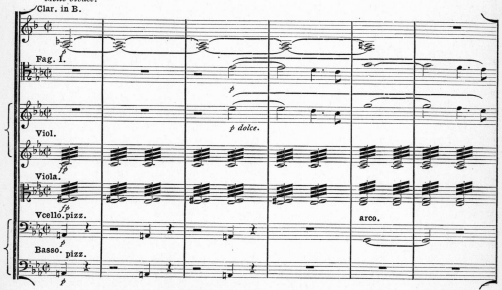

No. 41.   Der Freischütz: Act 1 — Scene I.

No. 42. Der Freischütz: Act I — Scene II.

No. 43. Der Freischütz: Act II — Scene II.

No. 44.   Der Freischütz: Act II — Scene IV.

No. 45.   Der Freischütz: Act II — Scene IV.

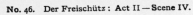

No. 46. Der Freischütz: Act II — Scene IV.

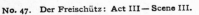

No. 47. Der Freischütz: Act III — Scene III.

BERLIOZ.

(Page 89)

No. 48. Symphonie fantastique: Rêveries.

No. 49. Symphonie fantastique: Scène aux champs.

No. 50. Symphonie fantastique: Scène aux champs.

No. 51.   Symphonie fantastique : Scène aux champs.

No. 52. Symphonie fantastique : Marche au supplice.

No. 53. Symphonie fantastique : Marche au supplice.

No. 54. **Symphonie fantastique: Marche au supplice.**

No. 55. Symphonie fantastique: Ronde du Sabbat.

No. 56. Harold en Italie: Sérénade.

No. 57. Harold en Italie: Orgie de Brigands.

MENDELSSOHN.

(Page 75)

No. 58. Midsummer Night's Dream : Overture.

Allegro di molto.

No. 59. Midsummer Night's Dream: Scherzo.

No. 60. Midsummer Night's Dream: Scherzo.

No. 61. Midsummer Night's Dream: No. 5.

No. 62. Midsummer Night's Dream: No. 6.

No. 63. Midsummer Night's Dream: No. 6.

No. 64. Midsummer Night's Dream: No. 6.

No. 65. Midsummer Night's Dream: Notturno.

No. 66. Midsummer Night's Dream: Notturno.

Con moto tranquillo.

238

WAGNER.
(Page 93)

No. 67. Die Walküre: Act I — Scene I.

No, 68, Die Walküre: Act I — Scene I.

240

WAGNER.

No. 69.   Die Walküre: Act I — Scene I.

No. 70.   Die Walküre: Act I — Scene II.

No. 71.   Die Walküre: Act I — Scene II.

No. 72. Die Walküre: Act I — Scene III.

No: 73. Die Walküre: Act I — Scene III.

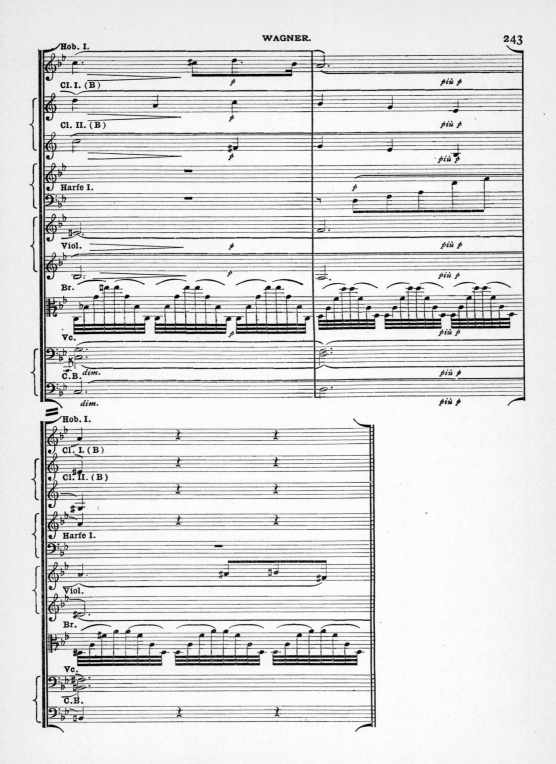

No. 74. Die Walküre: Act I — Scene III.

No. 75. Die Walküre: Act I — Scene III.

SAINT-SAËNS.

(Page 131)

No. 76. Le Rouet d'Omphale.

No. 77.   Le Rouet d'Omphale.

No. 78.   Le Rouet d'Omphale.

No. 79. Phaéton.

No. 80. Danse Macabre.

No. 81. Danse Macabre.

No. 82.   La Jeunesse d' Hercule.

TSCHAIKOWSKY.

(Page 155)

No. 83. **Symphonie pathétique : 1st Movement.**

No. 84. **Symphonie pathétique : 1st Movement.**

No. 85. **Symphonie pathétique: 1st Movement.**

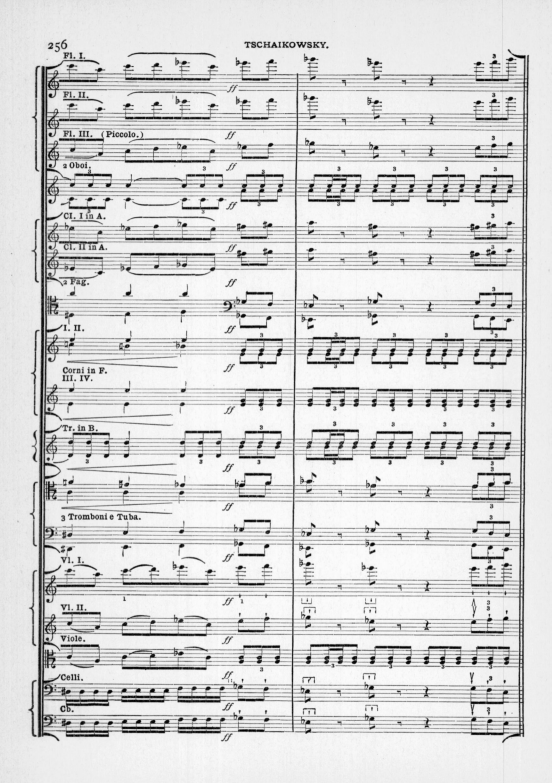

No. 86. Symphonie pathétique : 1st Movement.

No. 87. Symphonie pathétique : 2d Movement.

No. 88.   **Symphonie pathétique : 3d Movement.**

No. 89. Symphonie pathétique: Finale.

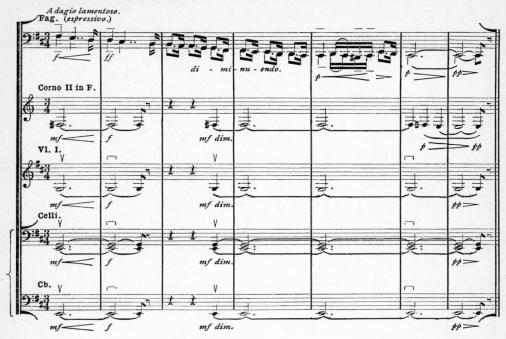

260

DVOŘÁK.
(Page 147)

No. 90. Symphony No. 5 in E minor: " From the New World."— First Movement.

No. 91.   Sym. in E minor: First Movement.

No. 92.   Sym. in E minor: 1st Movement.

No. 93.   Sym. in E minor: 2d Movement.

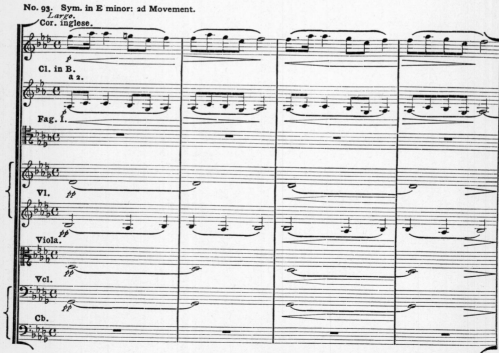

No. 94. Sym. in E minor: 4th Movement.

No. 95.   Sym. in E minor: 4th Movement.

No. 96. Sym. in E minor : 4th Movement.

RICHARD STRAUSS.

No. 97. Zarathustra: („das Grablied.") (Page 106)

No. 98.   Zarathustra: („von der Wissenschaft.")

No. 99. Zarathustra.

No. 101. Zarathustra.

No. 102. Till Eulenspiegel.

No. 103. Till Eulenspiegel.

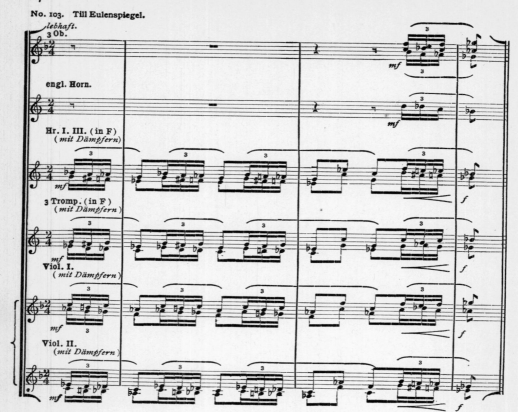

INDEX

"AN undertaking which," says W. S. HENDERSON, in *The Atlantic Monthly*, "will suffice for many years to come, and will remain for all time a monument to the learning, patience, and judgment of the editor."

A New Edition

Revised and greatly enlarged of

Grove's Dictionary of Music and Musicians

EDITED BY

J. A. FULLER MAITLAND, M.A., F.S.A.

In five 8vo volumes, each illustrated with a photogravure and twenty-four full-page half-tone plates, besides many illustrations in the text.

"Unquestionably the most valuable work of the kind in English, and at present superior to any other in any language, considering its encyclopædic character and the substantial quality of its most important articles." — *The New York Times*.

"The best and most comprehensive dictionary of music is still the pioneer one. . . . Grove's 'Dictionary of Music and Musicians' has become a standard work without a rival." — *The Review of Reviews*.

PUBLISHED BY

THE MACMILLAN COMPANY

SIXTY-FOUR AND SIXTY-SIX FIFTH AVENUE

NEW YORK

By DANIEL GREGORY MASON

Editor of "Masters in Music," Lecturer in the New York Normal College and in the Extension Department of Columbia University

Beethoven and His Forerunners

Four portraits and 25 plates. Cloth, $1.50 net

" Mr. Mason has brought the same clear thought, suggestiveness and philosophic spirit to bear upon this subject as he exhibited in his former volume, and the result is a treatment that will be found stimulating by all who approach music as something more than a mere sensuous pleasure." — *Richard Aldrich in The Music Review.*

The Romantic Composers

12mo, cloth, $1.75 net

The composers treated are Schubert, connecting link between Beethoven and the "romantic" school; Schumann, who created a new type of piano music; Mendelssohn, who anticipated the orchestral style of to-day; Chopin, the supreme master of the pianoforte; Berlioz, the pioneer of the dramatic symphony and a virtuoso of the orchestra; and Liszt, who contributed to music that form, — the symphonic poem, — most persistently cultivated by modern musicians.

" Mr. Daniel Mason is a critic of music whose deliverances one may not ignore. Since the appearance, four years ago, of his volume of studies in modern music, from Grieg to Brahms, he has been recognized as an uncommonly able commentator upon the most difficult and evasive of the arts. He has scholarship, he is penetrating and alert, and he is master of a style at once dignified and engaging, distinguished and precise." — *Bookman.*

From Grieg to Brahms

Cloth, $1.25 net

" A peculiarly sane and readable book, enriched and not merely bedecked with literary allusions, and at all times reasonable and sincere." — *Mail and Express.*

PUBLISHED BY

THE MACMILLAN COMPANY

SIXTY-FOUR AND SIXTY-SIX FIFTH AVENUE
NEW YORK

THE HISTORY
OF AMERICAN ART

EDITED BY
JOHN C. VAN DYKE

The History *of* American Music

By LOUIS C. ELSON

Illustrated with twelve photogravure plates and more than
one hundred text illustrations

Imperial 8vo, cloth, gilt, $5.00 net

In this "History of American Music," the second of the series, the
author has told of the beginnings, the foreign influences, the
changes, the methods, the personal endeavors, that have gone to
the making of our present music. Many of the events here nar-
rated occurred but yesterday or are happening to-day, and hence
have little perspective for the historian. It has not always been
possible to say a final word, even if that were desirable. In its
stead the widely scattered facts have been brought together and
arranged sequentially that they might tell their own story and
point their own conclusion.

CONTENTS

The Religious Beginnings of American Music — Early Musical Organi-
zations — Instrumental Music and American Orchestras — Musical
Societies and Institutions — Opera in America — The Folk-Music
of America — National and Patriotic Music — American Tone-
Masters — The Orchestral Composers of America — Other Or-
chestral Composers of America — Operatic, Cantata, and Vocal
Composers — American Song-Composers — Organists, Choir and
Chorus Leaders — The American Composers for Pianoforte —
American Women in Music — Musical Criticism and Authorship
— The Musical Education of the Present — Qualities and Defects
of American Music — General Bibliography — Index.

"At last the widely scattered facts which must be the basis of any competent
study of American Music are so brought together as to tell their own story and point
their own conclusion.

"Written in a kindly spirit by an able critic, it is without question the most comprehensive and the best of the works of its class." — *Chicago Record-Herald.*

PUBLISHED BY

THE MACMILLAN COMPANY

SIXTY-FOUR AND SIXTY-SIX FIFTH AVENUE

NEW YORK

The Art of the Musician: A Guide to the Intelligent Appreciation of Music

By Dr. HENRY G. HANCHETT

12mo, cloth, $1.50 net (by mail, $1.63)

The art of the musician is shown as an intelligent presentation of sounds and rhythms and inspirations into works displaying beauty or expressing emotion. It is by the handling of the materials of music that the composer proves the beauty of his vision.

"It should be the duty of every teacher (of music) to see that the work is in the hands of his pupils, for it will make things easier, clearer and more enjoyable."— *Musical Leader.*

Our Mountain Garden

By Mrs. THEODORE THOMAS (Rose Fay)

Cloth, illustrated from photographs, $1.50

This is not, like the above, a book about music, but one that must always remain dear to the many friends of the musician whose ideally beautiful summer home in New Hampshire it describes.

Music-Study in Germany

By AMY FAY

With a Preface by Sir George Grove and a Portrait

Eighth Edition. 12mo, cloth, $1.25

A series of lively letters from an American lady, written while a student of music in various cities of Germany.

How to Sing (Meine Gesangskunst)

By LILLI LEHMANN

Translated from the German by Richard Aldrich

Illustrated, 12mo, cloth, $1.50 net (by mail, $1.63)

PUBLISHED BY

THE MACMILLAN COMPANY

SIXTY–FOUR AND SIXTY–SIX FIFTH AVENUE
NEW YORK

Date Due

Date Due		
MAR 3 1920	MR 13 46	
JAN 24 1922	JAN 8 '56	
MAR 21 1923	DEC	
MAY 2 1925	JAN 25 61	
MAY 4 1925		
NOV 19 1925	APR 11 61	
FEB 24 1927	DEC 2 61	
	MAR 20 '63	
July 25 1934	MAY 6 '64	
38 S E N	5/21/64	
N 15 38	OCT 19 1997	
Ja 30 40		
My 7 42		
D 2 - 42		
D 10 42		
F 14 44		
APR 19 1980		